"GIRL"

(A Story for Every Les Being)

Christiana Harrell

Photography: H. Carter

Edited By: Christina Cosse'

Email the author: wordsRmylife86@yahoo.com

Third Edition

Visit: christianaharrell.com

ISBN-13: 978-1479168699

ISBN-10: 1479168696

Dedication:

There are four phenomenal women in my life that cannot be replaced and this book is for every last one of them because they have been there whether I have been up or down…

Bianca, thank you for pushing me and promoting me even when I got tired of doing it.

Sherrill, thank you for believing in me and keeping my head above water. I couldn't have been blessed with a better sister.

Nina, thank you for reading the same stories over and over and always being honest about my work. I love you pal!

Mommy I love you forever and a day. You are my strength.

Disclaimer

If you are looking for cheesy love stories and happy endings, this book is not for you. There is no glitter and there is no fluff. People will die, cheat, steal, kill and lie. You will see the word "nigga", there will be slang, there will be cuss words, and there is most definitely sex. Don't say you weren't warned.

Table of Contents

"A Hell for You"

*[9]Do you not know that the wicked will not inherit the kingdom of God? Do not be deceived: Neither the sexually immoral nor idolaters nor adulterers nor male prostitutes nor homosexual offenders' [10]nor thieves nor the greedy nor drunkards nor slanderers nor swindlers will inherit the kingdom of God. [11]And that is what some of you were. But you were washed, you were sanctified, you were justified in the name of the Lord Jesus Christ and by the Spirit of our God.-**1 Corinthians 6:9-11***

I slammed my bible shut and leaned back in the recliner of my living room chair, holding a picture of myself, my husband, and daughter. We looked like one of those greeting card families all cheesed up and dressed in red for the holidays. My husband was a very handsome man for forty-six. He stood six feet even, chocolate skin, teeth as white as chalk, shiny bald head, muscular body, and always well dressed. I considered myself the luckiest woman in the world being the misses to Reverend Mitchell Barnes. Our daughter shared his complexion, but her face evenly took on the features of us both. I smiled for a second but then my heart sank deeper into my chest as I wondered what the congregation, my family, and friends would think of me if they knew that their first lady was a closet dyke. I was thirty-two years old, questioning my sexuality all because of an intriguing young woman who set foot into our youth ministry program one Friday.

Tanya was 23. She had a head full of thick, jet black, layered hair. Her eyes were deep brown and her lips were full. She stood at exactly the same height as me, which was 5'7". 36-24-42 were the measurements of her body exactly. I got chills at the thought of my body pressing down on her warm, smooth, brown skin as she pulled me down on top of her to kiss me like it was the first time every time. I thought maybe it was her troubled spirit that had me drawn to her when she stepped into our place of worship that night, maybe God was telling me to give her special prayer. I watched her the entire night, as she teased her hair, clapped with the music, and praised our God. She was a sin in herself.

She approached me after the service requesting to speak to the reverend, but my husband was out of town visiting other churches. We had a guest reverend, but she did not want to speak with him. I should have let her walk away, but my Christian heart offered my assistance, introducing myself as Elaine, the wife of Reverend Mitchell Barnes. I guided her to my husband's office, so that we could talk more privately. She was beyond troubled. Tanya had just lost her job, car, and apartment, she was failing her last year of college and was at risk of losing her financial aid, and her grandfather was dying. My heart instantly went out to her. She was at her ropes end and she was thinking maybe she should take her own life. At that very Moment I was glad that she came to us, but saddened that God was her last resort.

Tanya had been walking from her grandfather's house to her college campus daily just so she wouldn't miss any of her classes. She also took care of her grandfather as well as she could and she studied when he slept. She kept what little things she had in trash bags in her grandfather's kitchen. His house was dim on the inside and cluttered. The only thing that I could think to do was take her into my own home and I did just that. We helped her pay to get her grandfather into a home, so she could focus more on school.

She had become a part of my family and my own guilty pleasure. My husband did not argue with kind gestures and my daughter was happy to have someone to entertain her when I or my husband was too busy to play Barbie.

I dropped Tanya off to school, when I left in the morning to drop off my daughter and run errands. Tanya would sit on campus to get as much done as possible, and then I would pick her up just before two. She would help me cook and clean to show her appreciation for allowing her to stay in our home, because she had nothing more to offer at the Moment.

I wondered to myself, at what Moment I could have stopped it all, and if I had really wanted to. The day of my deception played clearly in my mind. I picked Tanya up from class as usual. I had a little free time, so I decided to shower and relax since my husband was traveling again and my daughter was staying with her best friend to complete a project for school. I shut the water off to the shower, but I jumped as the door eased open. Tanya stood smiling at me.

"Do you ever lock this door?" She asked.

"No, why would I do that?"

"Privacy I assume."

I laughed. "I'm a wife and a Mother. There is no such thing as privacy. Can you hand me that towel over there?"

Tanya reached for my towel, unfolding it and stretching it out to wrap around my body. She walked over to me as I stepped onto the rug in front of the tub and wrapped the towel around my body. I froze as she held onto me a little longer than necessary. She stepped back, still smiling in my direction. "How old are you if you don't mind me asking?"

"Thirty-two. Why?" I responded.

"You look great for your age."

"Thank you."

"Do you work out?"

"When I get the chance, yes, I do."

"You should let me join you sometimes."

"Okay, I could use some company some days."

Tanya stood there staring at me lustfully. I held the towel against my body and waited for her to say something but she only stared.

"Was there something you needed, Tanya?"

"Um, I forgot. I'll come back when I remember."

Tanya stepped out of the bathroom, leaving the door open. I dried all the water from my body, wrapped the towel around me, and then sat on the toilet seat to moisturize my skin. I lotioned my feet first and worked my way up. Tanya walked by.

"I could lotion your back for you."

"Uh...ok...thank you."

I handed her the lotion and tilted my body while still seated. My toes curled into the rug and she had not even touched me yet.

"You should probably stand up and lower your towel so I can get your entire back. You can face the shower if it makes you comfortable."

I stood and lowered my towel, facing the shower and Tanya rubbed lotion into my back starting from the top and stopping right above my behind. I closed my eyes as her fingers ran across my back. She massaged up and down and grazed my neck a few times as she rubbed lotion into my shoulders. I was fully relaxed and forgot where I was until her hands made their way to my breast. I shrieked, dropping my towel, and spinning around.

"What are you doing?!"

"Shhhhh..."

"Tanya, I can't."

"You can't what? You're not doing anything, relax." Tanya pulled me.

3

"Stop it!"

I ran from the bathroom and into my bedroom, not understanding what had just happened. My body had never even reacted to my husband that way. I sat in my room for the rest of the night aroused, confused, and ashamed. Tanya stayed on my mind: her hair, her smile, her hands, and her laugh. The thought of her kept me wet. I thought maybe I should take another shower, but I refused to walk into the hall. I lay back in my bed and switched off the lamp. I opened my legs and placed my middle finger on my clit, massaging it until my juices released and I was sound asleep.

Tanya plagued, what I thought was a wet dream. I had not had one of those in years. My life was too busy to think about sex with anyone, especially a woman. My eyes fluttered opened and there was Tanya right beside me, tracing the inside of my thigh with her fingers. I didn't resist this time. She rolled me onto my other side, so my back could face her. She slid her fingers into my wet pussy, while squeezing my nipples with her free hand. She taunted me, pushing her fingers in and then pulling them back out, only to do it all over again. I let out soft moans as Tanya kissed my neck, back, and shoulders. I dug my fingernails into the sheets and bit down on my pillow as she went deeper and faster, whispering that she wanted to please me into my ear. Tanya said my name over and over again. No one had ever made it sound so sweet. Orgasm took over my body, my toes curled, and I began to cry while trying to fight how intense it was. Tanya whispered "let me feel you Elaine, cum for me," into my ear and I was done. My entire body was numb and my heart raced as I breathed heavily.

"Should I do the same thing to you?"

Tanya laughed. "No, you don't have to."

"Why not?"

She placed her hand over my lip, "You have a lot to learn about being with women. Go to sleep."

She held me close all night as I slept.

~~*~*

It had been seven months since that night and Tanya was now crack to me and without her I went through withdrawals. Every Moment I had away from my family I wrapped myself in her. I still had never made myself comfortable enough to please her the way she pleased me but she never complained. I was starting to believe she got off solely on pleasing me. We had sex a lot, but it wasn't the main factor in the relationship

4

that we developed. Tanya had become my best friend, my diary, and ironically my biggest secret. She never acted differently with my daughter or my husband, so neither of them suspected a thing, but sometimes we were caught being a little too affectionate with one another, but not affectionate enough to be questioned.

The last couple of days Tanya had been acting really different and only with me. She was getting angry with me about everything. If I was a few minutes late picking her up from school we fought, if I didn't answer my cell phone, we fought, if I couldn't hang out with her because I had to be with my husband for a function, we fought. She wanted all of my attention all the time, but that was something I could not provide.

It was 2:30pm and I could see the anger on Tanya's face as I pulled as close to the curb as I could get without blocking the way of other cars. She got in and didn't say a word to me.

"Hello to you too."

"Yeah…hey."

"Seriously? What's up with you? I haven't done you anything."

"You sure about that?" She snapped at me.

"What have I done, Tanya?"

She exhaled and then flipped, "I can't keep doing this with you! Everyday I'm right here listening to you complain, making love to you, and supporting whatever you do, while all I am is some well-kept secret of yours. How long are we supposed to be like this?!"

"I'm married Tanya, *married* and to a reverend at that!"

"That's not my problem neither is it yours. You're a grown woman and you can make decisions for yourself. Don't you want to be with me?"

"I don't know."

"Wow. You don't know? But you know when you want me to fuck you and hide away with you somewhere."

"Tee, please, don't do this right now. I like having you in my life."

"Like? Let me out of this car."

"No."

"LET ME OUT!"

Tanya grabbed for the steering wheel and we fought. I slammed on brakes and we slid into the back of another car at a crossing intersection. No one was hurt, but the other driver was pissed. He hopped out of his vehicle cussing and flailing his arms around in the air. He recognized who I was and calmed down. I gave him my insurance information and pleaded with him not to call the police. It took some convincing, but he got into his vehicle and left without a problem. I had my car towed before police showed up due to some nosey driver who may have called them. The mechanic who worked on our cars for years gave me a loner once I arrived and Tanya and I rode home in silence.

My husband was looking from the window when we pulled up. I was hoping he wasn't home so I didn't have to make up a lie so soon, but there he was opening the door for us to come in. "Where is your car?" he asked.

"I had an accident today."

"Are you okay?"

"Yes baby, calm down, I'm fine."

"Are you okay, Tanya?"

Tanya gave Mitchell and me an ugly look and stomped away.

"What's her problem today?"

"She had a bad day."

She stormed back over to us and shoved me.

"Is that what it is Elaine? I'm having a bad day? Are you sure it's not because the woman I love totally disregards me because she is too afraid to tell her husband that she's fucking me?"

My husband stepped back, "Excuse me? What is she speaking about, Elaine?"

"It must be the accident. I'll get her head checked in the morning." I grabbed her arm to walk her away.

She snatched away from me, "TELL HIM! Tell him the truth. Mitch I have been fucking your wife for the past seven months and I love her, but she is too afraid to love me back because of you."

"Tanya, STOP it!"

"Funny, you never say that when I'm fucking you."

I wanted to hit Tanya in her mouth. My husband grabbed my arm violently, while yelling at Tanya to pack her things and leave our home immediately. Tanya resisted at first, but then he threatened her with the police. She stormed upstairs and started to pack her things. My husband dragged me into his study and slammed the door.

"Let me go!" I yelled and snatched away.

"Elaine, what is wrong with you? Have you lost your mind?"

"No, I haven't but you have putting your damn hands on me."

"Watch your language."

"Oh stop with the holier than thou act! What do you want me to say, Mitch. I fucked up!"

"You sure did. Do you know what I'm going to look like to the congregation if this gets out?"

"You? That's all you seem to care about is yourself. When is the last time you took me somewhere that had nothing to do with church, when is the last time you complimented me Mitch, touched me?!"

"Are you saying this is my fault?"

"I'm saying that I finally feel alive and free. I'm experiencing feelings that I never have."

"That's unnatural, Elaine. God is frowning on you right now. You will burn in hell."

"I guess I'll see you there. You think I'm stupid? I know about you sleeping around when you're *out of town*, I hear the rumors about the women you screw in the church and I also know about you stealing. How do you think the congregation will feel about that huh? Is your sin less than mine?!"

"My sin? You're sleeping with a woman. You think the congregation will care more about what I do? It's your word against mine. Is this what you want? You want to go tit for tat with me? You'll lose. You have nothing without me. You *are* nothing without me. And if you want to make this really ugly, you'll never see our daughter again, so you better decide and quick."

Mitchell left the study, slamming the door behind him. I fell to the floor sobbing uncontrollably. My heart ached, just imagining Tanya walking out the door and it ached even more at the thought of never seeing my daughter again. I didn't know what to do.

~~*~*

I was still on the floor of the study when I woke up the next morning. I got up and walked toward the kitchen because my mouth was dry. Mitchell was having breakfast with our daughter and reading the newspaper. He looked up at me as if nothing had happened. "Good morning." he said calmly.

"Hey."

"You need to go get cleaned up and get dressed."

"Why? Where are we going?"

"Church"

"On a Saturday?"

"Yes, go get dressed."

I did as I was told. All I could think about was Tanya. I hoped she was okay. I hated the way we ended things, but I knew this was best. I had a family to think about and Mitchell was right. I was nothing without him. Tanya had nothing as well and nothing plus nothing is nothing. I dressed nonchalantly and walked downstairs with the same attitude. Mitchell was already waiting in the car. We dropped our daughter off at her friend's house.

"Why aren't we taking her?" I questioned.

Mitchell ignored me and pulled off. We pulled up to a church fifteen minutes later. There were about seven people inside once we got there. He pushed me in as I slowed my step. They stood in a circle with their hands joined together. One of the men spoke up.

"Come on Sister Barnes, we are here to help you."

"Help me? With what?"

"Don't be afraid sister. we all deal with trials and tribulations. It's God's way of testing us. We may fail, but we can try again."

"Mitchell, what is this?"

Mitchell spoke, "you're sick and you need help. They can help you. Tanya is here too."

"What the…"

Tanya emerged from the back with her head down. She looked up at me and I had never seen so much pain. At that very Moment I knew that it was Tanya who I wanted. I needed her. Everything in my mind, body, and soul yearned for her. It was time I took a stand for my own happiness no matter the consequence. My husband pushed me forward toward the other local pastors he had obviously called to put this whole show together. They sang old hymns and prayed out loud trying to cast out the "demons of homosexuality" in Tanya and I. This was a joke to me. How could people seriously believe that gays and lesbians were taken over by some sort of spirit? It's like saying attraction and desire is a disease and if that's the case, then we are all sick, gay and straight alike.

I stood still as they placed anointed oil on my head, pushing me one by one and praying. I could play along with this foolishness too. I threw my hands in the air, while rolling my eyes into my head and shouting thank you Lord. I pushed past the pastors, kicking off my shoes, and running through the pews of the church. I would apologize to God later for acting a fool in his house, but this had to be done. There was a cross in front of the podium at the front of the church, so I ran to it and pretended to pass out. They came over to me, fanning me and I could hear them saying to Tanya that she too could be freed. They lifted me up and carried me out to my husband's truck, lying me down on the back seat. The second he pulled off I sat up and burst into laughter.

"Did you seriously think that was going to work?"

"You are childish Elaine."

8

"Get a grip Mitchell. People are who they are!"

"So what, you're a lesbian? That's the life you want to live?"

"At least they live. You have me in a prison! Who goes to church four times a week? And on top of everything you're a crook, asking the congregation for money they don't have so that we can live this lavish lifestyle and call it all blessings. When God said to have an abundant life he did not mean anything materialistic. God wants ten percent, TEN, of our time, talent, and earnings, nothing more. You're a hypocrite, preaching to these people about their lives but just look at us. Way to throw stones Mitch. You want to do this right now Mr. Preacher man. I have scriptures for days!" I began to pound my fist into my hand, "Leviticus 27:30, Numbers 18:26, Deuteronomy 14:24, 2 Chronicles 31:5, 1 Corinthians 16:1-2..."

"You're the hypocrite! Sleeping with women you are supposed to be helping!"

"Maybe Mitchell, maybe, but you know what, she helped me. I don't have to be bonded by this life, pretending to be someone I'm not. God did not die for our sins and free us to enslave us. He knows that we are not perfect. For God did not send his Son into the world to condemn the world, but to save the world through him. John 3:17 Mitch!"

Mitch was silent. He could have argued with me for years to come about homosexuality, but in his heart he knew all things were measured on the same scale and at the end of the day we all die and are judged separately. We pulled up to our house and went inside. It was no longer a home. I went up to the bedroom and fell over onto the bed and laughed at myself for the way I acted in that church. Mitch left again and I was at peace.

Mitch had not come home for over a month. He called to say that he was fine and he'd be back as soon as he had all his thoughts together. Tanya and I had been talking and she was doing much better. Her grandfather had finally passed after being sick for years and he left her a great deal of money. She used it to get her life in order. She wanted us to be together and something inside of me wanted to be with her too, but I needed to deal with Mitch first.

Tanya and I were laughing at something that had happened to her at school when Mitch walked in the door. I asked to call her back and then hung up. He looked over at me as I sat on the sofa.

"You didn't have to get off of the phone."

"It's fine. We weren't talking about anything."

"You want to step into my office?"

I stood from the sofa and followed him into his study. I didn't feel nervous, but he was being to calm for me. I was used to Mitch being firm, demanding, and even cruel sometimes, but I sensed none of that at this Moment. He left the door opened as he took a seat at his desk.

"Have a seat."

"What is this about Mitch?"

He put his hands together and placed them in his lap, "Well, I had a lot of time to think while I was away and I think we should get a divorce." He pulled the papers from his briefcase.

"Are you sure?"

"Elaine if you aren't happy then I won't hold you here."

"Mitch—"

"Let me say this Elaine before I change my mind. Don't think of me as a reverend right now. I'm a man, a husband."

"Okay."

"You can leave, but you can't live in this state, because of what I have built here. You can have the property in Georgia. I will cover the mortgage, but you will have to pay all your own utilities. You can have your car since it's paid for. You will get all that you are entitled to as far as alimony is concerned and you can have our daughter every summer and any weekend that you want her. I still don't agree with how you are choosing to live your life and until our daughter is old enough to understand that, I feel it is best that I be the primary parent and residence for her. I don't want this to get ugly with lawyers and press."

"So that's my only option?" I asked.

"What else do you need?"

"What about Tanya?"

"What about her?"

"I don't want rules of who can and who can't come over."

"Elaine, you are a grown woman. I just want us out of each other's way. It has gotten ugly enough."

"What will you tell the congregation?"

"Whatever I have to, I am a man of God, so I will not slander your name if that is what you are thinking."

I leaned over the desk, pulling the divorce papers close to me and reading before signing my name to them. I slid them back over to Mitchell and stood from the desk.

"So that's it?"

"I guess so." He took a deep breath. "May I ask a question?"

"Of course Mitchell, don't become a stranger already."

"Did I make you this way?"

He looked as if he wanted to cry and it broke my heart for him to think that he had anything to do with why I loved a woman. I walked over to him and wrapped my arms around him. He tensed up a little then relaxed. We held each other for a long time in silence. I kissed his cheek, leaving my lipstick lingering. I looked into his familiar eyes.

"1 Peter 4:8 Above all, love each other deeply, because love covers over a multitude of sins. I love you Mitchell and I love Tanya. Nothing is your fault. This is just me and I'm happy and you will be happy one day too."

That was the last thing I said to my ex-husband before I packed my bags to start my new life. I placed the picture of us back into my bible and smiled. Tanya walked into the room and leaned down to peck my lips.

"What are you doing in here?"

"Just studying my bible, baby. Are you ready to eat?"

"I'm ready when you are."

I stood from my seat and followed Tanya out of the room. I grabbed her hand and turned her around to kiss her, pulling her body close to mine and kissing her passionately without any guilt in my heart. She was the best decision I had ever made. I saw no sin in the happiness she brought me and I would never understand how other people did.

"Pole Dancing"

That's right nigga throw mama's money on the stage. I dropped to my knees to lift each butt cheek separately as all these trick ass niggas dropped wads of cash on me. Rick Ross's "money make me cum" blared from the speakers of the club as I hopped up and then dropped back down into a split. I turned over on my back to make my ass clap while they all watched me, fantasizing about what it would be like to lick and stick this pussy. Them niggas could keep dreaming. They'd be lucky if they could smell it.

The name's Barbie, I know, not very seductive or stripper like, but it was a real name for somebody like me. I'm not like the rest of these stripper hoes. I have it all. I have everything that other bitches envy. I got book smarts and street sense, so it's more than difficult to pull wool over my Motherfucking eyes. The funny thing is that I don't have a sob story as to why I live this way. My parents were stupid rich, so I was born with a platinum spoon in my mouth, I went to all of the best schools, I wasn't raped or molested or none of that feel sorry for me bullshit. I'm just a trill ass bitch. I do me. I love the rush of the life I live and I wouldn't have it any other way.

I was seventeen years old when I set foot into Addiction. It was being run by this old as pervert Big Norm. He had a thing for young girls and when this fresh pussy stepped through his door, his dick stood taller than me. He licked his lips and took a seat. "So what can I do for you young thang?" he asked, drooling.

"I wanna dance."

"Here? Why? A pretty little thing like you should be in school doing something else with yourself. This place is for those whose options have run out. Where are your parents?"

"Look here you old fuck. I didn't come here for a lecture. I get enough of that shit at home. I'm a straight *A* student at my school and I am well aware of what I want to do with my fucking life. This life is nothing to me. I only get one and I'm going to do with it as I please. Now either you gon let me show you how I twirk this pussy or just let me stop wasting my fucking time."

Big Norm's eyes had gotten big. I guess no one had ever talked to him like that before, especially not a seventeen year old girl. He sat back in his chair with the "dick look" on his face. He motioned for me to follow him out of his office and to the stage. He took a seat and a few of his flunkies sat beside him. I threw my book bag to the side and stepped up onto the stage. He put on that old ass song by LL Cool J "Doin it Wild" or some shit. Fuck it, I'll work that shit anyway. I danced around the pole removing my clothes slowly. I climbed up the pole and slid down upside down with my legs spread eagle making my ass clap. I balanced myself on my hands and I slid to the floor. I was doing a handstand still clapping my ass. I flipped backwards into a split and then he motioned to me that he had seen enough. I hadn't even started fucking myself on stage yet. Oh, well.

Big Norm didn't want to risk being raided by the cops so he wanted me to wait until I made eighteen to start dancing officially. That was cool with me as long as he left those mama-Daddy speeches at the fucking door.

I walked through the dressing room with my bag as all the other strippers stared at me. Some had hate in their eyes because they knew I looked better and probably danced better than they did and others looked at me like a piece of meat, ready to be eaten. I sat my bag down in front of the mirror that was designated for me and I took a seat to make up my face. It was introduction time.

"So you're the new red bone that everyone was ranting and raving about huh?" a stripper approached me and asked.

"Excuse me?"

"Chill ma, I heard nothing, but good things. I'm Essence."

"Barbie."

"Nice to meet you Barbie, so what you doing in a place like this?"

"The same thing you're doing."

"Feisty! I like that. Well, I'm up next, so I gotta go. I hope you come and watch me dance."

Essence was dark as tar and she had two basketballs behind her. Why is it that darker women have to be referred to as Chocolate or Essence? That's some typical ass shit. I paid no mind to her after she walked away. She looked like that "everybody needs to know me" type chick, when in actuality she had no friends or admirers outside of the strip club. I continued to apply my make-up until the stripper next to me started to speak, causing me to fuck up my liner.

14

"Don't pay Essence any mind. She's an attention whore. You'd think she got tired of it with all the niggas out there grabbing her ass all night."

"And who are you?" I snapped.

"I'm Candy." She licked her lips.

Candy was a color I can't describe. She wasn't dark, and she wasn't brown. Her complexion lit up a room and it was clean and clear. She was probably the only stripper in the whole vicinity that had her own eyes, hair, and nails. She was all natural and that shit was appealing to me for some reason. Her voice was soft as she spoke to me. I had to stop myself from watching her lips. I wasn't into women and I didn't want to fall into that statistic that most strippers were gay or bi. I was neither—strictly dickly. Even though I had only had sex with one man, I knew it was what I wanted. They could have that pussy licking shit.

Candy was my guide for the night. She showed me what to do and what not to do. She told me who was who and what was what.

It was a busy night and I wasn't shy for shit. Candy amused herself as she watched niggas cum on themselves, while I gyrated my hips. I went home with three G's in my pocket that night.

~~*~*

Candy had become my best friend in and outside of the club. We hung out on a regular when we weren't taking niggas hard earned money from them. We were the two baddest bitches in the club. Niggas already put us on a pedal stool.

It was another Saturday night. Candy and I decided to leave early so that we could hit up some regular clubs. We were taking her car and we'd come back to get mine later. I walked out first, because she stopped at the bar to talk to the bartender. As I walked toward Candy's car a group of niggas were coming in my direction.

"Here we go."

"Say ma, you leaving already? Where you going can we come with you?"

"Not really."

"Damn why not. We got cake, if your time ain't free."

These niggas wanted more than to just hang out. To me every nigga in or around a strip club was just horny for any wet pussy. It didn't matter what face was attached to it, that's why it was so easy for me to take their money and not give a fuck. If they'd rather throw their hard earned money at me rather than their wife or girlfriend they had at home

15

giving up the pussy for free, then that was more than alright with me. I was getting annoyed by these drunk fools and I had the feeling if they didn't get what they wanted it was going to get ugly. Candy came out of the club and stepped up to meet me.

"What's going on here?"

"We trying to get ya girl to chill."

"She's with me."

All of their mouths dropped as Candy said that. I tried not to look too shocked myself since Candy obviously had some type of plan.

"She with you?"

"Nigga you heard what the fuck I said, she's with me."

"I like girls that like girls."

"Yeah, well that's all we like."

"I don't believe y'all."

He wanted a show and before I knew it Candy had her lips pressed against mine. Her lips were soft. She darted her tongue in and out of my mouth. I closed my eyes and got lost in her kiss.

"Aight, shorty, I respect that. I ain't gon break up ya happy home or whatever, but the dick will be here if y'all ever need it."

The crowd of drunken bastards walked off toward the club. Candy and I fell into laughter and continued to walk to her car. We hit up all the major clubs where the *ballers* hung out and then we headed back to her place. I was too drunk to do anything, but pass out.

The next morning I sat up with a major headache. Candy walked into the bedroom with coffee and a BC. I took it and I just stared at her. I felt a little weird once I was sober, because I remembered her kissing me. She must have sensed the awkwardness.

"Hey Barbie, about last night I didn't mean—"

"—it's okay." I cut her off.

"No, 'cause I know you're not like that."

"It's cool, Candy. At least you're a good kisser."

We both laughed.

"You are too. I um…I liked kissing you. I thought about doing again." Candy stated bashfully.

"Why didn't you?" I couldn't believe what I was saying. Before I could take the words back Candy was up on me kissing me. It felt even better now than it did last night. I sat my cup down on Candy's nightstand and started to kiss her the way she was kissing me. She squeezed my breast and played with my nipples through her fingers and then she removed my clothes. I removed her clothes too. Candy's face between my legs was the sexiest shit I had ever seen in my life. My toes

16

curled as she feasted. She stopped when I came and slid me down on the bed.

"I want you to taste me Barbie."

Candy knew what she wanted. She placed her legs over my face, sitting on it. I stuck my tongue out and Candy rode my tongue until she couldn't take anymore. I had never eaten pussy a day in my life and never intended on it, but after tasting Candy, I never wanted another flavor in my mouth.

~~*~*

I sat up in my bed reading the headline on the front page of the local paper 'Club Owner Found Floating in River.' My first thought was what the fuck? Then I tried to gather my thoughts. *Did that mean that the club was closed down?* I got up and got dressed so that I could pass by the club. We all knew that Big Norm had been involved in some illegal shit, but we never expected to find him dead. Apparently he owed some people some money and he refused to pay up, so they laid his ass out. They had to know a lot about Big Norm to even get close enough to him.

I pulled up to the club and hopped out. When I got to the door, it was unlocked. I walked inside and Peaches, one of the bartenders, was standing at the bar cleaning glasses.

"Hey Peach, wassup?" I approached her.

"Hey girl."

"You heard about what happened?"

"Yeah girl, they woke me up out of my sleep last night, everybody all fucked up about the situation."

"What's gonna happen to the club?"

"His daughter Deon is gonna take over?"

"He has a daughter? How old was the bastard?"

"Bitch who knows, Deon came about when he got one of his employees pregnant. Deon is just some spoiled ass dyke bitch who thinks she can talk to people any type of way. Big Norm just paid her mama to stay the hell away from him. He didn't want too much to do with her or Deon."

"She here now?"

"Yeah, she's in her Daddy's office."

"Oh, have you seen Candy today?"

"Nope."

I walked away from the bar and went to meet my new boss. I knocked and then pushed the door open. Deon sat at her Father's desk in an all white suit. She could not have been her Father's child. I guessed her Mom was a force to be reckoned with because she was a cutie. I lost my words as I stepped in.

"Um excuse me?" I knocked to get her attention.

"Hey, you are?" she looked up.

"Barbie."

"Oh, you're Barbie. Beautiful." she eyed me lustfully.

"Thank you. So you're taking over huh? I just thought I'd come in and introduce myself. I'm sorry about your Dad."

"Yep I'm the new boss and fuck him. He got what he deserved. All we had was a check to check relationship anyway."

Deon was harsh with her words. She clearly didn't give a fuck about nothing but money and bitches. Even though she had not met her Father, she definitely had his personality. She wasn't ugly like him, but that mouth would make you think twice. After I was done making conversation, I walked out of the office to see if I could find Candy. I hadn't seen her in almost three days.

As I walked into the dressing room I heard voices. One of them was Candy. I knew her voice from anywhere. I peaked in to catch the voice of the other person and when I looked in I saw Essence through a mirror. Candy spoke first.

"I told you I was gonna get that bitch, now give me my fucking money."

"We are too much alike. I hate you."

"You love me, now come here and gimme that mouth."

I didn't know what to think or how to feel. I had been played. These bitches made a bet on who would fuck me and I fell for their game. I wanted to beat the shit out of both of them right there, but I had to hear what else they were saying. Candy and Essence stopped kissing and Essence started talking.

"I hated you spending all that time with her."

"Essence, I don't have time for that jealous bullshit, we need to talk about this other shit."

"Now?"

"Yes now."

"Okay then, talk."

"Did you do what I told you to do?"

"I was going to, but Big Norm's daughter Deon is in the office. I didn't even know he had a daughter."

"What? Fuck! Well looks like I'm going to have to lay her ass out too. Big Norm was easy since he thinks with is dick, but this bitch is gonna give me problems."

"So what do you want me to do?"

"You know what to do."

Candy had lured Big Norm to a park and shot him in his car after learning all his safe codes and bank information. She and Essence were going to rob him blind and then skip town, but the stupid bitch didn't do her homework, because she didn't know that Big Norm had a daughter. Everything was switched over to Deon and she had changed the access codes and passwords, making everything inaccessible to Candy and Essence. It was now Essence's turn to do the seducing since it would be too obvious if Candy got close to the daughter as well. I eased back as quietly as I could because I didn't want to get caught listening. I didn't need to be added to their hit list. Those bitches were dirty.

~~*~*

Deon had decided that some changes needed to be made to the club and that included letting a few of the employees go. It seemed to me that she was getting rid of all her Father's people to put her own on. She decided that all the dancers should audition again, which was some bullshit if you asked me. I felt like she was just being a pervert like her Father. She had scheduled each girl to come in on a different day and today was mine.

I walked into Addiction and spotted no one in clear sight so I walked to the back into Deon's office. She was digging through a safe with her back turned to the door wearing only jeans and a t-shirt opposed to the suits I had been seeing her in. She was startled when I walked in.

"You don't know what knocking is?" she asked.

"Lock the door if you want me to knock."

She laughed. "Barbie right?"

"That would be me. Can we get this over with?"

"You in a rush?"

"Not really but I'd rather be at home doing nothing than standing in this dump."

"You work at this dump, watch it."

"And? Are you going to fire me?"

"They told me about your fly ass mouth." Deon smirked and walked over to me removing my overnight bag from my shoulder. "You're gorgeous you know that?" She said while licking her lips, circling me, and eyeing me from head to toe.

I stood completely still. "I thought I was here for an audition. You're wasting my time."

"Dance." She pushed up against me.

"Right here?"

"Yeah."

Deon was fucking with me and it was kind of turning me on. Her arrogance was more sexy than appalling, but no one beat me in the arrogant department. I grabbed her hand and pulled her toward her desk, pushing her back so she could lean on it. I turned around and pushed my ass against her and grinded slowly, while bending over. She placed her hands on my waist, but I slapped them away. "No touching the dancers."

I rocked back and forth as if a dick were inside of me and I was throwing it back. She bit her lip. I stood straight up, unbuttoning my jeans and pulling them down, right beneath my ass, so I could clap it for her. She was about to see why I was her Daddy's number one dancer. As I bent down further Deon grabbed my pussy from behind and rubbed my clit through my thong. I grabbed the chair in front of me releasing moans as she slid my thong to the side to feel my flesh against her fingers.

As we were getting deeper into our session the door swung open and there stood Essence's black ass, watching us. Deon rushed to the back of her desk and I pulled my jeans up, smiling at Essence because I knew that she was fucking with Deon. I picked my bag up off the floor and turned to walk out of the door. Essence bumped my shoulder her.

Bitch flew from my lips, but I wasn't salty. I kept walking. I walked to the end of the hall and Essence slammed the door. I kicked off my shoes and ran back on my tip toes to listen to their conversation. Essence was yelling.

"So, that's what you doing?"

"Essence, get back with all that!"

"No! That's so fucked up Dee. I thought I you was really feeling me and I told you about that bitch. She set up Big Norm and now she out to get you."

My mouth dropped. I was in disbelief. This bitch was about to pin all this bullshit on me. I walked back down the hall and put my shoes on just before walking out to my car. Candy was pulling up as I jumped inside my vehicle. I put my shades on and rolled my windows down, pretending that she wasn't even there. After Candy and I fucked she didn't say anything else to me and of course I had learned why and I wasn't salty about that either. I didn't expect anything more or less from a stripper with a dead body under her belt. She rolled down her window and yelled out to me.

"Wassup, Barbie?"

"Chillin."

"Why you acting?"

"I could ask you the same thing."

"I'm sorry ma I just been tied up."

"I feel you. I have to go though so, hit me up."

"You just auditioned?"

I nodded my head yes then backed out to pull off, but a light bulb went off in my head so I stopped behind Candy's car and she hopped out.

"You need something baby girl?"

"I need to holla at you about some shit real quick."

"Word?"

"Yeah, so how about you get in."

Candy hopped in and pulled out of the lot, making the block so I could talk to her without the risk of Essence coming out of the building.

"So, what you have to talk to me about?" she inquired.

"When I was leaving just a minute ago I overheard Essence telling Deon that you set Big Norm up."

"Are you fucking serious?"

"As Big Norm's death."

"That ugly, backstabbing, greedy bitch!"

"Yeah, I wasn't going to tell you at first since you've been acting funny with me, but I thought that was some real fucked up shit for her to be saying."

"Good looking out."

I dropped Candy back off at her car and pulled off with a smile on my face. Candy hopped into her car and her tires screeched as she sped off behind me and then passed me up to pull out of the lot.

~~*~*

Candy had disappeared off the face of the Earth. She had not come to work, she disconnected her phone, and her apartment was empty. Essence had been looking for her high and low, but was unsuccessful in her hunt. She was looking real stupid without her counterpart Candy to follow around. Essence talked to no one because her nerves were bad after we all heard the police were looking for Candy for Big Norm's murder and they stated that it was possible she had an accomplice because that same night his house was robbed.

I had done my final dance of the night and went to the back of the dressing room to collect all my things. I dressed and grabbed my bag to leave the club. Essence was standing outside talking to a customer who lingered after as I walked to my car. The nasty bitch was probably going to fuck him for some extra cash. As I opened my door I saw Candy run up on Essence and hit her hard across the face, knocking her to the ground. "Bitch you set me up! You thought I was going to let you get away with that shit ho?"

She sat on top of Candy coming down on her face over and over again as a crowd formed around them. Essence tried to fight back, but it was almost pointless as Candy rammed her head into the concrete. I called the police to report the fight and then I got out of the car to watch Candy beat Essence damn near into a coma. She had just added an assault charge to her murder charge.

Deon and her body guards came running over to stop the fight and the police pulled up, rushing to grab Candy before she could flee. Candy was beautiful, but the bitch wasn't that bright. Her fingerprints had been found all over Big Norm's car and a strand of her hair was found on his pants which meant the trick-bitch sucked his dick before taking his life. The cops arrested them. I stood to the side where Candy could see me and I winked and smiled at her as she passed me. I hoped the money she bet on fucking me was enough to put money on her books for the rest of her life. Basic bitch.

"Addictive Behavior"

A real woman doesn't give up. That's what I said over and over again in my mind, as Magic made it harder for me to move, squeezing me tighter and begging me not to leave. My arms hung stiffly at my sides, as I tried to wiggle my shoulders from her grip. *"Please, please, please,"* is what she whispered into my ear, but my sympathy for her had finally run out. I was sick of her anger, I was sick of being broke, and I was deathly tired of her drinking. I was addicted to her and she was addicted to alcohol. She said she loved me, but that was hard to believe. I pushed her off of me and continued to walk out the door, because I knew that if I didn't, I'd be right back in her arms, crying and telling her that she would be okay and we would be okay. It was the lie I had to tell to even myself just to make it through every day.

I unlocked my doors and opened them to toss my bags inside and whatever didn't fit was stuffed in the trunk. Magic ran up to my car opening the doors and pulling my bags out, "Lana please!" she yelled.

"Magic stop it!" I picked up my bags. "Why do you have to create a scene?"

"If I wasn't out here creating a scene you would think that I didn't give a fuck. I give a fuck!"

"It's too late. I'm leaving."

"I'm trying to change!"

"How many times have you said that? Get your shit together and get at me. Now stop pulling my shit out of the car before I call the cops on you. You know you already have two strikes."

"You wouldn't do that."

I pulled my cell phone from my purse to dial nine and one just to show her that I was serious. I'd press the last *one* if I had to. She backed away from the car and I replaced all my things. I got into the driver's side, started the engine, and took one last look at Magic before backing out of the driveway. She yelled I loved you and I stopped, taking another look at her. I pulled my sun glasses from my purse and pulled off without looking back. The trip down memory lane started instantly in my mind.

~~*~*

23

Six Years Earlier

I handed out water to all the people walking for National AIDS Awareness Day. My sister was supposed to be here doing this, but got called in last minute to work. She called and got me out of bed because I was off on Saturdays. When you did hair you could make your own schedule. I was still working on getting my license, so that I could work in a shop and get more clients. I eventually wanted to own my own shop, but I had a serious case of procrastination going on in my life.

I bent down to grab another bottle of water when I heard an enticing voice ask if I could get them a bottle from the bottom of the cooler. I looked up to see the most beautiful stud I had ever laid my eyes on. She stood about 5'8 and a half, her hair was brown and pulled back into a ponytail. She had skin the color of sand and her lips were thick and juicy. I dug down a little deeper into the cooler to retrieve a bottle of water for her and then handed it to her. "What difference does it make, if it's from the top or the bottom?"

"The ones at the bottom are cooler."

"I think you just wanted to be picky."

"Damn, are they giving you a hard time around here about the temperature of free water now?"

"No, just certain people."

"Lucky me then," she winked at me and laughed. "Did you do the walk?"

"No, my sister volunteers every year to keep the participants hydrated, but she had to work this year so here I am." I lifted my hand to block the sun from over my eyes. "You walk every year?" I asked.

"Actually no, this is my first time. I just lost a family member to AIDS and thought I'd support the cause."

"You had to lose someone to support it?"

"You really are giving me a hard time."

I smiled. "Well, I hope that water was cool enough for you. Enjoy the rest of your day."

She smiled back and poured the rest of the water over her head. "You do the same."

Magic walked off and I sighed deeply, needing to exhale because her sexiness too my breath, even walking away. I could see her toned and cut body through the shirt and basketball shorts that she wore. I shook my head and thanked God for his beautiful creations and allowing me to be alive to lay eyes on them.

As the crowd dwindled down I packed up what was left of the refreshments that my sister sent to the event. I carried as much stuff as I could, while dragging the cooler behind me to my car. I almost dropped everything in my hands, but Magic ran over to help me catch it all.

"Thank you." I expressed my gratitude.

"You're welcome, even though you were mean to me earlier."

I smiled. "I was not being mean."

She took everything from my hands and walked with me to my car, helping me to place everything inside. I popped my trunk to lift the cooler into it.

"Let me get that for you."

"Well, aren't you a gentle woman."

"I try."

There was an awkward silence between us as we smiled childishly at one another.

"Well I better get going it was nice meeting you, um…" I reached out my hand to shake hers.

She grabbed my hand. "Majorie Russell, but my friends call me Magic, and you are?"

"Lana Parker. Do I dare ask why they call you Magic?"

"I'm a boxer. It's just a name I picked up."

I thought to myself *that explains why you're so fucking sexy* while I eyed her from head to toe. I gave her one more smile and walked around to get into my car and she walked behind me opening my car door.

"This may be crazy, but are you free later?"

"Are you about to ask me out?"

"I mean, yes or no, depending on what you might say. I mean, I don't know your preference or anything. I just want to know you."

I blushed, "Where did you want to go?"

"Well they just opened this Mexican restaurant near my house and I wanted to try it, but I didn't want to go alone."

"Sounds good. Count me in."

"You want to take my number or give me yours?"

I pulled a pen from my glove compartment, and then dug for an old receipt in my car to write my number down. She closed my door for me and I pulled off smiling from ear to ear. It had been a long time since I was asked out on a date.

~~*~*

I had to pick Magic up for 7pm. I didn't want to over dress so I put on some jeans, a nice top that showed off my back and a little cleavage, and pair of simple black pumps. It took me over two hours to get dressed, but I had to look perfect or as close to it as I could get since she had seen me in my sweats, looking a terrible mess in my opinion. I didn't want her to know where I lived just yet, so I told her we would take my car.

I pulled up at Magic's door at 6:45pm on the dot. She still lived with her Mother and she was twenty-two. I gave her a free pass since I required anyone that I dated to be on their own at least by twenty-five. I gave people a hard time because I was twenty-two and on my own, but I learned that I had to cut people a little bit of slack. I cut off the engine and checked my lips in the mirror one more time before walking up to knock on the door. Her Mother answered smiling widely at me.

"Aren't you pretty! Come on in honey, Majorie, will be down in a second."

I stepped inside and followed her to the living room to take a seat to wait for Majorie. She still had fifteen minutes. Her Mother offered me every beverage under the sun. I smiled and said no thank you, using the manners I was raised with. Magic emerged from upstairs looking ten times finer than she did when she was all sweaty. I bit down on my bottom lip as I watched her come down in her black button down and jeans. I was impressed. She reached for my hand to raise me from the sofa, "Are you ready?" she asked.

"Yes." I said goodbye to Magic's Mother, kissing her on the cheek and then we walked out to my car. I handed Magic the keys.

"You're trusting me to drive?"

"You can drive, can't you?"

"Yeah."

"Well, I'm trusting you and besides you may as well, since you know where we're going and I don't."

Magic walked around to my side unlocking and opening the door for me then getting in on the driver's side. She leaned her seat back, adjusted the mirror, locked her seatbelt, and we were off.

The restaurant was literally up the street. We were there in a matter of minutes. She opened my door once again and at that point I was convinced that she was not pretending to be the chivalrous type just to impress me. My hands did not touch a door handle in her presence. She probably would have pulled out my chair once we were seated, but the waitress took us to a booth instead of a table.

There was a live band in the restaurant, singing in Spanish and playing mellow music, the service was great, and the food was even better. It was the perfect first date. We laughed, we talked about politics, we talked about family, we talked about religion, we talked about job security, we talked about children, and we talked about the possibility of us.

After dinner Magic and I took a walk on the river bend because we were not ready to part ways just yet. I was going to walk along the side where the water was, but she pulled me to the other side saying she'd rather her fall in if anything happened. Her gesture made me smile. She reached for my hand, locking her fingers between mine, waiting on me to protest, but I never did. I had butterflies in my stomach, and I had not had that feeling since I was teenager. Magic was the perfect nickname for her.

I dropped her off and she kissed my forehead before heading inside. She was definitely old school since she didn't attempt to kiss me on the first date. I was so used to women rushing everything. Magic was not that type of woman. She wanted something real so she wanted to take her time to make sure that she got just that.

I rode home smiling like I had just won the lottery. I switched on the lamp in my living room then checked my phone for missed calls. I had placed my phone on silent to give Magic my undivided attention and she had done the same. My phone read three missed calls, two of which were from my sister and the other was from Magic. They both had left voicemails.

New Message 1
Bitch why you not answering your damn phone? You never told me how the walk was and when I can come get the stuff that was left. You better call me in the morning. BYE!

New Message 2
Hey Lana, it's Magic. I know that you just left from here, but I just wanted to tell you that I really enjoyed our date and I would love to spend more time with you, but of course I don't want to rush anything so you let me know what works for you. We can go as slow as you want to. I don't know what it is about you, but I feel like you may be exactly what I've been longing for and this is just the beginning. I hope you sleep peacefully and make sure you say your prayers. Goodnight beautiful.

27

I hit nine on my phone to save the message. She was knocking me down and I didn't want to be picked up.

I woke up to a knock on the door. It was a delivery man holding a bouquet of pink roses. I signed for them and pulled the card out to read it, *'If actions speak louder than words then this is my way of shouting. I love you beautiful. I'll see you in a few. Magic'*.

It had been an entire year and Magic and I were as happy as we were the day that we met. She was moving out of her Mom's place and into mine. We wanted to wait before sharing our bodies with each other and that's exactly what we did. We kept ourselves occupied with other activities so we would barely think about it. We shopped together, wrote poetry together, enjoyed plays, concerts, movie nights, book readings, spoken word events, picnics, bars, pool halls, reggae clubs, occasional smoke sessions when she wasn't boxing, random slow dance Moments, lots of pillow talk, long make out sessions, and all night phone conversations when she was away. She was the woman of my dreams.

I taped up another box and sat it to the side as Magic walked into the room with more stuff that needed to be packed.

"To say that you only reside in one room of this house you sure do have a lot of shit." I teased.

"This stuff was in the basement."

"You really need all this?"

"Hush girl." she tossed socks at me.

It took us over four hours to pack and move all of Magic's things to my place. We fell out on the floor, tired, since we didn't have any help. There was no way that stuff was getting organized that night. Magic took her shower first and I went in after her. She sat in the bed reading, while she waited for me to join her. I walked into the room, wearing black shorts and a baby white t-shirt. She looked up from her book. "Are you trying to break me?"

I laughed. "How would I be trying to do that?" I said sitting on the bed next to her.

"You should have just come in here naked." she said while tossing her book on the floor and grabbing me around the waist and pulling. "Come here."

I pushed the covers from over Magic and straddled her, resting my arms on her shoulders and grabbing her ears. She looked up at me, "Give me a kiss."

I licked Magic's lips before pulling her bottom lip into my mouth and sucking on it. I slid my tongue into her mouth and kissed her slowly and she held onto me tight. I stopped and fell out laughing. She shook her head at me.

"You are such a tease."

"Whatever. Hey! You should teach me how to box."

"Alright ball up your fist." Magic held her hands up with her palms facing me.

I held my fist up in front of me.

"Hold them up higher. You have to protect your face and keep your chin down."

I raised my fist up, "What now?"

"Hit my hands as hard as you can."

I punched at Magic's hands.

"You hit like a girl."

"Well, duh." I laughed.

I hit her hands again and she tapped my face like she was slapping me. I sat with my mouth open then jumped at her. She rolled me over on my back and leaned over me. The smile on Magic's face faded as she locked eyes with mine. She leaned down, kissing me like it was the first time all over again. She eased her hand under my shirt while still kissing me, running her hands across my stomach from side to side. I breathed deeply and she stopped.

"I'm trying to resist, but you are so tempting."

"I wasn't trying to be." I said clearly lying.

"Can I just eat your pussy, please? We don't have to do anything else."

Magic had already started tugging at my shorts before I could answer. She took my silence as a yes and removed my shorts and panties from my love below. "Open up," she said while easing down to position herself between my legs. Magic bit the inside of my right thigh then licked in circles slowly. She bit down on my left thigh and licked in even slower circles. She sucked on each one of my lips, and then licked slowly to the middle. Her tongue slid up and then down slowly and my wetness leaked into the moisture of her mouth. I placed my hands in her hair, pulling as she vibrated her tongue on my clit. Her tongued flicked back and forth and then moved in circles. I moaned and my toes curled as I thought to myself that this was definitely worth the wait. Magic's tongue hung onto my clit until I orgasm-ed in her mouth. I grabbed a pillow, muffling my moans and biting down on it as my legs locked from the sensation that shot through every molecule that made me, me. She moved up wiping my juices from her face.

"You ok."

I tried to catch my breath, "Yes."

She laughed and then hopped out of bed to brush her teeth. She came back and snuggled against me, kissing the back of my neck. "You taste good. I'd lick you all night."

"I wouldn't stop you."

"Oh Yeah?" she slid her hand between my closed legs from behind, splitting my uncovered lips with her fingers and massaging my still wet pussy.

We couldn't resist. We made love.

~~*~*

The first six months of our domesticated life was amazing. We made love non-stop like two newlyweds. I loved having her there and I wanted us that way forever, but of course there is always that pivotal Moment when love is tested and today was that moment for us as Magic rushed in with a split lip, black eye, and busted knuckles. Vulgar language flew from her lips as she swung and kicked at the air. I stood from the sofa as she walked in and walked over to her.

"What happened to your face?" I grabbed her chin to make her look at me.

"Some stupid nigga, man."

"Baby, you're not supposed to fight on the street."

She slapped my hand down from her face, "Don't you think I fucking know that?"

"Don't get an attitude with me," I stomped back over to the sofa plopping down on it.

Magic went on a rant about going to see her Mom. Her stepdad was there and they did not have the best relationship. She had resented him from the time she was little because he used to molest her. He had moved out when her Mom found out, since that was his only other option if he didn't want to go to jail. He had just recently moved back in after learning that Magic had left. I didn't understand how her Mom would allow him to even come back after knowing something like that. The desperation of some women sickened me, but it was not my place to say a word about Magic's Mother, and I didn't.

She said that she walked in and he was sitting on the sofa with a beer in hand. She tried to ignore him when he called out to her asking if she couldn't speak and when she didn't respond he walked up behind her and grabbed her arm, trying to turn her around. She turned around and hit him and the scuffle began. Her Mother ran in to attempt to stop it, but couldn't so she yelled she was calling the police and Magic ran out of the house before they could get there. I shook my head as I listened to her yell.

"Did you really have to hit him Magic?"

"He shouldn't have grabbed me. Now my career could be over!"

"That's your own fault. You don't know how to avoid a fucking fight?"

"I don't need a lecture from you right now, Lana."

"I'm not supposed to tell you how irresponsible it was for you to be street fighting when you put everything at risk?"

"Shut the fuck up!"

"What? You want to hit me too?" I stood to get in her face.

She pushed me out of her way and headed for the door, "Move." She walked out of the door, slamming it behind her and I shook my head. I needed a cigarette and I had not smoked one of those in years. I couldn't go get one even if I wanted to because we only had one car — mine and she had taken off in it. I settled for the cookies and cream ice cream that was in our freezer. Since I couldn't indulge in nicotine I'd just indulge in junk food.

I sat up until three a.m., waiting on Magic to get home. I flipped through channel after channel and tried to read every book we owned, but it was hard to concentrate not knowing where she was and if she was okay. I hoped that she had not gotten into another fight. My worry started to turn into anger as I heard keys jingle at the door. I walked to the door and opened it and Magic fell over. She had clearly been sitting at a bar all night from the loud stench of alcohol seeping through her pores. She laughed after hitting the floor and grabbed at my legs to pull herself up.

"Hey baby, did you miss me?" She slurred.

I kicked her off me, "Don't touch me."

"Come here. I missed you." She stood to her and feet, pulling me.

Magic pulled me close to her and her breath reeked of hard liquor. She tried to stick her tongue in my mouth, but I turned my head, pushing for her to let me go. It was unattractive and disgusting to see her this way. She walked over to the sofa after giving up on getting me to kiss her and passed out fully clothed. I walked over to her, removing her shoes and as much of her clothing as I could, since she was much heavier than I was. I placed a blanket over her and left her to sleep. She'd pay with a hangover in the morning.

I woke up to Magic lying next to me with her hand in her boxers and someone knocking loudly at the door.

"I'm coming!" I yelled.

I hit the pillow a few times, aggravated at my lack of sleep and then walked to the front door. I opened the door to see two uniformed cops with their hands on their belts.

"I'm sorry to wake you ma'am, but does a Majorie Russell live here?"

"Yes, what's this about?"

"A domestic charge is being filed against her and we need her to come with us."

I took a deep breath and dropped my head, knowing that this would happen. I walked into the bedroom and shook Magic to wake her up.

"Baby, get up."

She fanned me away.

"MAJORIE GET UP!" I needed her to wake up and leave voluntarily so that the cops wouldn't come in and drag her out. Before I could finish my thoughts, the officers had come in and started to pull her from the bed. "I said I was getting her."

The officers completely disregarded me, pulling Magic from the bed and cuffing her. She didn't fight because she was in enough trouble. She looked at me and told me to call her Mom. Our happily ever after was shattering.

Court date after court date, I was drained, aggravated, disappointed, and depressed. They gave Magic two years, which was the max for a domestic charge in the third degree. She would have had less time had she not been a licensed fighter, but the judge expected her to know better and called himself making an example of her so, for two years all I did was cry, work, clean, eat, sleep, and write her letters.

In my mind every relationship had to be tested and this was ours. I just wanted to pass it. I missed her scent, her kiss, her sex, her voice on a daily, the touch of her hand, just the very essence of her. I stared at pictures of us often and sprayed our sheets with her cologne and every day it was hard to pull myself from our bed. Two years felt like a lifetime and today she would be released.

My heart pounded as I waited for them to release her from the gates. I had not touched her skin in so long. She never wanted me to visit her because she didn't want me to see her that way, so I suffered without at least her temporary presence. I jumped from the driver's side once she emerged and jumped into her arms. She held onto me tight. We embraced for a long while before pulling off to go home — home, that sounded nice.

I cooked Magic a large dinner and we sat around the table with candles lit, just staring at each other and eating. She looked into my eyes. "I missed you so much."

"I missed you too," I smiled. "So what now?"

"I guess I better start looking for a job, since boxing is over for me."

"Why don't you go back to school?"

"I thought about that."

"Well, I'll support whatever you choose to do."

"I don't deserve you."

"Don't say that," I wiped my mouth and stood from the table, walking over to straddle Magic and kiss her. She held me in her lap and my soul was at peace again.

~~*~*

Magic had changed. She was not the same ambitious girl that I had met who had it all together and figured out. She did get up to look for jobs the day after she was released and she even managed to land two within a year, but she lost them both; the first one because of her temper and the other because of falsified documents. Magic had not told me that she never graduated high school and had no diploma and to make matters worse she didn't possess a GED either. I had no idea who she was as she came home night after night drunk, trying to fuck her pain away into my flesh. It had become routine for me to undress her and bathe her. She never made it past the living room. I just started keeping pillows and blankets in there and every morning I handed her a BC powder and a glass of water to dead her headaches.

My tears were back and this time they were back because I was watching her fall apart and not because I longed for her. I had much rather been crying from void. This new addiction she had was tearing us apart. She was starting to just feel sorry for herself and make excuses as to why she couldn't make anything good happen in her life. She even went as far as saying that there was no God and that cracked my heart.

33

I got a break twice when she was locked up for violating parole. They gave her thirty days each time. The break was nice, but her court fees were killing my pockets. Our bills were backed up by three months and stress had become my first name, exhausted was my last. I was about ready to have it legally changed to *fed up*.

I spent hours at a time at my sister's apartment because I was starting to even dread going home. I had even started taking my clients over there. Today was one of those days that I had been gone all day and now it was time to go home. I pulled up to our house and there were cars parked in front and on our lawn. I had to park across the street. I unlocked the door and the house was filled with weed smoke and men screaming at the television, watching a boxing match. I was dog tired and aggravated just from standing on my feet and now I had to deal with this. I walked past all the noise and went into the kitchen to grab a bottle of water and there wasn't any. They had drank everything and eaten everything. She was really trying to set off my fuses. I took a deep breath and walked into our bedroom picking up a pillow from our bed and screaming into it. I sat the pillow down and placed all my things on our dresser. I undressed and took a long relaxing bubble bath. I brought the little CD player that we owned into the bathroom and laid back while Sade's No Ordinary Love soothed me. I slept peacefully that night.

I woke up the next morning ready to start my day. I was completely relaxed. I walked into the bathroom to brush my teeth and wash my face, but when I flipped the switch the light didn't come on. I flipped it over and over to make sure I wasn't going crazy. I walked into our bedroom and flipped the switch and that one did not come on either. Our lights had been turned off. There went my mood. I stomped into the living room and popped Magic on the legs to wake her up because of course; she was passed out from being drunk.

"Majorie, get up!"

"Huh? What?"

"Did you pay the light bill?"

"Shit, no babe, I'm sorry."

"Our lights are off. Where is the money?"

"I needed beer and food for the fight party last night."

"Majorie, tell me you didn't spend our fucking light bill money on alcohol and junk!"

"Babe, I didn't know it was due right away."

"Why the fuck does that even matter? I told you to pay it yesterday! You should have assumed that that was when it was due!" I punched her in the leg and stomped off.

I brushed my teeth and dressed in the dark and then left to continue on about my day. She could sit her ass in a dark house all day for all I cared. I went over to my sister's to wait on my clients and while I waited I called the light bill company to set up a payment plan. My sister loaned me the money to at least get the lights cut back on and told me to pay her back whenever I could. I stayed at my sister's house until one in the morning and I still was not ready to go home and look at Magic's face. Something had to give.

I walked in at almost two in the morning and to my surprise she was awake and sober. She stood as I entered.

"Can we talk?"

"About what?" I asked nonchalantly.

"Us…everything."

"I'm listening," I stood by the door.

"Come here," she reached out her hand from the other side of the room.

I walked over to her and we sat down on the sofa.

"Lana, I'm sorry. I know that you're stressed and tired of me not making any contributions."

"Keep talking," I said with an attitude.

"Please don't use that tone with me."

"What tone should I use?"

"This is still me Lana, beneath all this bullshit I've been dealing with, it's still me. I just have to get myself together again and I'm asking that you not give up on me just yet."

I sat silent and looked into her eyes. I knew that the woman I fell in love with still harbored inside of her, but I needed her to come out. "You have to go to AA or something for me to even believe you, because your drinking has turned abusive."

"Ok, I'll do it."

Magic pulled me into her and I wrapped my arms around her and started crying. She had not held me in so long, because she was always drunk and holding onto her bottle or the pillows on the sofa. I hoped that the person I fell in love with was here to stay and she wasn't just talking.

~~*~*

Present Day

I broke down into tears as I pulled off from the building where I had dropped Magic off every day for the last two weeks. She was not standing outside in her usual spot where I picked her up.

I had walked inside and saw the lady who conducted the meetings and she smiled at me.

"Hey, I haven't seen you in awhile."

"Yeah, I kind of come and go."

"What can I do for you?"

"I'm looking for Majorie, she wasn't standing outside."

"Majorie? I haven't seen her since the first meeting. Is there something wrong?"

"No, not at all. Thank you," I cracked a fake smile.

That was the final straw. Majorie did not want to change and I could not continue to enable her. I had made up my mind that there was nothing she could say to me to make me stay and if that wasn't confirmation enough I came home to an eviction notice on the door. She begged all night and cried but there was not a bone in my body that felt anything. I was angry.

I drove slowly. I didn't want to give up on Majorie but she had given up on herself. I came to a stop sign at the end of our block and already the idea of her absence was haunting me. I wanted the bad times to push down on the gas pedal and force me to keep going. Tears started to form and my heart got heavy. I whispered to myself, "don't look back Lana," while gripping the steering wheel. I looked into my rearview mirror anyway. That's not technically looking back is it? Magic was running up the street toward my car, waving her hands in the air and screaming "Lana please come back!" I put my car in park and opened my door and jumped out to run to meet her half-way. We grabbed onto each other tight.

"Lana I love you, I'm in love with you and I won't give you up. Please don't do this." she cried.

I had never seen Magic cry not even when she had went to jail. It did something to my heart and in a way it made me feel that maybe things could change and she was really being sincere. We walked to my car and she got in on the driver's side to bring us back to the house that we had thirty days to vacate. Our times were hard right now, but they were ours. Magic was my addiction and if the way she loved alcohol was the way that I loved her then only death would end us. This was my love and you don't give up on that right?

"The D in Drama"

I watched through my bedroom door as another stud fucked my woman. The woman I had lived to love for the last six years. We had been together since high school and for me it was love at first sight as this fresh face graced my presence. It was our eleventh grade year when she set foot in my classroom. I was sitting to the back with my head down as my history teacher lectured. That class was so damn boring, but when *she* walked in I could have sworn I saw a bright light. She was 5'6", shoulder length, jet black hair, pink lips, green eyes, just a bad ass redbone. Ma had it all. I thought I was dreaming. I sat up in my seat, wondering what her voice sounded like and what her hands felt like. Were they as soft as her look? She sat in the middle of the room and joined in on the lecture. I watched her as she dug through her backpack for a pen and notebook. She was graceful with everything that she did.

The next day in class I took a peek at the roll to see what her name was, Rose Anderson. She damn sure was just as beautiful as a rose. Pulling her wouldn't be a problem unless she was straight, but then again I was known for turning the straight ones out. They took one look at my light skin and hazel eyes and they were automatically curious. The lucky ones got to pull my dreads, which was few and far between.

Rose sat in her same seat and I sat in mine. I had a great view of her and those long legs.

Rose never said a word to me or even looked twice at me and before I knew it the first semester was over. I had given up on getting her because it was more than obvious that she was straight. Rumor had it that she was dating some dude in college and she was head over hills for the cat.

The first day of the second semester after the holidays, Rose wasn't in class in her seat like usual. It bothered me a little but I shook it off as I positioned myself to do what I always did in class —sleep. Fifteen minutes had gone by and nature was calling. I raised my hand and the teacher motioned for me to go use the restroom. He knew I wasn't listening anyway. I grabbed the hall pass and sprinted out the door to the restroom.

People were roaming the hall, as I ran through it. I had to go bad. Dudes looked at me stupid as I entered the girl's restroom. I had been going to school with most of these same cats since elementary and they still seemed shocked when they saw me walk into the ladies restroom to piss— fucking idiots. Just because I wore men's clothing didn't make me a man. Now if I had walked into the men's restroom, they'd all be behind me, staring like a bunch of fucking vouchers, and giggling like bitches, because I got a pussy between my legs.

I squatted to relieve myself, making sure not to touch the seat, wiped, and then flushed the toilet with my foot. I never touched the handle. I stepped out to wash my hands, and I heard sobbing coming from one of the stalls. I washed, rinsed, and dried, before knocking on the door where the crying was coming from.

"Hey, you ok in there." I asked.

"Yes, I'm fine."

"Don't sound like it ma. You want to talk about it?"

"Not really."

"I think you should. You might feel better."

"Is that right Dr. Phil?"

"Look, I'm just tryna help. You the dumbass, sitting in a stall, bawling like a bitch."

The door to the bathroom stall swung open and there stood Rose with bloodshot eyes. She had tissue in her hand and her hair was everywhere. She looked as though she had jumped straight out of bed and into her car without so much as brushing her teeth.

"Who the fuck you calling a bitch?" she charged.

"Man calm down, you got smart with me first and I was just being nice. I'm not usually nice."

Rose pushed past me and went over to the sink to flush her face with water. She stood to dry it and then turned back to me. "I'm sorry Snapps."

I was shocked that she knew my name. Everyone called me Snapps because I was known for going off on a motherfucka. I preferred it anyway because my Mom had to be smoking dope when she named me Sasha Adams, which was some girly ass shit. Maybe if she had known she was carrying a baby stud, she would have reconsidered.

"You're in my history class right?" Rose asked.

"Yeah."

"Did the teacher send you to look for me?"

"No, I had to piss."

"Oh."

"So, you ready to tell me what or *who* got you like this?" I inquired.

38

"My boyfriend broke up with me last night. I've been crying ever since. He says it's not me, but I know better. He's probably fucking with some bitch on his campus."

"Fuck that dude ma. He really isn't worth crying over. Any real cat can see what your worth and I'm not saying that because you're beautiful. I've just been paying attention to you."

"Really?"

"Yeah, I see all these dudes tryna get at you, but you don't budge. You stay true to that lame."

"Yeah, well, not anymore. He doesn't want me."

"If you ask me you're still being true. You're sitting in the bathroom crying, when there's a whole world out there."

"I guess you're right." she sniffed.

Rose turned back toward the mirror and grabbed for her backpack, pulling out a brush and makeup. She brushed her hair and then applied lip gloss to her full lips. I watched in amazement as she transformed. She was beautiful, even while she was down and out and that lip gloss did something to my soul.

Rose turned to me and smiled and I smiled back. She and I walked back to class together and we had been the best of friends since that day.

Rose conversed with other guys, but she never got serious with any of them. She had become my best female friend, because she understood me and she didn't ask annoying questions that curious bitches asked. She accepted me for me and chilled with me like I was one of her straight friends. She never disrespected me or let anyone else do it. When we went places people stared at us like we were a couple. Rose would grabbed my hand or kiss my neck just for amusement. It was like she was my girl, but she wasn't.

Our senior year was the best. She was my prom date and we had applied at all the same colleges. We didn't want to be away from one another.

On prom night it was a gang of us hanging. We had four rooms reserved at the Hilton and we had unlimited alcohol. I sat in the car waiting on Rose to walk out of the hall they had reserved for prom night, so we could drive to the hotel and get the real party jumping with our other friends. Rose jumped in the car ready and smiling hard.

"Snapps, someone likes you?" she blurted out.

"Who?"

"Someone we both know."

"Would you tell me already?"

"Okay, okay. Akeisha!"

I was hoping she would say that she liked me, but instead it was one of her fat ass friends. Don't get me wrong, big girls need love too, but that just wasn't up my alley, so they wouldn't be getting it from me. I half-way smiled and asked for details.

"She said she's been peeping you for a minute, but she didn't know how to come at you."

"How about...not at all."

Rose popped my arm and we fell out laughing. She tried to convince me to talk to her during the whole ride to the hotel. She told me how funny she was, how smart she was, how cute and kind she was, but all I could see in my head was her size. She was BIG. Most people swore I was into big women because I was 6'1", but I was not!

We pulled up to the hotel and Rose informed me that she had invited Akeisha to chill with us in our room. I looked at her like she had lost her damn mind. I already wasn't getting any that night and now she wanted to taunt me with the big girl. Rose went up to the room to wait for her friend. I stayed in the lobby to avoid her. She must have been waiting on us because Rose blew my cell phone up. I hit the reject button every time. I watched the elevators and finally Akeisha walked out. She exited the hotel and I was relieved. I went up to our room and Rose was heated.

"Snapps, you are so fucking wrong."

"Wrong for what?"

"I was calling you!"

"And!"

"You could have at least come up to talk to her! I should call her back up."

"You do that and I'll just leave again. Why are you playing cupid anyway?"

"She's single and your single and been single, that's why."

"Oh, so since she's single and gay you automatically assume that we are made for each other. FYI lesbians don't date each other just because they have gayness in common. We *do* have types, just like straight people!"

"Well, excuse me for trying to help your lonely ass out."

"Here's an idea. Don't!"

Rose and I had heated arguments often, because her ignorance pissed me off sometimes when she tried to *hook me up*. She sat silent for a Moment. She looked up at me and then spoke. "So what is your type?"

I paused looking at the opportunity that had presented itself, "You."

Rose fell silent again and this time I believed she was at a loss for words. I kneeled down in front of her and thought about how my friends would clown me for what I was about to do. They'd call me soft.

"Rose, you are the most beautiful woman I've ever seen in my life and since the day I laid eyes on you, I've wanted you. I accepted being your friend because it was the only way for me to be near you. After college boy fucked over you. You didn't want anything to do with anyone and I respected that, but shit it's been more than a year since then, he's moved on and so should you. You need to let someone in. Let me in."

Rose looked up at me and placed her soft hands on each side of my face. She looked in my eyes to see if I was being sincere. If only she knew how real I was being at that Moment. I swallowed back and then took the plunge.

Rose let me kiss her. She breathed hard as I worked her mouth with mine. I stopped and stood, staring down at her then she stood to meet my gaze, and unzipped her dress so that it could drop down to the floor. I unsnapped her strapless bra and threw it to the floor. Her breast pointed at me, so I grabbed them and then put one in my mouth making sure she felt me. I licked circles around her nipples and she moaned. I licked down the center of her body stopping at her belly ring and pulling off her thong. She squealed as I wrapped my lips around her pearl and sucked on it. Rose couldn't stand any longer, so I lay her back on the bed to continue what I was doing. I had to remove my jacket, tie, and shirt because it was about to get serious.

Rose let me beat it up from every angle. She moaned, kicked, and screamed and she never let go of my dreads. I was satisfied that she was satisfied.

That night turned into the life we had today. I had done my dirt, because of course, I wasn't a perfect stud and no relationship was perfect, but what the fuck had I done to deserve this? Rose had been my everything, but right now as this other stud smashed her from behind, she was just some bitch to me. How long had this shit been going on? It was taking everything in me not to get the burner out of my car and put a bullet in both of their pussies. I felt tears forming in my eyes as I watched and listen to this other bitch pleasing what belonged to me. Rose never even let me hit her with a strap, but here she was on hands and knees, taking that shit like a fucking soldier.

The day had felt wrong since I woke up that morning. Rose rushed me out of the house, and she kept asking me where I would be going throughout the day. That was also the day that I *balled* with my homies after work, but today I just wasn't up to it. I came home to be comforted by this female dog and she was in here with another motherfucka.

I walked out the door and got back into my ride, so that I could think clearly. I called Rose's fat ass friend Akeisha. The bitch had to know something.

"Hello," she answered before the phone could even ring on my end.

"What up Kei?"

"Snapps?"

"Yeah."

"What *you* want?"

"You busy?"

"Nah, not really, what you need?"

"Can I swing by?"

"Yeah, come through." she said with no hesitation.

This was too easy. Akeisha never stopped wanting me. She made passes at me, even after she found out about Rose and me, but I would never go there. I pulled up in Akeisha's driveway and she stood outside waiting on me. I knew she was going to want something so I prepared myself. It was nothing to fill her head up and make her think she was about to get something that she wasn't.

"So what brings your sexy ass this way?" she flirted and rubbed my arm.

"I need to ask you something."

"Ask then?"

"Is Rose fucking over me?" I questioned bluntly.

"Why you asking me that?" she leaned back.

"Because you're her best friend and I know you know!"

"I am that, and even if she was. Why would I tell you?"

I moved close to Akeisha, "Because I got something you want."

"Is that right," she grinned.

Akeisha rubbed my chest. But I pushed her away waiting for information first. "Well." I said and pushed her hands away.

She smacked her lips, "she met some chick online named Blaze, but all they do is talk from my understanding."

"You know her log-in info."

"Now you want too much."

I grabbed Akeisha's hand, "Come on Kei, for me. I promise it'll be worth it."

She blushed and then took me inside to her computer. She logged into Rose's *Yahoo* account like she did the shit often— too often. She

42

opened her saved conversations then moved out of the way for me to read one in particular.

StudsDream: *Hey you*

Pussywetter: *Hey, you miss me yet?*

StudsDream: *You know I do Daddy.*

Pussywetter: *Where your bitch at anyway?*

StudsDream: *Don't call her that and she's at work.*

Pussywetter: *You want to see me?*

StudsDream: *Now?*

Pussywetter: *Yeah now. I miss being inside you. You haven't been letting her hit my shit, right?*

StudsDream: *No baby, this is all for you.*

I couldn't read anymore. This bitch was the *grimiest* female I had ever come across. She had fucked up big time. I jumped up and pushed fat ass out of my way and went to my car. She yelled at my back as I ran out the door and hopped into my car to pull off. I reached beneath my seat and placed my gun on my lap. I stopped at a gas station and then went back to my crib. The bitch was still there. I took the gas can from my back seat and tucked my gun.

I poured gas on Rose's car and her bitch's car. I lit the blunt I had rolled after work and then threw a match on each car. I watched the flames go up. I got into my car and began blowing the horn like a crazy person. Both of their dumb asses were standing in the door watching their cars burn as I got out of my car to lean, smoke, and watch as well. Rose's bitch Blaze ran out of the house in her boxers and beater, trying run up on me, but as soon as she was close enough, I pulled out the burner under my shirt and placed metal in the middle of her head. Rose was next.

Rose ran back into the house, slamming and locking the door behind her. I stepped over her bitch's dead body and walked toward the door. I could hear her screaming and crying from the other side. I banged on the door with the end of my gun, but got no response. I was getting more pissed by the second. I hit the door harder, but Rose refused to open it. I knew I didn't have much time because my nosey ass neighbors were beginning to come outside.

"ROSE OPEN THE FUCKING DOOR!"

She screamed louder from the other side. I never stopped to think twice about what I was doing. This bitch was about to be six feet under. Her and her little bitch could spend forever together in their fucking graves. Since Rose refused to let me in, I shot the lock and opened the door myself. It was *my* fucking house. Rose ran to the bedroom— BAD

IDEA! I ran behind her and punched her in the back of the head. I tucked my gun in the back of my pants and then kicked Rose as hard as I could. She grunted from the pain. Tears continued to run down her face as she begged for mercy.

"Snapps, please, don't hurt me."

"Hurt you? Ain't that about a bitch!"

"Why Snapps, why are you doing this?"

I kicked her again, "Bitch, I gave you everything you ever wanted. I was there when nobody else was and you wanna know why?" "Was she worth it Rose? Huh? Was she? ANSWER ME!"

Tears began running down my face. I was starting to feel the pain now. Rose looked into my eyes and all I saw was fear. Images of everything that had ever happened between us, the good and the bad, replayed in mind, but only temporarily. The image of Rose moaning and enjoying the sex of another stud drowned out our memories. I couldn't take it. I came down on Rose's face hard with my fist, almost breaking her jaw. I kept hitting her until I saw blood. I stood and pulled her up by her neck, because my anger was now rage again. The same rage that had pulled that trigger a few minutes ago. I held my hands around her neck as she struggled to breathe. She tried prying my hands from around her neck, but she wasn't strong enough. Her life was slipping away and fast. I couldn't do it. I couldn't kill her. I let go of Rose and she hit the floor. I ran outside and hopped into my ride and I was just in time. Fire trucks and police cars weren't too far away as the sirens got louder, they got closer. A neighbor must have called the police.

I sped off and I had no idea where I was going. I just needed to drive. I beat on my steering wheel as I cried and cussed at myself— my stupidity. My lack in controlling my emotions that led to stupid decisions. I didn't know how to feel. I just knew that I was hurt, so hurt that I had taken a life that I had no right to. Somebody had to pay for this heartache.

Every turn that I made led me right back to where I started. I pulled up to Akeisha's house and the door was still unlocked from when I left the first time. I yelled through the house as I stepped in. "Akeisha! Where the fuck you at?"

"Snapps?" she emerged.

She came running like she was really worried about me. She reached for me asking what happened when she saw the blood on my clothes, but I slapped her hands away, "You did this bitch! You knew she was fucking over me and you never said anything. You probably encouraged it, you sloppy bitch!"

"Snapps, calm down."

"No, fuck that!"

I charged at Akeisha and slammed her up against the wall. I wanted to hit her so bad, but I couldn't. I knew it wasn't her fault. I needed and wanted to take my rage out on anyone in my way. I fell down on the floor and cried. Akeisha tried comforting me, even after I flipped out on her. I jumped up and left again. I had to get away. I had officially lost my fucking mind.

I decided to check into a hotel and tried to calm myself down for the night. I knew that I was looking at fifteen to life once I was caught.

*~*Rose*~*

"This one's alive!" the paramedic shouted. "Ma'am can you hear me? Ma'am?" he clapped and snapped, but his gestures were a faint sound to me.

My head pounded as my eyes fluttered open. I saw a face hovering over my body, but everything was still a blur. The lips were moving on the face, but I couldn't make out the words. I felt my body being lifted from the floor and placed on a cushion. I couldn't move. This was not my life. How could this be happening to me? Everything on my body ached, but the one thing that was filled with the most pain was my heart. I brought this on myself, bringing another stud into my bed. I had never seen Snapps that way. She should have killed me. I wondered where she was now. I had no right to even be concerned, but I was. Tears fell from my eyes as the EMT's worked on my bloody and swollen face. My hearing had finally come back to me.

It seemed like it took an eternity to get to the hospital and it took even longer for me to get a private room. I sat in that hospital bed just staring at the walls. My life was a complete mess and I had no idea how to clean it up. Snapps was missing and Blaze was dead. My thoughts got deeper and then they were interrupted by a knock.

"Come in." I said.

"Ms. Anderson, there are some detectives here and they want to ask you a few questions."

I didn't say anything. I just watched the door widen as a man and a woman walked in. The man was tall with blonde hair and blue eyes, and the woman was short and thin with flawless brown skin. They both wore suits and looked anal. I wasn't in the mood for this shit, but I knew I needed to co-operate.

"Ms. Anderson I'm detective Ryan King and this is my partner Shelby Stone. We need to ask you a few questions and you would be well advised to answer truthfully and to the best of your ability."

"Yeah, sure."

"Okay, we need you to tell us exactly what happened."

My eyes watered as I thought about Snapps and how she was leaned back on her car. She didn't say two words to me or to Blaze. She just pulled out her gun and blew Blaze's brains out, right there in front of our home in broad daylight. Everything was fresh in my brain, but I refused to talk, so I didn't. "I don't remember." I lied.

"Ms. Anderson you do understand that this is a homicide and if you withhold pertinent information you too could serve serious prison time. I understand that this may be difficult for you, but we need to know what you saw."

"I don't remember."

"Alright Ms. Anderson, I get it. I'm going to give you my card and when you're ready to talk give me a call."

The detectives left me to my thoughts. I was all fucked up. I couldn't figure out what had gone wrong. How could Snapps have known? What was it that could have made her so angry? Nothing came to mind. I reached for the phone next to my bed to call Akeisha. She was all I had right now and I needed her. I dialed her number and she picked up on the first ring. "Hello?" she answered sounding overly anxious.

"Akeisha?"

"Rose?"

"Yeah, girl you waiting on someone?"

"No, just feeling a bit on edge today. Where are you calling me from?"

"The hospital."

"The hospital! What's wrong?"

"Kei can you come to me, I don't really want to talk over the phone."

"Okay, I'm on my way."

It took Kei almost forty-five minutes to get to me. She had to lie and say she was family just to be allowed into my room after hours. That was some bullshit. She hugged me as soon as she saw me. She looked the way I felt— like shit.

"What happened, Rose?"

"Snapps killed her."

"Killed who? Blaze?"

"Yeah."

"What?"

I sobbed. "I don't know how to explain it. Everything happened so fast. Blaze and I were lying in the bed talking and then we smelled smoke and someone was blowing their horn like crazy. When Blaze looked out the window, she saw our cars on fire and she said my girl was standing outside. Blaze ran out before me. I should have gone outside first Kei, she'd still be here."

"Aww Rose, don't do that, don't blame yourself."

"But it is my fault. Snapps didn't say anything, she just shot her. I didn't think it would come to this."

*~*Akeisha*~*

How the fuck was I going to tell my best friend that I told her girl about her secret affair? I fucked this shit all up. I didn't expect Snapps to kill Blaze, if anything I just wanted her to see Rose for the lying cheating bitch she was and then come running to me.

I don't know what it is about people and big women. I'm a fly ass thick bitch if you ask me. if Snapps had fucked with me when I wanted her to, then all this shit could have been avoided. For years I've been the third wheel to her and Rose and I never complained even when they threw me off on studs that were bigger than me and ugly. What the fuck will me and another big bitch do together? Compare bellies? Fuck that!

I remember the first time I saw Snapps. She and Rose had just started hanging out after Rose and her college boyfriend had broken up. She brought Snapps with her to my mama's house for a barbeque for the 4th of July. I took one look at that pretty bitch, licked my lips, and made it my business to find out all that I could about her. I was confused that she was with Rose. I thought my best friend had gone and switched teams on me. If she had she was doing pretty well for herself stepping up in my mama's place with Snapps.

I pulled Rose to the side at the barbeque and grilled her ass.

"Who is that?"

"Who, the chick I got with me?"

"No bitch, the invisible bitch next to her."

"Don't get smart. That's my friend Snapps. We go to school together."

"I need to switch schools."

"Shut up stupid."

"So, are y'all fucking?"

"Kei, you know I don't rock like that."

47

"If I was straight and saw her, I'd rock like that. Look me in my eyes and say you're not attracted to her."

"I'm not."

"Whatever!"

"Okay, she's cute, but that's all. I wouldn't fuck her. What are me and another girl supposed to do?"

"Bring her ass in my room and you can stay and watch. I'll show you what they do."

"You nasty." I laughed.

"I'll be that. Introduce us."

Rose and I walked over to where Snapps was and she introduced us. I made sure Snapps knew that I was feeling her in that way. She never really showed me much interest, but that wasn't going to stop me. She could just be one of those studs who enjoyed being chased. When I saw something I wanted I went after it, no questions asked. I watched Snapps all night as she danced and laughed with my family. She was most definitely what I needed in my present and future.

Snapps and Rose were starting to hang out a lot and I figured that could work in my advantage if I got Rose to invite me out on their little ventures. Snapps would joke with me all the time, but there was never a romantic connection. I tried to figure out a way to create one, but every attempt failed. I could never even get her alone long enough. She followed Rose like a puppy.

I was starting to hate Rose, just being around the bitch lowered my self-esteem and I was a pretty cocky bitch. Sometimes I found myself asking why her? Why is it always her that gets what I want? Light-skinned bitch! I wondered if she only hung with me because she knew she looked better and could take all the attention. My thoughts were getting the best of me and I conjured up evil plan after evil plan to get to Snapps and make Rose out to be exactly what she was— a hoe.

Now I sit next to her in her hospital bed, holding her hand as she cries, being what I have always been— the fucking friend. I had no idea what I could do. I was a little amused at the thought that Snapps had come to me, but this was not the time to have that on my mind. I needed to get to Snapps before the police did, but where would I look?

*~*Snapps*~*

FUCK! FUCK! FUCK! FUCK! I thought. I had to calm down. I pulled into the parking lot of a cheesy motel, making sure to park toward the back. I walked toward the front to pay for a room, so that I could get myself together. There was a little foreign lady sitting at the front desk. She stared at me, waiting for me to speak.

"How much for the night?" I asked.

"35.99 plus tax." she stated plainly.

"I'll take it."

"You pay with cash?"

"Yeah."

I gave the little Indian looking lady forty dollars and snatched the key from the desk. I knew this place was as low budget as it got, she didn't even ask for I.D. I went straight to my room and turned on the television. I was sure my face was all over the news by now. My legs wouldn't stop shaking as I waited for something to pop up on the fuzzy screen. It took about ten minutes for the screen to clear. Just as the television cleared, the news anchor announced that a new report had just been released on where I had laid Blaze out more than a few hours ago.

"Here in a local suburban area it was reported that gun shots were fired and local residents smelled smoke. Emergency vehicles arrived to find one unidentified female lying in the street with a gunshot wound to the head and another female now identified as Rose Anderson in critical condition. Police are in search of the owner of the home, Sasha Adams, who was said to have been spotted fleeing the scene before Police arrived. Neighbors say that Adams and Anderson were quiet residents and never really had company up until a few months ago when the vehicle you see torched behind me showed up. Rose Anderson is in the hospital in stable condition. The police are not releasing any more information at this time, back to you Karen."

They rambled on about the story for a few more minutes and then it was on to the next. I sat at the end of the worn down bed, with my hands under my chin. I heard everything that the reporter said, but *months* stuck out to me the most. How long had she been fucking that bitch? I felt myself getting angry all over again. There is nothing like an unanswered question to piss you off. I had a lot of unanswered questions, and the only person who could answer them was Rose.

I dozed off in my trifling room when I heard a hard knock at the door. My heart pounded a mile a minute in my chest. All I could think was that, I was found. I heard the little Indian lady from the opposite side of the door and I was instantly relieved. She was just doing her rounds. She said a few words, none of which I understood, and then I shut my door.

I checked my cell phone in my pocket and I had a missed call from Akeisha. *What the fuck did she want?* I wasn't sure if I wanted to call her back. She might be trying to set me up, but then again if she wanted to turn me in she would have done it already. I decided I'd call her back, because I knew that she had probably been in contact with Rose. The phone rang once and Akeisha picked up.

"Snapps! Where are you? Police are all over searching for your ass!"

"I think I know that, Akeisha."

"Why did you just leave like that?"

"Um, I don't know, maybe because I killed somebody! What the fuck do you want?"

"I want to help you."

"Help me what?"

"Get away."

"And go where Akeisha? I'm not running."

"So, you're going to turn yourself in?"

"Yeah, but not until I talk to Rose."

"She don't wanna talk to you."

"Bitch, did I ask you that?"

"Snapps, you gon stop talking to me like that!"

"Or what? What the fuck you gon do. I'm already going to jail for life bitch. I can add some more years. You just find a way for me to talk to Rose."

"How? She got cops surrounding her."

"You kept the fact that she was fucking another stud behind my back for months to yourself. I'm sure you can manage a fucking phone call."

"Fine."

I hung up the phone and decided I needed to take a shower. I had a few things in my car. I went out to get them, so I could wash my ass. I made sure that there were no police in the area, because those bitches had my exact description from a photo they took from my house.

That shower did nothing for my nerves at all. I sat at the end of the bed just gazing at the television. I could feel myself starting to daydream, but my phone snapped me out of my trance. I looked over at the night stand to see it lighting up. It was my Mother.

"Hello," I answered nervously.

"Sasha?"

"Yes Mama."

"Why is your fucking face all over the news?"

My Mom didn't let me get a word in. She tore into my ass. I had one of those real hood mamas too. I guess you can say I got my attitude honest. I've seen my Mama stab men, bust windshields, stalk her old boyfriend's new bitches — Mama was off the wall for real. I never really understood why she went through some of the shit that she did, because she was a pretty woman and she never really depended on no man.

"Mama—" I tried to cut in.

"Is this about that girl? I never liked that bitch. I told you that from day one. She looked like trouble. All those pretty little young girls are nothing but trouble. If you would have listened—"

"Mama."

"If I were you, I would have killed that bitch too. You better tell me what happed, before I get really upset, because the news is making you look like some type of monster. An armed and dangerous criminal. I didn't give birth to no damn criminal..."

"MAMA!"

"What girl? You better have a good reason to be constantly calling me and interrupting me!"

"I'm trying to tell you what happened, but you just keep running your mouth."

"Are you disrespecting me right now? I know you're not playing with me. I'll find your ass before the police does and prison will be the least of your worries. You understand me?"

"Yes ma'am."

"Now, tell me everything."

I ran the whole story down to her. I even started crying, because it had just hit me how much I was really hurting behind the fact that Rose played me all the way to the left. I had no idea how to feel. I was pissed, hurt, and still wanting to hurt someone. I wanted everyone to hurt because I was hurting. My Mom tried to ease my mind a little, but her words only calmed me temporarily.

I had fallen back on the bed and dozed off without realizing it. I woke up in the middle of the night in a cold sweat. Blaze's face popped into my head and so did the bullet that I put through it. I had never killed anyone before and now I was wishing I hadn't. If this was how I had to sleep the rest of my life. *How could I lose my control like that?*

*~*Rose*~*

Snapps was all that I could think about. Most would say that I was stupid for what I did, and they would come down on me for missing her right now. I know, the nerve of me right? I just wanted to hear her voice and tell her everything. I wish I had known that she would lose it, because now a life was lost and I was lying in a hospital bed, half-dead and lonely. Akeisha had left in the middle of the night. I was sure she thought I was sleeping, but how could I sleep with all that was going on right now? I wanted to call Snapps' Mother, but that woman hated me and I'm sure if anyone had talked to Snapps, she had. She never spoke to me when we went over to her house and she always gave me dirty looks and right about now, I could only imagine what she wanted to do to me. I was safer right there in the hospital bed, than anywhere that woman could get to me. She was mad ghetto and I never hesitated to show my disgust in how she was. She already hated me, so there was no reason for me to act as though I fancied her. Ms. Adams was a loud woman, with tattoos all over. I had no idea how she held a job down at a hospital for so many years, looking and acting the way she did, but surprisingly people loved her everywhere she went.

She never complimented me or had anything nice to say to me or about me. I just assumed it was that parental jealously that most parents had behind their children.

I must have thought about her too much, because just as I was about to sit up and call a nurse, Ms. Adams walked in.

"Ms. Adams, what are you doing here?" I asked.

"Surprised?"

"Yes and no. How did you find me?"

"I do work in a hospital."

I hung my head low at my own stupidity and then prepared myself for whatever was about to come next. I knew this wasn't one of those friendly 'how are you' visits.

"Why did you do it, Rose?" she pursued.

"Do what?"

"Oh, now you want to play stupid. You know exactly what I'm talking about."

"Ms. Adams, I honestly don't have an answer for you."

"You better find one. My baby is about to go to prison because of your trifling ass. You know, I never had a problem with her lifestyle. I never cared who or what she did until the day she brought you home." Ms. Adams walked closer to my bed, making sure that I heard every

52

word she said. She pointed her finger directly at my face, tightening her mouth, trying to restrain her festering anger. "There was always something about you — too beautiful for your own fucking good. You had Sasha blind, but you never fooled me. I was exactly like you once — young, beautiful, and careless, but there is also something that separates us."

"And what's that? I'm classy and you just some ghetto trash?"

Ms. Adams slapped me and grabbed me by my throat, slightly cutting off my air supply, and lifting me from the bed. She hovered so close I could feel her breath on my nose.

"No, you little bitch. I have respect for the people who dared to love me. Sasha loved you and what did you do? You took it for granted."

Ms. Adams released my neck, letting my head fall on my pillows. She didn't utter another word. She just shot me a look that would have killed me and started for the door. Before walking out she mumbled, "She should have killed you too," and the door closed.

The tears fell fast as soon as the door was shut. I wasn't crying because I was hurt, or for Blaze or Snapps, but because Ms. Adams was right. I took Snapps for granted. I underestimated the love she had for me. *How could I? When did I become this person?* I held my hand to my throat and I just let tear after tear fall down each cheek.

*~*Snapps*~*

BOOM BOOMBOOMBOOM

I jumped up fast. My heart was going a mile a minute. I didn't want to answer. It could be the police. *What to do? What to do?* That's the only thing that was going through my mind as I panted and pushed shit around the room.

"Sasha, open this damn door!"

"Ma?"

"Yes, now open up!"

I opened the door and grabbed onto my Mom for dear life. It could have been housekeeping; I would have hugged them too. I was just happy to see that it wasn't the police, coming to drag me out, kicking and screaming.

"Girl, get off of me. I'm bringing you to turn yourself in."

"What? Mama I was going."

"When?"

I just looked at her. I had no idea when I was going to go. I had enough money saved up to stay in that motel for another ten years at least. I should have never told my Mama where I was.

"Come on. Put your shoes on. The longer you wait, the worse you'll make it on yourself. You created this mess and now you have to face the consequences of your actions. I raised you better, hiding in hotels and shit. Bring your ass."

I gave my Mom everything that I had with me except for my driver's license. I wanted to cry, but I had done enough of that in the past three days and I was also afraid that my Mama would back hand me for being a pussy about the situation. I wasn't that sure she would though, because I could see the hurt in her eyes as we pulled up slowly in front the police station. I stepped out of the car after we were parked, taking a deep breath. My Mama came around to my side and grabbed my hand. I felt like a kid again as she said 'come on baby, let's get this over with.

I walked up to the front counter and before I could get my name out, two female officers surrounded me with cuffs ready. I had become a local celebrity obviously. As soon as the cuffs were locked around my wrist my Mom broke down. I knew it was coming. She had kept a level head long enough. An officer went over to escort her to a private room for questioning and I was dragged the opposite way.

Prison was the worse place I had ever been in my life. I wouldn't wish that shit on my worst enemy. The food was awful, the beds were uncomfortable, privacy was non-existent, and you were basically told when to do everything. Shockingly, I had only been in two fights in my first year. I was given fifteen years, and was eligible for parole after five. After the trial and all the details were laid out the jury was kind of easy on me.

Rose had begun to write me after the second year.

Hey Snapps,

I know I'm probably the last person that you want to hear from after everything that you and I have been through. I feel like this is all

54

my fault. I've thought of a million ways to apologize to you for what I've done that caused you to do what you did. You probably hate me, because I hate myself, but I've never hated you. I know that you have some unanswered questions and so do I. I figured you should know everything, so that the blank spaces in your mind are filled. I hope that you don't cringe from seeing this name or at anything that I will write. Well…Blaze and I met through Akeisha. We saw each other a few times and chilled over at Akeisha's every now and then. I have no idea when the relationship turned sexual. I never intended on it going that far. I really just liked her attention when you weren't around. I try to think of when I could have stopped myself and then I realize that I always tried. Akeisha had been telling me that you were probably doing the exact same thing because no stud as attractive as you would be faithful to one girl. My head was all fucked up and times when you wouldn't answer the phone it pushed me to believe that Akeisha may be right. Akeisha broke down a few months ago, confessing everything about how she really just wanted to break us up. She had no idea it would get this far. I was sickened by all that she said and how she conjured up this whole mess. She and I aren't friends anymore. I've been staying to myself lately. Your Mother has finally stopped hating me. I went to her because I had nowhere else to turn. I told her everything and she said that she forgave me. I hope that you can find it in your heart to forgive me as well and maybe even write me back so that we can have proper closure. I've always loved you and I'm very sorry Snapps.

Rose

I had a lot of regrets now knowing all that I knew. I should have killed Akeisha's ass, but I'm more than sure that she will get whatever is coming to her. I don't want any more trouble. I just want to do my time and get out, to get back to whatever is left of my life. I decided not to write back to Rose, because there was really nothing to tell and I still wasn't exactly ready to be pen pals. I loved her and that would probably always remain, but we were much better off without each other. Akeisha tested our bond and we failed. There was no way to rebuild on that foundation and I accepted that every night as I stared at the walls of my cell.

"Dirty Laundry"

I leaned in to kiss Des one more time, before my Mother flipped on the light to the front porch just to see if I was in before my midnight curfew. Des had the softest lips and her lip gloss always tasted sweet in my mouth. Sometimes, I would open my eyes as she kissed me, to admire her long lashes and watch how much she was into kissing me.

Des was wearing a short denim skirt and I placed my hand on her inner deep caramel thigh and tried to slide up, but she grabbed my hand, stopping me and her other hand tugged at my long sandy brown hair. She smiled a little as we kissed at my failed attempt to molest her one more time. I leaned back toward the window and I rolled my eyes as I opened the car door to get out. I said goodnight and slowly walked to my front door and before I could make it to the final step, my Mother was swinging the door open and glaring angrily at me.

Des was my best friend turned lover. Our Mothers were best friends and had been best friends since they were little. They had us around the same time and they kept us close to one another by always keeping us in the same schools and programs. We went on our first dates together and everything and we quickly learned that our attraction toward each other was much stronger than what we felt for boys. Des' Mom knew that we were in an actual relationship and it was the first secret that she had ever kept from my Mom in the thirty-six years that they had been friends. My Mom wasn't exactly gay friendly and she made it more than clear every time we walked past a gay couple, by expressing her disgust.

I'm sure she would be more than sickened, to know that my best friend was also someone who I gave head regularly. I'd like to say that I was turned out, but unfortunately, I initiated the relationship with Des, making the first move on a night that she had gotten her feelings hurt for the first time.

Des called me over to her house one night, needing my shoulder and girl talk, when her and the first guy she had ever taken seriously had broken up. He decided he was too young to be serious and just like that, Des didn't matter anymore. She sat on the bed crying for hours, taking the break-up as a serious devastation. I, on the other hand, looked at it as an opportunity. I wiped away her tears with my fingers as each one rolled.

"Des, look at me."

She reluctantly looked up in my direction and then put her head back down. She was even beautiful when she cried. I couldn't resist. I, myself had never been with a woman, but I had touched myself enough to know that I didn't want a man plunging in and out of my private parts. I lifted Des' face up by her chin and held it there, so she couldn't look down anymore.

"I need you to listen to me. You are beautiful. Anybody who doesn't want you has to be stupid. I never thought he was good enough for you anyway. There is someone out there who can treat you way better."

None of that was a lie. Des was beautiful. She was the only girl that I knew who wore her hair natural and barely put on makeup and could kill anyone in a room with her features alone. She was 5'6" and very shapely. She had no idea how beautiful she really was. She responded with an attitude.

"Yeah, like who?"

That's the question I needed her to ask. I froze for a minute just staring at her entire face. There was only one way to answer her question, but I needed to see that I wouldn't be rejected or slapped. I didn't want to lose our friendship or make her uncomfortable, but I didn't want to hide who I was any longer. I kissed Des and waited for her to respond. She didn't kiss me back right away and she didn't pull back. After a few seconds she closed her eyes and kissed me back. I still felt nervous, but after that moment Des was mine.

I snapped back to reality, as my Mother burned me with her eyes. My entire demeanor changed whenever it was time for me to set foot in that house. All of a sudden I felt as though the world was on my shoulders.

"Sonya, you are really pushing it little girl."

I didn't bother saying anything back because arguing with my Mother was pointless. She was one of those, *what I say goes* type of people and when she didn't get her way, there was hell to pay. Some days my Mother treated me like I was the light of her life and other days I was the scum of the earth. We were only sixteen years apart and I was to blame for her having to grow up way too fast instead of the irresponsible thought to open her legs to a dude who wouldn't stick around anyway.

I tried desperately not to take some of the things she said or did to me too personally, for the simple fact that she sometimes was still learning about life herself.

I walked right past my Mother, not even acknowledging her comment, but nothing was ever that simple with her. It was obvious that tonight she was in one of her moods because she usually waited on the sofa, but tonight she met me at the door. I heard the door close as I walked toward the hall that led to my room. I was more than sure that my Mother was right behind me. Before I could turn the knob to my door she was standing right there, breathing down my damn neck.

"I cut you a lot of slack, letting you stay out until midnight. My Mother wanted me in by nine."

"I pulled up at 11:58."

"You know I go out every Saturday and you know I'm not leaving until you get here."

"I really don't get the point of this conversation."

"The point is that you're abusing your freedom. I think you intentionally push your curfew to the minute just to fuck with me."

"Okay, Mom."

"Would it kill you to come in a little bit earlier on Saturdays, sometimes?"

"Would it kill you to tell me that you want me to come in a little earlier sometimes?"

"Just be more considerate. I'm leaving. Don't have anybody in my house."

My Mom slammed the door behind her and I let out a big sigh. Maybe she had a bad day or maybe it was PMS. She just loved to hear herself talk. I grabbed my cell phone to call Des. Her phone rang a few times before she answered.

"Hey baby, you good?" she answered.

"Yeah, she fussed about nothing."

"You should be used to it by now."

"I am. I just wish she would say what she really means when posing an argument. She came in here talking about, I intentionally push my curfew to the minute just to fuck with her. All she had to say was she wanted to go drink early and find her dick for the night before church in the morning."

"Baby, stop it."

"Ugh!"

"That's still your Mother."

"Unfortunately."

"Okay Sonya, have an attitude."

"I'm sorry. She just really gets to me sometimes. I can't wait to get out of this house."

"You need to just tell her about us and maybe she'll ease up some. She is only hard on you, because she doesn't want you to make the mistake she made, getting pregnant early."

"Des, don't start this."

"You have to tell her. I'm tired of her thinking we're just best friends. We've been more than that for awhile and I know it's killing my Mom keeping a secret from her best friend. She's been respecting the fact that it's your business to tell."

"Your Mom knows that mine is nothing like her. She'll trip hard on me and you know it!"

"You don't know that. This is the twenty-first century."

"My Mom has nothing nice to say about gay people. We are talking about a woman, who will ask to be reseated at a restaurant if she is placed by a same sex couple. She moves to the other side of the mall when she sees them holding hands and yells that's a damn shame. Are you serious right now?"

Des was not pleased with my response at all and decided she didn't want to talk anymore. Now I had my Mother mad for no reason and Des mad because I didn't want to be attacked for being who I was. She had no idea how hard it was dealing with a homophobic parent. I could think of all the times I was out somewhere with my Mom and we would see gay couples. She would throw her slangs and I would just stand there wanting to defend them, but I didn't have that kind of courage. My Mother was a pain in both my ass cheeks, but I still loved her and respected her enough to keep myself in my cluttered closet.

I did try on many occasions to tell my Mother about my lifestyle and I always tried on the days that we got along really well, but I knew it would go bad. I wanted to cherish the happy Moments while I could and just tell her after graduation. She could hate me and disown me once I was able to take care of myself.

The sunlight came in through the blinds covering my window, shinning brighter than I cared for and I turned over groaning at how it burned my eyes. My Mother opened my blinds every morning to wake me up, because she knew I couldn't sleep in a bright room. She was blasting gospel music through the house and I knew automatically she was up getting dressed for the second service at church. I hopped out of bed, knowing she would be sticking her head in to make sure I was up getting dressed as well. I moved as slow as I could, like I always did on

Sunday, hoping she would leave me home for not being ready on time, but of course, it never worked. She would sit on the sofa and wait a lifetime before she let me miss church. I had to give that to her. She was a faithful servant, whether she had a hangover or not. She would never miss out on a chance to admire our *attractive* and newly divorced pastor.

I showered and dressed as fast as I could, so she wouldn't come in my room acting like she had a mental problem. She never really yelled or fussed on Sunday's though. She was a fairly decent person on that day, so decent that everyday should be Sunday.

I put on a simple dress and some low heels. My hair still hung nicely around my face, from the fresh roller rap that my Mom had just done to my hair three days prior. I grabbed my bible and my money for offering and I walked into the living room, where my Mother was waiting.

"I'm ready."

She stood up and gave me a half smile. I guess that was her way of saying that I looked nice. She turned to walk toward the front door and I followed. I never cracked a smile and I drug my feet.

We pulled up in front of the church in less than fifteen minutes and searched for an available parking space. She pulled into an empty space on the side of the building and in we went. The service always lasted longer than I needed it to, but it always uplifted my spirits no matter what I was dealing with and to make it even better, Des and I had a lunch date once I made it home. I sat there thinking of what to wear as the pastor made his closing remarks.

Des sat across from me staring at me like she was seeing me for the first time. She had a goofy grin on her face and her arms were folded across her chest.

"What?" I asked.

"You're just sexy, that's all."

She reached her hand across the table, motioning for me to give her mine and I complied like a good little girlfriend. She held my hand in hers and rubbed her thumb across each of my fingers.

"Is there something on your mind?" I looked in her eyes.

"No. Why?"

"I was just asking. You're acting like you love me today with all this public affection."

"I love you every day." Des leaned down and kissed my hand and all I could do was smile. We sat in silence just smiling at each other until we received our food. It was a very pleasant lunch. I wish that every day was like this one. My Mother wasn't on my ass about some bullshit and I had the most beautiful person I've ever met in my life, sitting right across from me and she loved me and only me.

I paid for lunch this time and Des and I walked to her car. A guy pulled up as Des and I walked to the passenger side together and I opened her door for her. The strange man stopped to watch us with a confused look on his face. Des smiled at him and then pulled me into her, to kiss me. We knew that his dumb ass was watching because we never heard his door open and close after he parked. I pulled back and made her get into the car. He had seen enough femme on femme action for the day. I closed her door and walked around to the driver's side so that we could leave. Once I sat down and closed the door, Des turned to me and pulled me to kiss her again. She was messing with my hormones, badly. She stopped and I started her car.

"My Mom isn't home. We can stop at my house before I bring you back," she suggested in a naughty tone.

I didn't respond to Des. I knew exactly what she wanted. I pulled out to make my way to Des's house. She kissed on my neck and licked the rim of my right ear while I drove and I felt like I wasn't making it to our destination fast enough. It was rare that Des got like this, but when she did, I took full advantage.

I didn't even bother to pull into her garage. Des was out of the car before I could cut off the engine and I was behind her shortly. I followed her to her room, once inside the house. I closed Des' room door behind me and turned around, to her right up on me, pulling up my shirt over my head. Des straight up attacked me, licking from my neck to my nipples. She undid the belt on my jeans and unbuttoned them so that she could easily slide her hand in, to massage my clit. She held me to the door by my neck with her free hand and I moaned, while barely standing. I wanted to fuck her, but she pushed my hands away, taking total control. Des pulled my jeans down from around me and threw them to the side. She got down on her knees and pulled one of my legs over her shoulder. I lost my mind as she worked my clit with her tongue. I pulled her hair, begging her to stop, but she wouldn't, gripping my ass with her hands and pulling my pussy as close to her face as she could get it. I tried to push Des' head back because I was getting ready to cum and I would never let it go in her mouth, but she held on.

"Baby stop. I'm cumming."

"I want you to come in my mouth this time, Sonya."

"You sure?"

"Yes, now quit stopping me."

Des continued to wreck my clit. It didn't take long to get me back to where I had stopped her. My body shook as I felt the sensations of orgasm running through my body. This one was more serious than any others that I had before. I couldn't control my screams and I pulled harder on Des's hair, while releasing the stresses of my week into her mouth. I pushed her away from my sensitive clit. I wanted to attack her like she attacked me, but I failed.

"Aw babe! Come on!"

"I can't."

"Why?"

"That time again."

"Are you serious? That's so messed up!"

"Oh, shut up."

"This isn't fair."

"Fair for me. I've wanted to fuck you since I picked you up. You looked really good today baby."

Des laughed and then walked out of her room. I searched for my clothes, so I could put myself back together, before going home to my Mother and whatever mood she would be in.

We left Des' house and I sat on the passenger side of her car this time, leaning back with a smile on my face. She held my hand and glanced at me every second that she could look away from the road.

We pulled up in front of my house and I leaned over to kiss Des goodbye like I always did and as we both closed our eyes, the glass where I was sitting shattered. We both screamed and before I could duck or cover my face, I was pulled through the window by my hair. I fell hard onto the grass as my Mom yelled as loud as she could, calling me everything, but a child of God.

"You trifling bitch! You will not be this way in my house!"

I grabbed my Mother's hand trying to loosen the grip she had on my hair. I could hear Des screaming for her to stop, but my Mother screamed at her too, calling her a dike and spitting in her direction. I could feel the hair coming from my scalp as my Mom pulled me across her lawn. I kicked, trying to break free, but she refused to let go. She came down hard on my face with her fist over and over again. I could taste blood in my mouth after a few punches. Des was hysterical still screaming at my Mother as she constantly hit me and dragged me up the stairs. My skin burned from my Mother dragging me. I was helpless as I screamed and cried. Des' Mom pulled up and hopped out of her car charging at my Mother trying to pull me from her grasp. Des helped now, pulling me in her direction. Des' Mother screamed.

"Let her go! Are you trying to kill her!"

I wished that I would stop breathing at that very moment. My Mother finally let me go to engage in a heated argument with Des' Mom. They cussed back and forth at one another, as Des cradled me in her arms. I had blood everywhere. I held my shirt to my face to stop my nose from bleeding. I had not realized that damn near everyone on our street was now outside, watching the show. Des' Mom had sold me out and told our secret. I had no idea how to feel, but one thing was for sure. I was hurt. The tears wouldn't stop falling. Des' Mom came over to us and pulled Des from over me, saying they had to leave. My Mom grabbed my arm, pulling me from the ground and yanking me toward the house.

"Go clean yourself up. You brought this all on yourself and I dare you to dial 9-1-1."

I rushed to the bathroom and tried to stop myself from crying. This was not happening. I leaned over the sink, spitting out blood. I grabbed a towel and dabbed at my face with peroxide. There were cuts on my back and sides. I took off all of my clothes and stood in the shower pouring peroxide down my body. I showered and walked to my room naked. My Mother had taken my television, laptop, cell phone, iPod, and MP3 player out of my room. Everything was turned upside down and inside out. The only thing that was perfectly intact was my bed and in the middle was a bible. I grabbed a shirt and some pants from my bedroom floor and put them on and flopped down on my bed. My Mother called me into the kitchen and I went reluctantly. She motioned for me to sit across from her and I did.

"You do know that you're going to hell right?"

I dare not respond. I just put my head down and cried on the inside. This is what I was afraid of.

My Mother sat up half the night reading from the front of the bible to back and she dared me to nod off even a little. I pinched myself when I felt my eyes getting heavy.

"You will have nothing, Sonya, you hear me? NOTHING! I have given you everything that you could possibly want and this is what you do? You ungrateful, nasty bitch! I should punch you in the face again. How dare you embarrass me like this? What am I supposed to say to the people at church? At work? Go in your room and stay there until I feel like you should leave. You make me sick to my stomach and don't even try to go to school looking like that, just stay in your room."

I stood from the table and went to my room. This woman was going to make my life hell on Earth, so I may as well be there. I was more than sure it had to be better than this.

I closed my door and fell back onto my bed. I dozed off thinking of different ways to end my life and then I heard a tapping noise. I opened my eyes to see what it was. I went over to my window and Des was on the other side with tears in her eyes. I opened my window as quietly as I could. She grabbed me, holding me as tight as she could without hurting my already injured body and whispered to me, "Are you okay?"

"No."

"Come with me, please."

"She'll know I'm with you, Des."

"We can go somewhere else. You're not safe here, Sonya. Look what she did to you."

"What about school?"

"We'll figure that out later. I'm not leaving you here."

There were two clicking sounds. My Mom stood behind Des with her gun and a flashlight, flashing on us.

"You want to go to hell early? Huh?"

We stood still. My Mother was obviously not thinking clearly. She didn't come closer or point the gun toward us. She just held the flashlight at us and the gun at her side, waiting for us to answer her question.

"Sonya, is this what you want? This is the life you want to lead?"

With hesitation I said, "Yes."

"Then leave. You are not my daughter."

I leaned back into the window to grab a few things to take with me, but my Mother stopped me.

"No, go just like that. The things in that room are for my daughter, not you. Leave before I lay you out permanently."

Des helped me out of the window. I walked barefoot to her car and got in. My Mother watched us pull off. Once we got to the stop sign, I broke down, because I had no idea what to do next.

~~*~*

Des sat up all night with me the night that my Mom forced me to choose. She held me and rocked me, trying to get me to calm down

65

before I ended up in an emergency room. She rubbed my back and handed me water to sip.

"Sonya, listen to me."

I choked on tears.

"Are you listening?"

I nodded my head yes.

"I know you just made a hard decision, but you may have to make a harder one and go back home at least until you graduate. I was wrong I was being selfish and missed you. I shouldn't have come."

"How will I see you?"

"We'll figure something out. You'll have much of nothing if you stay here. I can help and you know my Mom will do what she can, but it won't be anything compared to what your Mom can do as your legal guardian. Just sleep on it, okay? Whatever decision you make I will stand behind you and do all that I can to make sure you are okay." she kissed my forehead.

I nodded my head in agreement. I knew that she was right. I had to be logical about this, but logic just didn't seem fair to me in this situation. Why did I have to lie about who I was just to receive the perks of being a teenager? In elementary they tell you to be who you are and to accept that you are different from one another, but what they don't teach are the consequences of being yourself. What they don't teach is that you could even be attacked by someone you love just for being you. I knew that if I didn't go back home my Mother would try to make it as hard as possible for me to live. She was spiteful like that.

Any dignity I had left was gone as I knocked on my Mom's door. Des sped off to keep from having another episode. She opened it and scowled at me.

"Can I help you?"

"I want to come home."

"You don't have a home here."

"Mom, please."

She looked around outside to see if anyone else was out there, then she moved aside to let me walk in. "You will not live that lifestyle under my roof."

"I understand."

"No female company, no cell phone, and church twice a week."

"Okay."

"We're going to see the pastor tomorrow. Go to your room."

66

I walked to my room and fell across my bed, exhausted, upset, lonely, and frustrated. Other kids were stressing out about graduation and what college to go to and I was struggling to live.

I woke up to gospel music bumping through the house. I walked into the kitchen and my Mom was sitting at the table eating cereal and doing the games on the back of the box. She had a bowl sitting on the other side of the table so I joined her.

Get dressed when you're done so we can go see Pastor Haines. She never looked up from the box. I ate quickly then went to my room to throw on some clothes. I didn't wait for my Mom. I sat in her car on the passenger side until she came out. We rode in silence.

We pulled up to the church and went to the Pastor's office. He sat reading with his glasses on. He stood and smiled as we entered the room. He shook my Mother's hand and then walked around to hug me. We all sat down. My Mother spoke first, "Thank you for seeing us on such short notice pastor."

"You know I do what I can to help my members." He smiled.

I'm the sinner to them, but they were clearly having sex with each other mentally. My Mom had me reading the bible enough before she put me out so as they went back and forth with words Matthew 5:28 circled my mind. Damn them both to hell. I rolled my eyes waiting to be back-lashed and slandered. I cleared my throat as the flirting escalated and the pastor adjusted himself in his seat.

"So Sonya, I hear you have some things going on in your life that could use some prayer. I want you to know that, you are not the only person going through this and you can be delivered. We have helped many in your same situation."

I thought about those many members he claimed to have been *delivered* and how nothing about them had really changed. They just learned to keep their lives private enough to not embarrass the church. Hell even some of his deacons were gay and it was clear as day, but as long as they had a woman on their arm, no one questioned it.

We sat in his office for two hours as he quoted verse after verse and told me how I could miss out on blessings by living this life. I let it all go in one ear and out of the other. I loved Des and there was no question about that, and there was nothing he or my Mother could say to change my mind, but I would pretend as long as I had to.

~~*~*

My Mom pulled up in front of the school to drop me off for my first day. I was supposed to have my new car for my senior year, but I knew that was out of the question, now that my Mom didn't trust me to go as far as the corner, without thinking I'd meet up with Des. I hopped out and walked into school. I knew that my Mom would be at home thinking all day about if Des and I would be doing things at school, but she couldn't just keep me from getting my education. I'd go to the police on her ass.

Des and I had the same first period. I had not seen her in almost two months. I ran to her and hugged her and she hugged me back. She looked different to me, but I knew it was due to the long period of time that I had not seen her.

"How was the rest of your summer?" she asked.

"Miserable. How was yours?"

"Lonely. I was kind of down, because I wasn't sure your Mom was going to let you come back here."

"She wasn't, but it's hard to transfer seniors."

"Thank God for that." she hugged me again and we entered the classroom.

She sat right next to me, "I'm so ready to get this year over with."

"Who are you telling?"

We passed notes all of first period. It was the only class we had together and we couldn't have lunch together because both of us had early release. She had to be at work and of course, my Mom was sitting outside waiting for me. Des parked at the back of the school, so I never had to worry about run-ins. I hopped into the car.

"How was school?"

"It was okay." I was shocked she asked.

"You ready for the year?"

"I guess so." I was not in the mood for her small talk.

"There is someone that I want you to meet. They are coming over for dinner tonight."

I knew there was a reason behind her sudden case of niceness. I smiled a cordial smile and said okay. She told me that we had new neighbors and there was a boy my age that I might like, so she invited them over. He would be going to school with me and she wanted me to show him around. This woman was clearly delusional if she thought I'd go to sleep and wake up straight. I'd let her believe it as long as she liked, if it kept her off my back.

I sat in my room as my Mom yelled my name. I pretended not to hear her the first time, because I knew what she wanted and that just was not important enough for me to move. She came into my room and asked if I heard her calling me. I simply replied no. Come meet the neighbor's, girl. We walked into the living room. She pulled me forward so she could play perfect Mother.

"Baby this is Lisa, and her son Tony. Don't be rude, speak." she nudged me.

"Hey."

My Mom rambled to Lisa about how I and her son were the same age. Had she not said son I would have thought he was a girl, because he looked better than me. I stood there feeling goofy as they chatted. Tony stood against the door. My Mom called me rude, but she didn't even ask them if they wanted to sit down. I turned to go back to my room. My Mom motioned for me, "Bring Tony with you. Let us women talk. I'll call when dinner is ready."

My Mom talked to us both as if we were five and not seventeen. That woman had real issues. Tony reluctantly followed me to my room. Once inside he flopped down on my bed. He stared at all the pictures of famous women posted on my wall.

"What's your name?"

"Sonya. Why?"

"I just wanted to know yours since you knew mine."

He stood and walked over to my closet and opened it, looked around and then closed it. He was getting too comfortable for me. He saw that I was giving him an ugly look so he sat back down.

"I think my Mom is trying to set us up." he finally said.

"I know mine is."

"Why? You're a pretty girl, I'm sure you can get a boyfriend."

"Men aren't exactly my type."

His mouth dropped open more dramatic than it needed to, then he crossed his legs and changed his entire tone, "Girl, you're gay?"

I laughed. "Yes."

"Honey me too! My Mom and Dad aren't having that shit though, so I have to act *trade* around them. You know all hard and shit."

"Wow, well you do a good job."

He popped my leg, "We can help each other out."

"What do you mean?"

"We can pretend to be in a relationship," he stood like he had just had the idea of the year. He placed his hand on his hip and began to pace. "This is too perfect. My prayers have been answered." he threw his hands in the air.

"Shhh, keep it down."

"Girl, I'm sorry."

Our Moms called us to the kitchen for dinner and asked us question after question, to see if we had gotten to know each other a little. They had no idea.

~~*~*

It was smooth sailing after that. Tony was my *boyfriend* as long as we were around our parents. We held hands and pecked on the lips just to keep them thinking it was official, but once we got to school we were ourselves and on the weekends we pretended to be on dates with each other, but we were with Des and his boyfriend Rico. Des thought it was hilarious the way we played our parents.

Tony and I had gone to all the dances together. We took a set of pictures together for our families and another set with our partners for ourselves and each other. Tony and his boyfriend had planned to go away to college together after graduation. Des wanted to take a year off and I didn't have a plan, but I needed one, quick.

I walked through the door and my Mom tossed pictures off Des and me from prom at my face. She screamed and she yelled. She called me names and she wanted me out for good. I called Des and she came to pick me up. There was only two months left in the year. I would not cry this time about her not accepting me. The real world was right in my grasp. My birthday was coming up in a week and I'd be making eighteen, so I didn't need her anymore. I would not continue to live in the closet. It was time I aired my dirty laundry. I was prepared this time. Des had some of my things at her house just in case she pulled another stunt like this. I hopped in on her passenger side and we went to her house. I had not seen her Mom in so long. She lay across the sofa as we came in.

"Hey, Sonya."

I waved.

"I haven't seen you in so long."

"Well, I'm back until graduation."

"Your Mom again?"

"Of course."

"Well you know you're welcome here."

"Thank you."

Des and I went into her room and fell out on her bed laughing.

"You're handling this so well."

"I guess it has finally gotten old to me."

"Have you put thought into what you want to do after graduation?"

"Well, I know my Mom won't do anything else for me after this, so I decided on the military."

Des sighed hard and touched my face. "I'll write you every day."

"Promise?"

"I haven't broken one yet have I?"

"No, you haven't," I smiled.

"How are you feeling right now?"

"Free."

"Infuriated"

After two years of being separated from the woman I loved, we were back at it. Things between us had gotten intense and out of control. Basically, to make a long story short, money was low and stress was high. We were young, and the only thing that mattered to us was having fun and being with each other. Responsibility came at the bottom of our list. We decided to walk away before we hated each other and get our lives together. Felicia, but known as Flex because of her toned body, was now a semi-pro ball player and I was finally putting my accounting certification to use for a company that I will not mention for the sake of my job.

Flex was six feet even, tanned, one hundred eighty-five pounds. She had the sexiest dimples one person could wear on their face. Her hands were big enough to grip a male's basketball and soft enough to make me melt when she touched me.

I, however, was the exact opposite of Flex. I was petite and short. I wore heels with Flex all the time, because she hovered over me by six inches and looked odd together when I wore flats like I was her child. We had the same complexion and our smiles were similar. People often told us we looked related, but what couple doesn't after years of being together?

'Moving Mountains' by Usher sounded over and over on my cell phone, which was the ringtone of any number that wasn't locked into my Blackberry. It would have been easy to ignore if whoever it was would have just stopped calling. It was four o'clock in the morning and I wasn't due to be up until six, so I tried with all my might to just lie in bed and pretend that my cell wasn't ringing. After the fifth call, I decided maybe it was something crucial. I threw a miniature tantrum, rustling through the sheets and covers on my bed, before reaching to yank my cell from the charger. The number looked familiar to me, but I couldn't put my finger on who it could possibly be. I didn't bother to think on it long, I picked up and my attitude roared through the phone with a simple hello — exclamation point.

"Damn, I miss you too."

"Who is this?"

"Has it been that long?"

"Flex?" I said catching the tone of the now familiar voice.

"Yeah, baby, the one and only."

I sat up in my bed now wide awake from the shock of hearing her voice for the first time in two years since we separated. She broke the silence that had awkwardly crept up.

"Well, how have you been?" she asked.

"Fine, I guess. What about you?"

"The same, I miss you though, and I want to see you."

"Um, wow… I don't know what to say."

"Say you will meet me for lunch… or dinner."

"Why are you calling at four in the morning?"

"Tracy, don't change the subject. I want to see you."

"You don't know if I'm with someone."

"I don't care about another bitch. You'll always be mine."

"I knew you would say that."

Flex and I talked until it was time for me to get dressed for work. She finally convinced me to meet her for lunch during break. I tried to remain as calm as possible, not to look so anxious. I had remained single after Flex and I split because she was really all I wanted. I convinced myself that we would eventually be together when the timing was right. I kept the same number, waiting on the day for her to call. Even all of my profiles on the internet were public and easy to search, but she didn't need to know all that.

I changed several times that morning wondering if she would still find me as beautiful now as she did five years ago when we met through a mutual friend. Much about me had not really changed. I was maybe about five pounds heavier, but still slim, and my hair was now natural and died auburn.

It was hard for me to concentrate on my work when I finally made it to the office. All the numbers on my computer screen looked like Chinese symbols and I called everyone by the wrong name. My nerves were clearly getting the best of me as I sat reminiscing about everything that led Flex and I to this point again.

The one thing that stood out in my mind was New Year's Day, 2007. I sat in a chair beside our bedroom door flipping through channels. Flex paced back and forth through the house, doing only God knows what. She came into the room and stood in front of the television and I just looked at her.

"Would you move?" I scolded.

"I need to tell you something."

She turned around, lowered the volume on the television, and came to sit across from me on our bed. I sat in a chair, leaned back, waiting for whatever it was that she needed to say.

"Tracy, I love you, and we have been through a lot together. I've been pacing and thinking all day, well... actually... I've been thinking for awhile, and I think you should marry me."

I laughed at Flex and smacked my lips, but she didn't crack a smile. She moved from the bed to the floor on both knees and she placed her hands on my hips, while keeping eye contact with me. "I'm serious Tracy. Marry me."

"Get up and stop playing girl." I popped her arm.

"Tracy. Marry me... please?" her eyes watered.

I looked in her eyes searching for a hint of doubt, but there was none. The instant I sensed her sincerity, tears formed in my eyes and started sliding down my cheeks. I had always wondered as a little girl how someone would propose to me and here Flex was asking simply and sweetly. I placed a hand on each side of her face and choked out the word *yes* as best I could. I had never seen her smile as big as she picked me up from the chair to hug me. I wrapped my legs around her, and we embraced for a long time.

I wore her ring for a long time after she slapped it onto my size seven finger, but struggle kept us from the alter.

Eleven o'clock came faster than I wanted it to and I was on my way to TGI Fridays to meet my ex-fiancée for lunch. She and I pulled up at the same time and parked right beside one another. I took a deep breath and opened my door to get out. I watched her as she walked over to me with that familiar smile and those dimples. She pulled me into an embrace, and I inhaled her cologne and allowed her to hold me as long as she liked. She stepped back to have a look at me.

"Well aren't you all grown up and still beautiful."

I blushed, "Thank you. You look okay. " I laughed.

"You have always been my number one hater," she joked.

We went inside so that we could be seated and catch up. The butterflies in my stomach intensified as I took a seat across from her. We engaged in small talk until our food came then things got heavy.

"Tracy, there is a reason I wanted to see you."

"Oh boy."

"Don't do that."

"Okay, so what is it?" I asked, placing my hands beneath my chin.

"I really missed you and these last two years have been empty without you. I think we should try again, now that things are better in our personal lives."

"Flex I—"

"Let me finish. I want to pick up where we left off, only without the drama. I want you to be my wife. I really need you in my life."

"I don't know Flex, it's been so long. I'm not sure we are still the same people."

"Then we'll get to know each other again. Just think about it."

Flex spent the rest of my lunch break explaining why we should just go ahead and get married. Neither of us was getting younger and we had already gone through hell and back together. With every statement she made I agreed inside my mind that she had a point.

After lunch we embraced and when I tried to walk away she pulled me back and kissed me passionately. I almost lost my balance when she let me go. She got into her truck and sped off and I watched just blinking. I forgot what it was like to kiss her and I forgot how good it felt.

I spent the rest of my day thinking about it and that night I said to myself, what the hell.

~~*~*

It took Flex and I four months to plan what most people planned in a year. It was easy when you had the money to pay for everything. It was a civil union to the world, but a wedding to Flex and me. A stupid sheet of paper doesn't determine what a marriage is or the true definition of commitment.

The day before the wedding we had a dinner party at Houston's for all of our friends and family members. My sister stood to give a toast, directing it toward Flex. She raised her glass. "I've watched my sister and the way she looks at you, and I can honestly say that there is nothing but love in her eyes. I always knew that you were the one and I'm glad that you two have found one another again. Other girls may have had some, but they just lost one. You're *the man,* Flex. I know things will be different this time."

Everyone laughed and clanked their glasses. At that very Moment I should have objected to my own wedding, because everyone laughed but Flex and me. A feeling of discomfort shot through me suddenly and Flex did not look the same to me anymore as she stared off into space.

The dinner went on smoothly for everyone else as they laughed and engaged in conversations about sex, love, marriage, and kids. I could see everyone's lips moving, but they were silent to me as my thoughts spoke loudly inside my head. I figured maybe I just had cold feet and it would pass over while I slept. I smiled and laughed best I could for the rest of the night so the feeling of doubt wouldn't show on my face to my family, friends, or Flex, who wasn't paying attention anyway.

Everyone hugged and kissed and went their separate ways after dinner. We made it an early night since the wedding was the next day. I tossed and turned that night until it was time for me to wake up and get ready to become Mrs. Tracy Watson.

When I woke up the next morning the exhaustion showed under my eyes. It was a good thing that my sister had handled everything. All I had to do was sit and get my hair, nails, make-up, and feet done before six o'clock.

My sister filled me up with coffee so that I could keep my eyes open as I got pampered. Her cell phone rang constantly as people called making sure they were placing things in the proper places at the garden that our ceremony was being held in.

Six o'clock came quickly. My sister zipped the back of my silk, off white, fitted, strapless wedding dress and placed the veil over my pint up hair. She handed me my bouquet and lightly kissed my cheek before opening the door for my Father to come in. He smiled widely and told me that I was beautiful while holding out his arm for me to wrap mine around.

My Father led me around the side of the house that sat behind the garden so no one would see me before they were supposed to. 'Ribbon in the Sky' by Stevie Wonder blared from the speakers as I walked around. An announcement was made that I was getting ready to enter and the song switched to Stevie Wonder's 'You and I'. Candles were lined along the trail that led to the alter, where Flex stood with all her *groom's women,* in all white tuxes and soft pink ties that matched the dressedof my bridesmaids. Some people smiled at me while others cried, and the photographer snapped my every step. It was dark outside and calm. I walked slowly so that no one missed me.

Flex reached out her hand to take mine after my Father guided me forward and kissed my cheek — a symbol of his approval as he handed me over. I wore my veil behind my head because there was no reason to pretend I was a virgin. She looked into my eyes and I looked into hers. The pastor spoke his piece and then Flex and I exchanged our vows.

Felicia "Flex" Watson	*Tracy Moss*
Tracy, you know that I love you with all my heart and I'm not that great with expressing myself, but I can stand here today and say to you that I always knew that you were the one for me and I have never stopped loving you or thinking about you. Everyone probably thinks that we are crazy for suddenly making this type of commitment, but nothing is crazy when you are sure. I'm not interested in what anyone feels. All I want to do is make you happy and love you for the rest of my life. We made promises a long time ago to die in each other's arms. My arms are open and I'm ready to keep that promise. I love you and you will always be mine.	*Felicia my lover, my best friend, the first woman that I have ever given all of me to, I love you with every breath in my body and I have not been able to breathe without you. My heart races at the sound of the telephone, I am mute at the sound of your voice, I can't sleep at night from the thought of you, my heart and feelings have created an emotional barricade that can't be touched by anyone but you, I call everyone your name, and I fall at your feet because you are my "king" ...I do all of this because I'm in love and I have been in love since the day that I saw you, kissed you, been held by you, and confided in you. I found myself in your eyes and I want to stay there forever. I love you.*

We both cried as we spoke and then we kissed, and just like that we were married.

The reception seemed to have more people than the actual ceremony and there was plenty of food. Flex and I had our first dance as a married couple to 'For You' by Kenny Latimore. Everything was perfect.

We didn't plan a fancy trip for a honey moon, because we had to get back to work. Our limo dropped us to the Hilton Hotel where we booked a suite for the weekend. It would be the first time in two years that Felicia and I would make love again. Felicia carried me over the threshold of our room and we laughed at the silly tradition. The hotel gave us complimentary champagne and fruits and a bunch of other stuff that we probably wouldn't even use, but it was nice. I walked over to the window and stared over the lights of the city. Everything looked so small from high up, but beautiful.

Felicia walked up behind me and cut my dress from my body with scissors, right down the middle. She grabbed my hands and pressed them against the window. I stood wearing only black laced boy shorts and a black strapless bra. She sucked on my neck with vengeance with her cold tongue from the ice she held in her mouth. Her fingers slid between my legs moving my shorts to the side. She rubbed my clit while holding me against the window. The melting ice in her mouth ran down my shoulder splitting evening over back and breast.

Flex snatched her tie from around her neck and pushed my hands together to bind them. She grabbed two more pieces of ice and ran them all over my body. The hair on my arms raised and I jumped from the chill. She licked all the places where she slid the ice and the warm/cold sensation drove me insane. I wanted to grab her, scratch her, pull her, push her, *damn these tied hands*. She pulled my shorts down past my ankles then unsnapped my bra, throwing them both to the side where my cut wedding dress lay on the floor. She lifted me up and wrapped my legs around her waist, inserting her fingers inside of my pulsating walls.

Flex wore a size eleven ring, so that'll give you an idea of what was happening inside of my body as she moved slowly in and out, quicker and harder. My back and bare ass was pressed against the window and I was sure someone could see me being fucked from another building, but I didn't care. It felt so good. My tied wrists dangled behind Flex's head as she pressed into me, muscles bulging from her arms, holding up my weight, and fucking me. I felt bad for anyone who could hear my loud moans as I came all over Flex.

It was a honeymoon to remember because we never stopped.

~~*~*

Between working and fucking a year passed. Flex and I had found a house together and we were renting to own. We could have easily just moved into one of the houses one of us already lived in, but we wanted

79

to avoid that this-is-my-house argument. We didn't want anyone to have more power than the other one.

Everything was good until Flex flew in from an away game one night. That entire day had just been a bad day. I was looking forward to relaxing, cuddling up to Flex and forgetting about my day. I walked inside and it was pitch black. I tripped over something as I walked in and walked over to flip on the light. I jumped because Flex was sitting in the corner with red eyes. It was her bag that I tripped on. She had a bad habit of sitting things down as soon as she walked in and leaving it there. I walked over to her after sitting my purse down.

"What's wrong baby?"

"I can't play ball anymore."

"What? Why?"

"I lost my temper and I got ejected."

"You... how... what happened?"

"This stupid ass girl elbowed me on purpose. To the point that I fell and could barely move, so when I did, I got up and punched her and then I cussed out the ref for the piss-poor call he made."

"So why can't you play anymore?"

"It's not the first time it happened. I had one more time to get ejected."

"Well, why didn't you control yourself? You should have been the bigger person."

"I don't want to hear all that right now."

"I'm just saying."

Flex jumped up and punched the wall. I jumped back and just looked at her as the sheet rock cracked.

"Calm down, it's not that serious."

"Not that serious? That's all I know how to do. It's all I've done all my life!"

"You can get a job like the rest of us."

"Doing what?" she punched the wall again.

"Flex, seriously calm down. You're scaring me."

Flex started to breath heavily and tears fell from her eyes. I backed up out of fear and I shook a little. She punched the wall a few more times and yelled cuss words. I didn't know if I should try to hug her to calm her down or just allow her to knock down the wall in our house. I had never seen her this way.

"Would you stop punching the wall?"

Flex punched the wall again and I walked to grab my purse and car keys. I was not about to be in the house with her until she calmed down.

I reached for my keys and she snatched me by the wrist holding my arm in the air.

"Where are you going?"

"You obviously need to be alone."

"You're going to just leave me here? You don't give a fuck about me."

"I didn't say that Flex. Let me go. You're hurting me."

"Where are you going to go?"

"Over to my sisters'."

"Why? So you can talk about me and tell her all my business."

"No, stop putting words in my mouth and let me go!"

Flex let my arm go and I reached for my keys again. This time she grabbed my neck and slammed me against the wall. She stood close to my face while squeezing my neck. "You're not leaving me here. I need you."

I tried to pull her fingers from around my neck, but she squeezed tighter. When she finally let me go, I fell to the floor to catch my breath. She sat down on the floor with me and wrapped her arms around me. She apologized constantly and she rubbed my hair. I had no idea who she was.

I should have left that night, but I didn't. I convinced myself that it would never happen again, after she explained in extent what happened at the game. I thought maybe it was a spill of emotions and they had been released at the wrong time. I covered my bruises with foundation so that I could be presentable at work and I didn't tell anyone what happened because I didn't expect it to happen again. People fight and these things happen, right? Flex had never put her hands on me before, so I knew it had to be the game that made her react that way.

~~*~*

Flex lounged around the house day after day. I got the internet installed so she could search for jobs online and I bought her a newspaper every day. Some days when I had enough time at work, I highlighted the things that she may be interested in doing. She said that she had been on a few interviews, but for some reason I didn't believe a word that she said. Money was getting tight between us since I was the only one working. Feeding Flex, was like feeding three men. I was cooking, cleaning, working, finding time to fuck her, and doing all the shopping while she laid on her ass. I just wanted one minute to myself and some support.

Flex was laid out across the bed in nothing but boxers and a wife beater when I got out of the shower.

"Flex, get dressed. You're going to make us late."

"I don't feel like going."

"Are you kidding me? My sister is renewing her vows. Get up. You aren't tired. You didn't do shit all day."

"I'm trying."

"How? I called Ms. Martin and she said you never showed up for that interview."

"You checking up on me?" Flex got up from the bed and walked over to me. She stood really close and my face was to her chest. She put her finger to my head. "I'm not some fucking kid. Don't check up on me."

"Don't act like a kid and I won't check up on you." I pushed her hand.

Flex backed up and slapped me hard across the face. My jaw cracked and a sharp pain ran through my face. She looked at me like she was waiting for me to say something. I ran at her swinging as hard as I could, knowing I was unmatched. Spit flew from my mouth every time Flex's hand landed on my face. It felt like she was hitting me with the inside of her wrist, but it didn't stop me. I called her every stupid bitch that I could think of as blood leaked from my mouth. She grabbed my arms and held me down on the bed. Her weight pressed down on me and I couldn't move. She balled her fist and held it up like she was going to punch me. I closed my eyes tight and turned my head, but she didn't hit me. I burst out into tears and lay in the bed crying after she got off of me. I was officially afraid of my own wife.

Flex dressed and left and I just lay there. She knocked down lamps and pictures frames as she walked out. I missed my sister's ceremony and my phone rang off the hook, but I ignored it.

Flex crawled into bed with me in the middle of the night and wrapped her arms around me. I tried not to jump because I didn't want her to know I was awake. She whispered I'm sorry and held me tightly. She snored in my ear and I stared at the wall in front of me until I dozed off.

Flex was gone again when I woke up the next morning. I walked into our bathroom and flipped on the light. The light hurt my eyes and I squinted until they adjusted. My face was hurting and I could barely open my mouth. When I looked into the mirror the entire left side of my face was swollen and my eye was cut. I couldn't go to work like that. I cleaned the cut and then called my job.

"Heeey, Judy? This is Tracy I won't be coming in today."

"What? Tracy? You never call off. Are you okay?"

"Yeah, I'm fine. I ate something and had an allergic reaction and now my face is swollen."

"Oh, okay then girl. I'll tell Mr. Benson that you won't be in. I'm sure you have a million hours of sick time." she laughed.

I forced out a fake laugh as my eyes watered. Judy made small talk and then let me go. I ended the call and the tears fell harder. This was not who I was. *"Shit, shit, shit,"* was all I could say as I cried. Our room door opened and I silenced myself. I grabbed tissue and ran water to throw on my face before going back into the bedroom.

Flex was standing there with uniforms in her hand and a bag of ice with a towel. She laid the uniforms on the bed and walked over to the bathroom doorway where I stood, placing the bag of ice to my face. "I'm sorry, Tracy. I'm just dealing with a lot and I don't know how to handle all of this. I'm sorry I'm taking all of it out on you. Please don't leave me. It'll get better and I'll try harder. You believe me?"

I nodded slowly.

"I got a job today. I won't be making much since it fast food, but it's a start. We can pay the lights, cable, and water or whatever with my checks."

She hugged me and held me close.

~~*~*

It had been almost a month and Flex had not had any temper tantrums. She worked daily from six a.m. to three p.m. and most days she was too tired to say or do much of anything.

My sister had not been speaking to me since her ceremony. I guessed she was pissed at me for not showing. I couldn't tell her what happened that night. It would make an already bad situation worse. I had been helping my sister look for houses, because her and her husband wanted to relocate since they had more children and they needed more space. I called one more time to see if she would pick up and she finally did.

"What?"

"Sharee, don't be mad at me."

"You're my sister. You were supposed to be there, Tracy."

"I know, and I'm so very sorry."

"You better have a great excuse."

"I was called into work on an emergency," I lied.

"More important than me?"

"I could have lost my job. I know you don't want me and Flex living with you and Justin. I'm wearing my pitiful face. You can't be mad at this face."

She laughed and finally forgave me. I pulled the paper from my purse that I had printed out with housing information on it and started telling her about the properties I found.

I walked into the kitchen and sat at the table as I explained everything about each house. It was so nice talking to my sister. She asked how the married life was going and I gave the sugarcoated version. My sister always knew when something wasn't right with me, and she could tell even on the phone. She pressed the issue when my tone changed, but I insisted that everything was fine. She knew not to push me too much. We hung up so that I could start dinner before Flex made it home. I sat my phone down on top of the real estate papers and proceeded to cook.

I was half way done when Flex walked in throwing her hat and bag to the floor. She walked into the kitchen and kissed my cheek and lifted the lids on each pot to see what I was cooking. She sat down at the table and then stood back up holding the real estate paper.

"What the fuck is this?"

"It's for Sharee."

"You and Sharee haven't been speaking. You're fucking lying to me."

Flex charged at me and I ran around the kitchen table while trying to explain the paper.

"I called her today baby. She finally forgave me."

Flex knocked over a chair. "You're trying to leave me!"

"No, I'm not. It's not for me!"

Flex jumped up on our table and over at me, pushing me onto the door of our pantry. She grabbed my neck with both hands and started lifting me from the floor. My feet dangled beneath me as she choked me. Flex cried and screamed, *'you're not leaving me'* into my face. Snot ran from her nose as she choked back on tears. She yelled, *'I'll kill you'* into my face and that's when I knew that I had let things go on too long. Flex was now making physical threats on my life and I was afraid. She removed one hand from my neck and pulled me as she walked over to get my cell phone. Flex scrolled through my phone and called my sister. My sister answered on the first ring and Flex started yelling.

"SHAREE, SHE'S TRYING TO LEAVE ME. TELL HER SHE CAN'T LEAVE ME!"

"Felicia?" I heard her say.

She continued to cry. "SHE DON'T WANT ME NO MORE."

I screamed loud enough to shatter glass. "HEEEEEEELP!"

Sharee yelled. "WHAT THE HELL IS GOING—"

Flex ended the call.

As soon as she dropped the phone I cocked back and punched Flex in the left eye. She screamed, but that lick didn't loosen her grip on my neck. I hit her in the opposite eye harder with my left fist. She let me go and grabbed her face. I ran and she ran behind me. She jumped on me and we both fell to the floor. Flex's nails scratched my arms as I struggled with her. She placed her entire hand over my face and held my head down as she tried to unbuckle my jeans. I screamed and fought her.

"STOP!"

"You're not leaving me Tracy. You're always going to be mine."

Flex pulled my jeans right beneath my ass and pushed her fingers inside of my dry walls. I screamed as I felt her nails scratch me. I had no idea who she was or why she was hurting me. It was little things that set her off; things that had nothing to do with her at times. I didn't remember her being this way the first time that we dated. Somewhere in our two year gap, something had to have happened. I had to get away or one day she'd kill me for real. I wasn't sure what was worse, being physically abused or it being done by a woman and I couldn't do much to defend myself.

~~*~*

I sat wrapped up in a blanket in my sister's guest bedroom jumping at any sound I heard. It had only been three weeks and the images of what Flex did the last time I saw her still replayed daily in my head. I had taken a leave of absence from my job to get my head together.

My sister had become worried, after Flex called her so suddenly from my cell. She called her husband. They came over to my house and when they heard me screaming they kicked in the door. Justin pulled Flex off of me and her soiled fingers exited my sore vagina. It felt like my lips had been punched. My sister helped me from the floor and pulled my underwear and jeans up. Justin held Flex and tried to calm her down and snap her out of whatever trance she was in. He was the same height as her, but bigger, so it was easy for him to restrain her. My sister walked me to my bedroom and told me to grab whatever I needed. She wasn't giving me a choice.

85

I could see everything that she was thinking all over her face. She was disgusted and very angry. I grabbed clothes and placed as much as I could into an overnight bag.

"You want me to call the police, Tracy?"

I sniffed. "No."

"How long has this been going on?"

"A while."

"Why didn't you tell me?"

"How was I supposed to tell you that my wife was in here kicking my ass?"

"Tracy."

"I would look weak."

"No, you wouldn't. Domestic violence isn't just a crime that happens between a man and woman. Flex can kick a man's ass as big as she is. You should have told me."

"I thought she would stop."

"Stop? Did you look at her? She looks like she's out of it. She needs help."

"I know."

"She could have killed you."

"I know that too."

"You need to press charges on her Tracy."

"I can't do that. She'll lose her job and she's trying to get back into the league."

"Wait, she's not playing ball anymore?"

"Nope, she got ejected for her temper."

"Oh, my, God. You used to tell me everything, what happened?"

"I'm grown, Sharee. I can't gossip about my own wife. I wanted to help her."

"Help her? She needs to help herself."

"I don't need a lecture right now. I just want to get away from her right now."

Flex sat on the sofa with her face in her hands. We took one last look at one another and then I left. The reality of everything had hit me when I went to take a bath and I removed my panties. There was blood inside and my menstrual wasn't due for another two weeks. I was raped by my own wife and even worse I wasn't going to report her.

~~*~*

86

Flex called constantly in the past three weeks, but I would never answer. She left countless voicemails apologizing and saying that she would get help. She cried, she professed her undying love, she recited her wedding vows, and she recorded her daily activities so that I would know exactly what she was doing every minute of every day.

My sister knocked on the door before entering and then joined me on the bed with a tray of food.

"You okay in here?"

"Yeah, I'm fine."

"She still calling?"

"Yep, and I don't think she will stop anytime soon."

"You want to talk about it?"

I nodded my head up and down. "I don't know what happened, Ree. One minute we were fine and the next she was someone else."

"When did it start?"

"After she was kicked out of the league. She was so mad that night. She had this look on her face like she wanted to kill somebody. I should have left then, but I just loved her too much."

"Love doesn't hurt sis."

"I know, but I just couldn't leave. It's easier said than done. We were together three years."

"But separated for two"

"Something had to happen to her while we were separated. Nobody just snaps like that."

"You don't have to sacrifice your life trying to figure it out, Tracy. It's her burden. Has she ever tried to kill you?"

"She held a knife to my throat once."

"And you stayed?"

"I was scared Sharee. You don't understand the power of fear."

"Well you're safe now and she better not come up in here or I'll bust a cap in her ass."

I laughed at my sister's poor attempt to be a thug and she hugged me.

~~*~*

I sat out of work for five months. I could take up to six, but I was going to go crazy just sitting in my sister's house. It was time for me to get back to my life. I still wore my ring because I didn't want people at work asking questions. As far as they knew I was injured in a car accident. I got my Father to create a police report for me for my boss to file and that was all there was to the situation. I was welcomed with open arms, and I was ready to work so I could regain my independence. I missed Flex like crazy. I had to learn to sleep alone and do everything for one instead of two. She knocked her daily calls down to once a week. I still didn't answer when she called and she still left a voicemail.

She said that she was getting help and understood why I had to leave her. She wasn't angry with me. She claimed she felt like shit for what she did to me, and she would spend the rest of her life making it up to me if I gave her the chance one day. She said would wait however long it took for me to come back to her. I could have easily deleted her voice messages without listening to them, but a part of me still needed to hear her voice. I was starting to believe that I needed help too because I should hate her, but I didn't. I wanted to embrace her and be there for her. I knew she was the only one who could remove the pain I felt daily inside my chest, but I had to stay away. I *needed* to stay away.

My first day at work wasn't so bad. They had done a potluck to welcome me back. My boss brought me up to speed on everything that was going on. Judy handled most of my clients while I was out and she did an excellent job.

I took a long drive before going back to my sister's house after work. I pulled up behind her car and my cell phone rang. It was Felicia. My body felt heavy and weak just seeing her name on the screen, yet again. It probably wasn't a good idea, but I answered, "Hello."

She was silent.

"Hello."

"How have you been?" she finally asked.

"Okay."

There was silence again.

"What do you want Flex?"

"Nothing really, I didn't even expect you to pick up."

"Oh, well, I was just on my way in. I'll go now."

"Wait."

"What?"

"Will you have dinner with me?"

"That might not be a good idea."

"Why not? I won't do you anything, I promise. You can come in your own car and tell your sister, please."

I thought about it for a moment. "Just dinner?"

"Yes, just dinner. With your wife."

Call me stupid, but I accepted. Something in me knew that Flex and I were not done and I strongly believed that people could change. I knew who Flex really was and she definitely wasn't an abuser. I couldn't see her for the person she had become. All I could see was the person that I met who loved me more than anyone in the whole world.

I sat up the rest of that night, looking at old pictures of Flex and I: all the holidays that we had spent together, our random trips to the zoo and the aquarium, our late night walks on the river, me sitting on the sidelines of her basketball games, family cruises, us just laying around our old raggedy apartment, and finally our wedding pictures. Each photograph tugged at my heart, reminding me that we were meant to be together and this was just something that we had to go through. I jumped up and went to my sister's room.

"What's wrong, Tracy?"

"I'm going back home."

"Home to… Flex?" She looked puzzled.

"Yes, please don't judge me right now."

"I'm not judging you. I can't do that. I'm not God and you're grown. You make your own decisions. Just be careful. When are you leaving?"

"Now."

"Are you sure that's what you want to do?"

"Yes, I have to try again."

"Okay, well, call me if you need me, Tracy, I'm serious."

"I will."

I packed up all of my things and placed it inside of my trunk and on my back seat.

It was midnight when I pulled up to my house and instantly all the painful memories came back to me. *What the hell am I doing?* I ignored the thought and got out to walk up to the door. I pulled out my key and turned the lock and the knob at the same time. I had a gun pointed in my direction as I walked in.

"It's me! Tracy!"

Flex lowered the gun. "Tracy?" She flipped on the light.

Flex tucked the gun behind her into her pants and then pulled me into a tight embrace. She kissed me all over my face slowly and then kissed my lips. Her tongue slid into my mouth and she kissed me as though she had never kissed me before in her life. I could taste our tears as we kissed and all of our emotions exploded into each other. Flex pushed the door closed with her foot and carried me to our bedroom. She laid me down in our bed and started to remove my clothes, then stopped suddenly.

"We don't have to do this if you're not comfortable."

"I'm okay," I whispered.

Flex kissed me as long as she could before sucking on each breast and circling my nipples with her tongue. She licked slowly as if she were savoring the flavor in her mouth. She licked down the center of my body just before tracing my panty line with her tongue. Flex's tongue was long and thick, just like her fingers. I felt she was afraid that I would have a flashback so instead of penetrating me with her fingers; she pushed her tongue inside of me and massaged my clit with her fingers as her head moved back and forth. Every now and then she would stop just to lick upward hitting my clit.

"Baby stop, I'm going to cum in your mouth."

"I want you to."

I came in Flex's mouth and it was intense. My body fell limp. Flex started talking to my pussy and I laughed.

"You know I love you right? I'll never hurt you again." She kissed my pussy and then lay beside me. "What made you come back?"

"Stupid pictures, I missed you. I missed us."

"I missed us too. I'm really sorry, Tracy."

I placed my fingers over her lips. "Can we just sleep?"

Flex held me all night and we just slept.

~~*~*

The holidays were coming up and it was time for us to do some shopping. My sister still wasn't fond of Flex, but she had agreed to meet us at the mall so we could all sit down for lunch and do some shopping. Sharee and her husband were buying gifts for the kids, and I was picking up things for people in the office and my sister's kids. We had been in the mall for hours. We got there around twelve and it was about seven. My sister and her husband left, but I was still looking around when Flex ran up to me telling me about a shirt she wanted to buy.

"Baby, it's just $150.00."

"It's a shirt."

"I just need $75.00."

"I'm not giving you $75.00 dollars."

"You just spent a hundred on your boss alone and you can't give me $75.00?"

"It's my money."

"Yours?"

"Yes, *mine*. Nobody told you to piss yours away on stupid shit."

Flex grabbed my arm and pulled me from the register just as I was paying for some shoes. She drug me by the arm to the car.

"Are you fucking serious right now Flex? I'm not in the mood for one of your tantrums."

She snatched the bags from my hand and threw them into the back seat. She opened my door and pushed me. I sat with my arms folded, pouting like a child as she walked around to the driver's side and got in.

"So, we have to leave the mall, because you can't have a fucking shirt?"

Flex punched the steering wheel. "You are so fucking selfish when it comes to me!"

"I'm selfish? It's my fucking money and I told you what we were coming to the mall for. Not once did I say hey let's get Flex a $150.00 shirt!"

"I didn't even want you to buy it. I asked for half."

"You just got paid! Just take me home because I see you're about to start acting crazy."

"Crazy? I'll show your ass crazy."

Flex started the engine and sped from the lot. Her face was scrunched and she talked to herself angrily as she drove. Flex pulled into a vacant lot next to the bridge and hopped out. She started to pull the bags from the back seat and toss them into the water one by one. I hopped out and jumped on her, trying to stop her. She pushed me to the ground and I hit the back of my head on the concrete. Flex stood over me and grabbed my shirt collar.

"Are those motherfuckers more important than me, huh? HUH?"

She slammed my back into the concrete and I held my neck up to keep from getting a head injury, or worse, becoming unconscious. I felt rocks push into my skin each time she would lift me and slam me down. Flex stood and continued to toss bags. I jumped up from the ground and started to run as fast as I could while screaming help, hoping maybe someone would hear me. She ran behind me and caught me before I got too far. She picked me up from the ground and I kicked as she carried me back to the car. I tried scratching and biting her, but it didn't faze her. She put me inside the car and slammed the door. I leaned back against my window and as soon as she got in the car and closed her door, I kicked her hard in the face at least four times and her mouth started to bleed. She touched her lip and saw her own blood and jumped at me, but decided against attacking me. Instead, she started the car and sped to the interstate. I pulled out my cell phone to text my sister to tell her where I was and what was going on just in case something happened to me.

"Who the fuck are you texting?"

"None of your business!"

"Give me that phone!" Flex reached over trying to snatch my cell from my fingers, but I gripped it tight and pushed her head as she drove. The car swerved a little and she let my phone go. Flex pushed her foot down on the gas and we went up to ninety miles. An eighteen wheeler passed and she tried to swerve into it, but I pushed the wheel.

I screamed, "Stop the car! Let me out!"

"You want to get out? Jump!"

I had to think fast. It was time to show this bitch what crazy really was. I looked around the car and then pushed the clutch up to park while we were still moving. Metal clanged together and the car started to slide forward. Cars passed us quickly blowing their horn as we slid across the lanes. I held on to my seat and held my breath. My heart was beating faster than it ever had. Flex held on to the steering wheel, trying to keep from being hit. She pressed on breaks and the car rolled slowly to the side until it came to a complete stop.

"You broke the fucking car!"

Flex jumped out of the car and started screaming and cussing. I locked the doors once she got out. She started walking up the interstate just throwing her hands in the air and swinging. My sister texted telling me she was on her way. I texted her and what exit I was sitting close to. I jumped when I looked up and saw Flex standing right by my window staring at me. She yelled through the glass.

"WHO THE FUCK ARE YOU TEXTING?" She punched the window. "Open the door!"

"Leave me alone!"

"Open the fucking door!"

I sat thinking I was safe until someone got to me. I would hope she wasn't stupid or reckless enough to break the glass on her own vehicle, and of course, she wasn't, but she was smart enough to carry a single, spare key in her pocket. She unlocked my door and I pushed the locked back down. I held it down and she ran around the car until she could pop one. I dialed my Father's number and he picked up, sounding as if he were sleeping.

"Daddy, come get me." Tears started to roll down my face.

"Where are you?"

"On the interstate going west, Fe-Fe-Felicia is hitting me. I'm so scared Daddy please, come get me."

"You see any cops?"

"No."

"Calm down and breathe. I need you to tell me exactly where you are, so I can radio an officer to you."

I told my Father where I was, as best I could and then we hung up. I was terrified as Flex finally swung the door opened and snatched me out by my hair. It was dark and there was nothing but trees surrounding us. She pushed my face into the window and it shattered, but the glass didn't fall. I swung at her and the hit stunned her, and she let me go. She caught her balance and then ran up on me again, pushing me into the car.

"I'll fucking kill you, Tracy! YOU HEAR ME I'LL FUCKING KILL YOU!"

Red and blue lights flashed as she pulled me from the car to the side where there was a ditch and water. She was about to push me down into it, but the cops jumped on her restraining her. My sister and my Dad pulled up behind the cop car and ran over to where I was standing. Flex was not the girl I had met and it was time for me to let all those old memories go. I was pressing charges and moving on with my life without looking back.

After a year and a half of counseling and court dates, I was finally able to move on with my life and rid myself of anything that had something to do with Flex. My sister and my Dad hated her and didn't even want her name mentioned. She tried calling me from jail a few times, but I changed my number. I sold everything in our house and moved into my sister's house. She bought a five bedroom and she wanted me to stay there.

Felicia had to do two years in jail and pay a $10,000.00 fine. She begged me to drop the charges, but I refused. I figured jail would be great therapy for her and maybe some people could beat on her for stupid shit for a change.

I pawned the ring she gave me and I went back to living my life. I was not interested in being in another relationship for a while. I was more focused on putting the word out in the LBGT community that domestic violence is very real and they should tell someone if they are being abused. People tend to think it's fair game just because it's two men and two women, but I'm here to tell you that it's not when you're only 5'4" and maybe 130lbs standing against someone twice your size, who just might have a mental hold on you as well. They know you love them and they know their power.

I wished that I had told my sister sooner or anyone for that matter. I wish that I had left the first time. I wish that I had fought harder. I wish that I had realized that I was stronger. No one should be scared for their life and I'd never be afraid for mine again.

"Teacher's Pet"

Twenty-nine years old and here I was, the principal of the same high school that I graduated from. I wasn't sure I would get the job but I did and I couldn't be happier. I celebrated with my family and a few close friends, but I had a lot that needed to be done if I was going to hold my position and earn my respect as the youngest principal in my district. I wasn't stopping there because I had a bigger goal at hand. I was eventually going for Superintendant and nothing would stand in my way.

I felt like I was on top of the world and I had everything one black woman could ask for, even someone to share it with. If it's not hard enough being a black professional female, try being a lesbian strictly into feminine women. I was never into the whole online meeting and dating thing and I barely attended gay/lesbian events because I had been too afraid to run into some of my students, the parent of a student, or worse, a co-worker. Even though I'm more than sure, if I saw someone I worked with at an event like that my secret would be safe with them. I just wasn't too fond of having people in my personal life like that. I was up shits creek when it came to dating. The few gatherings that I did attend yearly were filled with heterosexual, married couples or single women who were hard to read. Being a femme myself I knew how easy it was to blend with the straight crowd. I loved the look on people's face when they do discovered that I was a lesbian and then following the expression came, *well you don't look like one.* I mean, exactly what does a lesbian look like, a male impersonator, white, rough? There is no one way to be a lesbian, so FYI, we all come in different shapes, sizes, and colors too.

I loved to hear my parents rant and rave about my love life. My Mother would often ask when I was going to meet a nice young man. She had it stuck in her mind that my attraction to women was a phase. She would say that my beauty would just go to waste and my ovaries would rot. I'll admit that I am beautiful. I spend a lot of the time in the mirror admiring my mocha colored skin, my full lips, my almond shaped eyes, and my toned body — thanks to my gym membership because without it, I'd be overweight. My favorite thing about myself is my naturally curly hair. I had no idea where it came from because both of my parents as well as my grandparents have what you would call *bad hair*. I believed that somewhere down the line my Mother stepped out on my Father with the milk man or at least that's the joke I cracked.

My Father on the other hand was in complete and utter denial about my lifestyle. I had to come out to him every time that I saw him. He would always ask me about the one boyfriend I had in high school and he would inquire about why it didn't work out. If he wasn't my Dad, I'd give him the same answer that I gave everyone else, *"because he had a dick,"* but unfortunately, I couldn't say that to my Dad. Instead I would just tell him that he and I didn't have anything in common and he found someone else who could give him what I couldn't.

I loved my first and only boyfriend very much, but the idea of sex with him or any man was just sickening. There were a few times that we almost got to that point, but I would always stop him with false panic attacks, asthma attacks, invisible periods, cramps… shit, you name it and I've faked it. We stayed together until after our senior prom and then he never spoke to me again. I was single for a long time, because I knew I didn't want to be with another man and I was too scary to try women.

It wasn't until my junior year of college that I had my first sexual encounter with anyone. Her name was Amalia Sanchez.

Amalia was Latino, tall, and thick. She had long, wavy, brown hair, and green eyes.

She wasn't afraid to try me.

She and I both were education majors and she was my roommate. We had a lot of classes together, so we spent a lot of time with each other by default. She would often make passes at me and her heavy Spanish accent would draw me in, but I brushed her off because she always made me nervous. Amalia was wild and partied a lot. She was the exact opposite of me. I didn't reveal my body, I didn't socialize, my hair was always in a ponytail, and I was very shy, quiet, and focused on school. Opposed to Amalia, who always had her cleavage showing in some way or her legs out with her hair hanging down. She did just enough in school to get by, because the way she looked at it, whether she was head of the class or not, we were all getting the same degree. I would sit and watch her get dressed on Friday nights, which was party night for her. There was something so sexy about the way she applied her lip gloss and flipped her hair. She would always come and stand over my bed after she was dressed.

"Natalie, you like my dress?"

"Yes, it's cute."

"Cute? I'm changing."

"Why?"

"Because you were supposed to say sexy. I don't want to be cute. Cute is for puppies."

"Okay then, you look sexy."

"Nope, too late, you should have said it the first time," she walked away.

I shook my head, "Seriously. You look good."

"Would you try to talk to me in this dress?"

I shifted in my bed, "I can't answer that."

"Yes, you can. It won't make you a lesbian if you do."

"Of course, I would. You really look amazing."

"Thanks chica," she blew a kiss in my direction.

It always took Amalia hours to get ready. I would just watch her continue to do things even after she was dressed already.

"You should come out with me."

"I need to study."

"We have the same classes and I'm passing so what are you studying?"

"I have two papers that are due."

"Ugh! Natalie. You need to get out honey. You're young."

"I do get out."

"Yeah, to the library. Come out with me. I'll use force if I have to."

I laughed.

"Okay, I'll make you a deal. You come out with me tonight and you never have to go again."

"Alright, deal."

"And I have to dress you."

"You're pushing it."

"Come onnn," she clasped her hands together as a plea.

"Fine."

Amalia found the shortest and tightest dress in her closet to put me in. She pulled my hair from the ponytail it was in and put moose on my already curly hair. She applied make-up to my face, which was something I had never worn and she handed me a pair of heels to wear. I almost didn't recognize myself after she was done. She smiled widely at me once she was finished and then she whistled at me like men do and started dancing around the room at her own work. I grabbed my wallet and we were out.

"So, where are we going?"

"A club."

"Does it play Spanish music?"

"Sweetie no, I like R&B and hip hop."

It took us about fifteen minutes to get to the club. We paid to park and then headed toward the line, which was wrapped around the building. I hopped in behind the last person and Amalia grabbed my hand and pulled me past all the people waiting. Girls turned their noses up at us and whispered, while guys hissed at us and tried to get our attention.

The bouncer at the front of the line let us right in after kissing Amalia on the cheek. She started dancing the second we were in. I just looked around. I felt like a sheep in a room filled with wolves as men winked and licked their lips at me. Amalia pushed me to the bar and we were handed two free shots. I assumed this was her regular spot since she was getting VIP treatment. She got two more shots and we threw them back and then I was pushed to the dance floor. I stood completely still as Amalia grinded up against me and ran her hands up and down my body.

After a few shots I started to feel the music a little more and opened up. I danced right along with Amalia as others danced around us and some watched. Amalia would get so close to me that her lips would brush across my face. She looked beautiful under club lights as sweat formed across her brows. A random guy came and danced between Amalia and I and I decided to use that as a restroom break. I danced away from the crowd and tried to catch my breath. It was hard being tipsy and trying to hold myself up over a toilet. I hated public restrooms, but the liquor wanted out of my body.

After I was done I walked out and looked around the club for Amalia, but I couldn't spot her through all the people. As I started to walk forward I was pulled back and then pushed into a dark corner against the wall. Amalia pushed her body against mine and laughed as she leaned into me to talk into my ear.

"Who told you to leave me with that loser?"

Before I could answer two guys walked over to us and yelled over the music to get our attention.

"Are you two sisters?"

Amalia answered, "No, we're lovers."

"That's bullshit."

"Why is it bullshit?"

"Y'all are too beautiful for that dyke shit."

"That's why we're dykes. She's beautiful, I'm beautiful, so we figured hey, two beautiful people should be fucking each other."

Amalia looked me in the eyes and then kissed me. Her lips were soft and her kisses were slow. I closed my eyes and got lost in her. My arms hung limply at my sides. I wanted to touch her, but the fear in me said no. Amalia was not shy as her hands traveled from my waist to my ass and to the seam of my dress. Her fingers trailed my thighs and I wanted her. Once she stopped the two guys were gone. I'm sure they were pissed off. Amalia leaned into my ear again. "Did I make you uncomfortable?"

I shook my head no. Amalia grabbed my hand and pulled me toward the exit. I was a puppy now, willingly following her lead and waiting for her next move. People watched as we left holding hands, now looking more like a couple than just two friends out for a night. Of course, it didn't stop men from trying, but Amalia ignored them as we walked by, looking back at me with a smile every other second until we made it inside the car.

"You're a really good kisser," she smiled.

I cleared my throat and put on my seatbelt. "Thanks."

Amalia started the car and backed out fast to speed down the exit ramp of the parking garage. She turned the music up loud and sang along until we made it back to our dorms.

Amalia leaned on me as we walked back to our room. Her arms held my waist and her head was on my shoulder. She was finally winding down after dancing half of the night. We made it into the room and she fell across her bed. I removed her shoes and placed them neatly to the side. I unzipped the back of her dress and lifted her a little bit to take it off. She turned over to watch me put away her things.

"You look really good in my dress," she said with her face pressed against her mattress.

"Thanks."

"Come here," she patted the empty space on her bed.

I sat on the edge.

"Do I make you nervous or something? You're always so tense."

I laughed. "Kind of."

"What can I do to relax you?"

I sat still.

"Can I...kiss you again?" She sat up behind me, placing one leg to each side of me.

I nodded my head yes.

Amalia brushed my hair to the side with her hands. She pulled the dress strap from my shoulder and kissed my bare shoulder the way she would kiss my lips. She trailed kissed up to my ear and then turned my head, by pulling my hair, so that she could stick her tongue deep inside my mouth. She unzipped my dress as she kissed me and it fell exposing my breast and hard nipples. I stopped kissing Amalia and jumped up covering my breast by folding my arms across my chest. She wore a seductive grin on her face as she looked at me.

"Oh...my...goodness. You're a virgin." She stood up and walked toward me, "Relax." She pulled my hands from my chest, pulling me into her.

She pushed the dress from my waist to the ground and then pulled down my thong. I stood completely naked, shaking, with my arms by my sides. Amalia stepped back and unsnapped her strapless bra and then removed her pretty laced black boy shorts. She pulled me over to the bed and laid me down on my back, while never taking her eyes from mine. Amalia laid her naked body against mine. Her skin was warm and smooth.

She whispered in my ear. "Touch me."

I placed my hands on her back, but I didn't move them, because I was afraid I may do something she did not approve of. Amalia moved my hands from her back to her ass. She shifted her body so that one of her legs was position between both of my thighs and then she began to grind on me. Her thigh pressed against my clit as she moved up and down slowly. Her skin felt so good up against mine. I moaned as quietly as I could, but Amalia was not happy about that.

"Don't hold anything in," she grinded a little faster.

I moaned louder and Amalia rubbed up against me and squeezed my breast. Amalia had awakened something in me. She stopped, took my hand, and placed it between her legs.

"You did that to me."

Amalia was soaking wet. I played with her juices on my fingers until she lifted my hand and licked her own away. At the sight of her licking her own wetness from my fingers, my clit began to jump. I was amazed and completely aroused. She looked into my eyes no matter what she did. I jumped as she placed her hand over my pussy and spread the lips.

"This may hurt a little," she whispered. "Relax."

I sucked in air as she penetrated me with her middle finger. She moved in and out slowly until I was relaxed.

"More?"

"Fingers?" I breathed heavily.

"Yes."

I nodded my head quickly and Amalia inserted another finger inside of me. I moaned even louder now as I felt my walls expand. I closed my eyes tight and exhaled. My eyes watered from the sensation building in my body.

I struggled to talk. "Wha-what are you doing to me?"

"Massaging your G-spot. Shhhh...just enjoy it."

My toes curled as Amalia taught me things about my body I would have never had the guts to learn on my own. She stimulated things I had no idea could be stimulated and on top of that I had multiple orgasms.

I lay exhausted next to Amalia as she stroked my hair. I had a million thoughts running through my mind, but the one that stood out to me the most was the thought of how Amalia tasted. I wanted to please her the way she pleased me. I turned to face her.

"Teach me what you just did."

She laughed. "Honey you're a woman. You already know, you just don't realize it."

"Well, can I?"

"If you want to. No pressure."

"I want to."

I sat up and moved down to Amalia's pussy. The scent of it made my mouth water and without asking her another question I wrapped my lips around hers. I was a natural at eating pussy. I got a little cocky as Amalia jumped and moaned. She cussed and told me when I hit her spot. I could do this all night.

Amalia transferred schools after that semester and just like that it was over. We tried to keep in touch, but she had gone to another state, so it was pointless. Amalia was too wild for me anyhow. For the remainder of the time that we were fooling around I had become too serious and she just wanted to have fun. It was a match made in hell. I was kind of relieved after she left because I needed to get back on track with school.

Everything had become Amalia. I wanted to be around her all the time. I wrote her letters that I had never given to her. I doodled her name on every notebook. I got mad when other girls would talk to her and I always wanted her full attention. I was head over hills for someone who only saw me as a good time. I dated other women after her, but none of them tasted the way she did and none of them could hypnotize me the way she could, so I kept my eye on the prize: graduation, become a teacher, become a principal, and then a Superintendant.

Amalia and I reconnected ten years later, when three positions opened that needed to be filled before the start of a new school year. I wanted the spots filled with only the best. My high school was known for its academic excellence and I wanted that to continue. Filling the positions for Spanish and Math was a breeze since only one candidate for each had shown up for the interview. They each had very impressive resumes and came from other great schools. They were highly recommended from their references and each could teach multiple subjects.

I had one final interview for the day after seeing several other people to teach AP English. I crossed them all out with my red pen, while talking to myself. I had already seen everyone, but this last applicant had come in last minute. She was recommended by the school board, so I squeezed her in.

"Boring, not enough experience, too young, blah…"

I couldn't say those kinds of things in front of anyone else, because I could be sued, but I knew exactly what I was looking for and none of those teachers were it. They all just looked like they wanted a paycheck. I needed people who actually cared about the future of young adults. This wasn't just a job for me.

I buzzed my secretary. "Has the last person shown up yet?"

"Yes, she's waiting out here."

"Did she complete the application?"

"Yes, Ms. Hester."

"Okay, send her in."

I made a few more notes on applications as my door swung open and when I looked up, there she was, all grown up.

"Natalie?"

"Amalia?"

We both screamed like little girls as we embraced each other. She looked so good in her black pencil skirt and soft pink button down. She hadn't aged much at all. She had gained a little more weight, but it looked amazing on her. My eyes lit up and butterflies entered my stomach as I glared at the woman who had turned my world upside down.

"How have you been, Ms. Sanchez?"

"Oh stop it Natalie. We've seen each other naked."

"True. Well, how have you been, Amalia?"

"Better than most, worse than some, so I can't complain really, but look at you though, Ms. Principal."

"Yeah, well."

"Don't be modest. You always said you wanted to get this far and here you are."

Amalia's smile melted my heart as she boasted about my achievements, by pointing at plaques on my wall. She expressed how proud she was and then we talked about what she had been up to lately. Amalia was very successful herself, getting her masters in English Literature and being recognized by different organizations as teacher of the year. The interview lasted almost two hours as we played catch up. I ended up giving Amalia the job, more so for my own personal enjoyment, rather than the fact that she was actually qualified.

I showed Amalia around the school and I walked her to the classroom that would be hers. Our conversations kept venturing to the past and what we had been up to. I was more interested in what she had been up to and how I could fit in now that she was older and more mature. I wanted Amalia to see how different I was, but for some reason I couldn't be as aggressive with Amalia as I was with other women I dated after her. She made me weak. I handed over all of my power just from her looking at me. Every time she opened her mouth to talk I would say things in my head like: *ask her out, now, do it. She wants you to. You're a pussy Natalie Hester.* I just could not and would not muster up the courage to take control of the situation.

We walked back to my office, so that I could grab my briefcase and then walk her to her car. It was great just having her in my presence.

It was a good thing that classes hadn't started just yet, because it was so clear how I felt about Amalia and the students didn't need to see that. Amalia and I hugged once more before she got into her car. I closed her door for her and she started her engine. She rolled her window down and yelled at me just as I was walking away.

"What are you doing tonight?"

"Making myself some dinner and watching a movie maybe."

"Mind if I join you?"

I stuttered, "Uh su-su-sure."

She smiled. "What's your address?" She pulled a pen from her glove compartment.

I rattled out my address and Amalia was off. I didn't have a damn thing in my house to cook, so I had to make a store run. It sounded nice when I said it to Amalia, but now I actually had to cook something. Spaghetti was the simplest thing that I could think to cook. Little did I know that, that one simple dinner would be the start of our lives together again.

My alarm clock went off at 5:30am. I rolled over and Amalia was out of bed as usual. She got up before me every morning to make us coffee and breakfast. She would take her shower too so that I could have the bathroom once I was up. I walked through the dark room and into the bathroom, where I switched on the light and stretched. I turned on the water, grabbed my toothbrush and tooth paste and proceeded to do my daily routine. Amalia came into the bathroom as I turned on the water to the shower.

"Morning you." She walked over and kissed me.

"Hey, baby." I kissed her back and wrapped my arms around her. "Why are you in a robe?"

"I haven't taken my shower yet."

"Why not?"

"I thought I'd wait for you." Amalia untied her robe and dropped it.

She removed my clothes and then we got into the shower for some early morning lovemaking. There was nothing better than that. I preferred Amalia wet anyway. She pushed my head back under the water and bit down on my neck, while sliding her hand down, my dripping wet skin until she reached my pussy. She stroked my clit, while the fingers on her other hand dipped in and out of my mouth. Amalia loved when I sucked her fingers. I spread my legs a little further as she kneeled down to massage my clit with her tongue. Amalia's tongue slid back and forth and then she pulled me forward, while pushing her tongue as deep as she could get her tongue inside of me. I placed my hand against the shower wall as I felt my knees buckling beneath me. I wasn't going to let her have all the fun. I yanked Amalia up hard by her hair and turned her around, pushing my fingers through her walls. She yelled out "*Jódame Natalie, no jódame con fuerza hasta queyo cum*". I never had a clue what she was saying when she started speaking Spanish, but it turned me on and made me more aggressive with her. Amalia came and then we washed each other's body. She got out and I lingered under the water a little longer. It was always hard to get me out the shower. I would just stand there and enjoy the temperature of the water running down my body. After about thirty more minutes I got out and dried off.

"Babe have you seen my Chanel button down?!" I yelled through the house.

"I'm wearing it!" she yelled back.

I decided to wear a simple dress after discovering that my girlfriend had jacked me out of my shirt for the day. She looked sexy in my things

104

so it didn't bother me. Amalia was the main reason I was so attracted to femininity. She always smelled like something from Victoria's Secret, she had nice curves that she never hid and killer legs. Amalia had a certain poise and I loved it. I'm not a stud basher or anything, but to me women in men's clothing kind of defeated the whole purpose of female attraction. They hid everything under those baggy clothes. I wanted to see ass and I wanted to see titties and my woman would get the same from me. I'm sure it was more of a comfort and style thing for studs, but femmes was and always will be my preference.

I dressed and then went into the kitchen to have breakfast and coffee with my lady. She had made pancakes and sausage and she had the newspaper already sitting in my chair. She kissed me as she sat my food in front of me and then she walked off to get her own plate. We had the perfect life together. She really fit into my world perfectly and she was definitely different from the Amalia I had met ten years ago.

There were many nights that we just stayed home and cuddled on the sofa or played games. She chose me over the party for a change. I would have never thought I'd see the day when Amalia Sanchez would settle. I wanted every day to pass by quickly while I was at work just so I could lie next to her at night. I thought I had fallen for Amalia back then, but now I realize that was just infatuation because she was my first. Now I could say that I truly loved her because we have shared more than just sex. She was my companion, my life partner.

"Babe?" I looked up at Amalia.

"Yes, baby?"

"What were you saying in the shower?"

She giggled. "Fuck me Natalie, fuck me hard until I cum."

"Why did I ask?" I sat with a naughty smile on my face.

"Eat, I'll tell you more dirty things later." She winked at me.

I ate my breakfast and then got up from the table. Amalia ate slowly, so I was always done first. I grabbed both of our briefcases and made sure we had all that we needed for work. Once she was done, I cleared her plate for her so she could grab her shoes. We walked out to the driveway after setting the alarm and I kissed her before she got into her car. We had to take separate cars to work so that we wouldn't look suspicious. I didn't need anyone talking or creating rumors when I was so close to being superintendant. There was no way they'd give me a position like that being a lesbian. Times have changed, but not enough.

"I'll see you around four?" I smiled.

"No, I have a meeting with a parent tonight."

"Having trouble with a student?"

"Yeah."

"Well, call me when you're on your way home, so I know your okay. I love you."

"I love you too."

We kissed and then we were off to start another day. I felt good inside. Life was good, everything was good.

The day went by quickly. Amalia had called at ten minutes 'til five to tell me she would be home soon. I knew she would be tired when she arrived home so I started dinner for her and ran her some bath water. She came in after about thirty minutes.

"Baby!"

"In the kitchen."

"I was just letting you know I was in here."

"Okay, I ran you some bath water, but it's probably cold, so just wait a second, chill out."

I heard her dropping her things at the door. Whenever Amalia had a bad day, she would drop everything right by the front door and then plop down on the sofa and turn on the television. I dried my hands and walked into the living room where she was sitting.

"Bad day?"

"Yeah."

"Want to tell me about it?"

I sat down next to her and pulled her feet up onto my lap. I removed her shoes and rubbed her feet as she told me about her day. Catering to Amalia was second nature to me.

"This girl in my class, Toya Logan, is such a fucking brat. She talks out of turn, she's loud, she's always chewing gum, she's always late, and she's barely passing."

"Why haven't you sent her to me?"

"Because I figured I could handle it. She's just an unruly teenager."

"That doesn't belong in my school."

"Babe, please."

"Okay, I'm listening."

"I met her parents today and they aren't any better. They think she is just a perfect little angel."

"Baby, I can deal with it if you want me to."

"No, I'll just have to change my methods and be a little harder."

"Well, I'm here if you need me. Send her and her funky ass parents right to me."

Amalia kissed me and I continued to rub her feet. Whenever she had a day like that, she never said much, so I did anything I could to make

106

her feel at least okay. She dozed off as I rubbed her feet, so I eased off the sofa and went to warm up her bath water. I woke her up and walked her to the bathroom to give her a bath. I did everything from undressing her to bathing her and then drying her off to redress her. I laid her in the bed and then left her to sleep her stress away.

~~*~*

Amalia had been coming home late for over two and a half months. She was detaining the girl that had been giving her trouble. I decided that it was time for me to deal with this myself, so instead of going home I decided to intervene and sit in the detention with Amalia and this pain in the ass little girl. I wanted to find out what her problem was and why she was misbehaving. I needed any reason to kick her out of the school, so she could be someone else's problem. My baby wasn't being paid to be a fucking babysitter.

I stepped into the classroom and Amalia was sitting at her desk looking over papers.

"Where is the headache?"

"I didn't keep her today. I'm behind on some papers that need to be graded."

"Anything I can help with?"

"No baby, I got it."

"You look mad. Are you okay?"

"Yes, I'm fine. I just have a headache from looking at all these words."

"Sit back for a second."

Amalia placed her pen down and sat back to smile at me. "Did I tell you that you looked beautiful today?"

I stood up and turned her chair to face me and leaned over close to her face. "No. Did I tell you that you look beautiful every day?" I brushed a piece of her hair behind her ear.

Amalia blushed. "Kiss me."

I did as I was told, forgetting where I was. Our tongues twirled around in each other's mouths. Amalia always placed her hands on each side of my face as she kissed me and sometimes I would open my eyes just to look at how beautiful she was and how into me she would get while kissing me, then I'd closed them to venture back to the place where she is lost with me. I started to undo the button on her blouse. I always wanted to fuck on the desk in a classroom and now I had the opportunity with a beautiful woman. The door to the classroom swung open and Amalia and I jumped.

107

Amalia stood. "Toya! What are you doing? I mean why are you still here?"

Toya grinned. "I left my bag behind my chair. What were you two doing?"

"Get your bag and stay out of adults business."

"Well, I'll tell my parents about this, they're adults."

"Little girl…" Amailia walked toward Toya and I grabbed her.

I pulled Amalia to the side. We had fucked up big time. I couldn't let this interfere with my chances of becoming a Superintendant.

"This will be all over the news if she tells her parents."

"I'm supposed to kiss her ass?"

"We have to do something. We'll both lose our careers."

"No puedo creer que quieres que arrodillo a un niño. Ella es una adolescente con problemas, ¿quién carajo va a creer en ella de todos modos? Estás siendo ridículo! Debí haberme quedado fuera del estado. Juro." She spoke loudly and fast while throwing her hands around and pointing at Toya.

"Lower your voice Amalia and speak English! I don't understand a word you're saying."

Amalia and I debated as Toya stood and watched with an evil smile on her face. This little seed of Chuckie was going to blackmail us if we didn't give her what she wanted.

~~*~*

I had a week to decide whether or not I was going to meet Toya's demands. This little brat wanted straight A's, to be excused from ever getting detention, weekly report of good behavior sent to her parents, and basically permission to skip any class that she pleased. There was no way in hell that I could do all of that without it looking suspicious. She was a trouble maker, so it would be impossible to make her look like a saint in a week.

I pulled up to the school building and grabbed my briefcase from the passenger side. My hands were tied. People were exactly accepting of out lesbian teachers and principals. I could lose so much behind this. I was so angry with myself for being so careless. I was good at separating business from my personal life. I walked into my office and Toya was sitting at my desk with her feet kicked up.

"How did you get in here?"

"I told them you told me to wait for you, so have you thought about my offer?"

"I have."

"And?"

"And that's almost impossible for me to pull off. You have to be more reasonable."

"Fine, I'll just go to the papers then."

"Wait, give me one more week. I'll think of something."

She smiled her evil little grin and then exited my office like she had just won the lottery. I threw my face into my hands and decided I would not make it through the day. The assistant principal could deal one day without me.

I went back home and called my Mom. I already knew that I was in for a lecture, but she was the cleverest person that I knew besides my Father. I hopped she had some great advice for me or that she would at least say something that would influence my decision without putting my job and reputation on the line. The phone rang twice.

"Hello sweetheart. Why aren't you working?"

"Mom, I need advice."

"Oh, this sounds bad, let me turn off my soaps sweetie." She came right back to the phone. "What's the problem?"

"Mom, I messed up bad."

"Tell me."

"A student caught Amalia and I making out after hours in her classroom." The phone was silent. "Mom?"

"I'm still here."

"Say something."

"I don't know what to say other than that was irresponsible of you, Natalie."

"Mom, I didn't call for a lecture. The kid is blackmailing us."

She laughed. "How old is she?"

"Fourteen, I think."

"You are kidding me. Are you telling me that you can't outsmart a fourteen year old? How on Earth did you become a principal? Does she have proof?"

"Only what she saw."

"Then it's her word against yours. Is she known for being a troublemaker?"

"Very much so."

"Then I'm not exactly sure what the problem is. Let her say what she pleases. It will all just be a rumor. Children start those all the time. Be smart Natalie and don't look so suspicious."

My Mother was right. Toya was just a child and she was not about to push me around as if she and I were on the same level. I called Amalia.

"Hey sweetie I heard you left early."

"Yeah, the demon was in my office first thing this morning. She can't be on time for class, but she can be on time to blackmail me."

"What have you decided?"

"I'm not doing a fucking thing she says."

"Good I was hoping that you wouldn't. Well, next period is starting and she's in it. I'll see you later?"

"Yeah."

"Okay, I love you."

"I love you too."

*~*Amaila*~*

The bell rang and everyone ran out of final period happy to be free. Toya winked at me as she walked out, but I kept my composure not to expose myself. One of my other students stayed behind. Her name was Jane Dennis. She was always quiet, always did her work, and always sat up front in my class. She was teased for being the "teacher's pet" so to speak and she looked like a nerd with her glasses and clothes that never matched. She never usually stayed behind so I figured something was wrong.

"Jane, is there a problem honey."

"I need to talk to you."

"About what?"

"Can you close the door?"

I walked over to the door and shut it and then sat down at my desk.

"Tell me the problem."

"Are you a lesbian?"

I sat up straight in my seat and reached for the bottled water on my desk before I started to choke.

"Jane—"

She cut me off. "It's okay if you are. Actually, if you are then I'm really happy to know someone else who is."

"Are you a lesbian, Jane?"

"Yes ma'am, I am, or at least I think I am… but that's not what I wanted. I know what Toya is trying to do to you and Principal Hester."

"She told you?"

"No, she's an idiot; she was chatting in an open room about it calling you guys dykes and stuff. I wanted to help you."

"How can you do that?"

She laughed her nerdy laugh. "I just told you she's an idiot." She stood up and handed me her cell phone. "Here look at these."

There were numerous pictures of Toya beneath bleachers having sex and giving blow jobs to boys at the school. My mouth hung open as I scrolled. Times had changed so much since I was in high school. I couldn't imagine licking or sucking on anything at her age. "How did you get these?"

"I'm quiet, but I don't miss anything and after I heard what she was doing it made me upset. I like having you as a teacher and I won't let her get you fired."

"What do you want?"

"I don't want anything."

I stood and hugged her tight. "If you ever need anything you tell me. I'm serious."

"Okay, Ms. Sanchez," she smiled.

"Can you email these?"

She pulled a folder from her bag. "I printed them for you and have copies on demand."

I laughed. "Thank you. Do you need a ride home?"

"I'd like that."

I dropped Jane off to her place of residence and then drove home so that I could tell Natalie the good news. She was in the kitchen cooking as always. I ran to her and kissed her hard.

"Hey babe, good day, I see." she grinned.

"Great day! I have something that is about to make yours great."

"Give it to me."

"Bam!" I handed her the folder.

She flipped through them. "Where did you get these?"

"A fellow rainbow member. I'm not sure if I can tell you."

"I don't even care. I'm just happy!" She lifted me on the counter and kissed me.

We'd celebrate by making love that night.

*~*Natalie*~*

My week was up and Toya was in her usual spot waiting for my answer. I didn't even bother to tell her to get up from my seat. I pulled the folder with the pictures of her from my briefcase and spread them across my desk for her to see.

"Hmmm, looks like you have a few secrets of your own young lady or should I say tramp?" I said not caring that she was a student. She wanted to get in the ring with grown-ups, she was going to have to take the punches.

"Oh my God, how did you get these?"

"Oh my God is right and wouldn't you like to know." I leaned down in her face, "You can walk out of my office and go back to a child's place and study like everyone else to pass and behave or these pictures can get placed in every locker in this school. You will get teased so badly that you'll have to move to another country, because I can promise they will hit the internet. Boys just love to show the girls they banged and what they love even more than showing off who they've been inside is who swallowed their babies. Try me." I said through closed teeth the way my Mother used to as she reprimanded me.

Toya started to cry as she stood from my desk and walked to leave my office without a word. I'd never be that careless at work again. I didn't know or care where Amalia got the pictures. I was just grateful that I could keep my life the way it was, go after my dream of becoming a Superintendant, and Amalia wouldn't have to deal with that unruly teenager again.

We'd both be more careful now.

"185 Days"

I slid my cell phone up to light up the keys because I needed to see what time it was. The time read 2:30am. The club would be shutting down soon and my friends were nowhere to be found. I looked around the club to see if I could spot any of them, but it was entirely too crowded since it was around the 4th of July. I was tired of hearing that loud ass music, I was tired of unattractive ass women trying to talk to me all night, and I was tired of people bumping into me and not saying excuse me, but then giving me the eye when I pushed their dumb asses. I had not been enjoying myself. I was ready to leave before I had even gotten there. It was just a waste of twenty dollars that could have gone towards something I could use for more than a couple hours like a vibrator. I checked the time again and it was now 2:33am. Time was fucking with me bad. I decided to push my way through the crowd to find one of my friends.

I spotted Angelique and Vince waiting in line to use the restroom and I pushed my way over to them. Vince yelled over the music. "Where you going bitch?"

"I'm leaving! It smells like hot ass in here. I'm bored and all the females in here are ugly!"

"Eww bitch, let me pee first, then you can drop me off too."

"I didn't volunteer my gas to bring you across town."

"I'm not going home. I'm going get me some dick bitch, owwwe!" Vincent started dancing with one hand in the air, while snapping to the music and laughing at his recent comment.

I shook my head and smiled for the first time that night. I waited a few more minutes for Vincent to finally use the restroom, and then we headed to the first level of the club. I checked the time again and it was now only 2:45am. I exhaled, aggravated because I wanted to be at home and people were moving slowly down the steps, but as soon as I looked up from my phone I saw the most beautiful woman I had ever seen in my life. I had never believed in love at first sight until that very Moment. Yes, I've heard all that BS about it not being real and people just lusting, but this had to be something more. She locked eyes with me and it was obvious that she felt whatever it was that I was feeling. The stud that she was with pushed her up the stairs because she had stopped in her steps.

People continued to move slowly down the stairs and I followed, letting the rail guide me because I refused to break glances with whoever this mystery girl was.

We passed each other and she grabbed my hand, but the crowd forced us to separate. She smiled at me as her eyes followed me down the stairs and mine followed her up. A club to me was the last place to meet anyone and/or take them seriously, but I wanted her bad. She wore baggy shorts and tight, fitted, plaid, button down shirt. Her hair hung straight and stopped right at her shoulders. Her skin was the color of dark wood and she had deep grey eyes, so it was obvious that she was mixed with something. She motioned for me to wait for her when I got to the bottom of the steps, so I moved over to the side away from the crowd and Vincent followed.

"Bitch, what are we waiting for?"

"You didn't see that girl grab me?"

"Ew, real fish? No! I'm trying to get out of here girl, my man waiting on me."

"You can walk."

"Walk! Not with these $300.00 shoes on ho. I sucked some serious dick for these."

"I hope you get lockjaw."

Vincent shoved my shoulder and laughed still waiting. It only took her a few seconds to get back down the stairs and when she got up close I couldn't stop myself from smiling. She stood close and extended her hand to me.

"Amelia, and you are?"

"Celeste."

"I think you are beautiful, Celeste."

"So are you."

"Would you mind if I called you sometime?"

"What? You actually want to call me and not text?" I laughed.

"Texting hurts my fingers," She laughed.

Amelia pulled her phone out of her pocket and handed it to me. I programmed my number into her phone and she called my phone so that I would have hers too.

"When do you want me to call?" she asked.

"Whenever you want to."

"Well, I'm calling as soon as I leave here. I don't want to take up too much of your time so I'll let you go now."

As I walked off Amelia pulled me back and hugged me and whispered talk to you later into my ear. Her words went right through me and the hairs on my arm stood up, as she turned to walk away and made her way back up the steps. Vincent pushed me toward the door, pretending to be irritated.

It took me less than ten minutes to drop Vincent off. My cell phone rang as soon as he shut the door. I smiled widely and picked up. "You were serious weren't you?"

"Very. I don't have time for those 'I'll call her in two days so she won't think I'm *jocking* her games,' I'm very much so sweating you, so where are you?"

"On my way home."

"Already?"

"Yes, where else is there to go this time of morning."

"You can come have breakfast with me."

"You're not tired?"

"Are you setting me up to turn me down? I'm not taking no for an answer."

"I'm just a little tired."

"Tired? Sleeping is overrated. Come eat. I'm paying so you can't argue with me. I'll beg."

"You always take strange women from clubs to breakfast."

"Just the ones named Celeste, so are you coming?"

"Fine," I blushed.

I met Amelia at *IHOP*. She was already seated and waiting for me to arrive. When I walked over to her table she stood to hug me again and then pulled out my chair.

"I didn't know what you were drinking so I got you water, orange juice, cranberry juice, and apple juice."

"Aren't you thoughtful?"

The waitress came over to the table with a menu for me and I placed my order. I sipped from each drink just to mess with Amelia. We stared at each other without a word until our food arrived. Amelia broke the silence, asking me a million and one questions, simple ones like my favorite color, all time favorite song, my dream car, how many siblings I had, my middle name, schools I attended, etc. I answered all her questions and then some. We sat in *IHOP* over two hours just talking and taking advantage of free refills. I had to go home eventually.

"You're not tired?"

"Nope, but I'm assuming that you are."

"Very much."

"I guess I can let you go. What are you doing later?"

"Nothing that I can think of at the Moment, I'm off from my piece of shit job today and I don't have to go and visit my parents until next weekend."

"Can I come do nothing with you then?"

"When are you going to sleep?"

"I'll sleep. When do you want my company?"

"Uh, how is one or two? We can go rent movies and do lunch."

Amelia handed me a napkin to write my address on, so that she wouldn't have any issues getting there. I was terrible with directions so I was happy that she was up with technology and possessed a GPS system.

~~*~*

Amelia arrived at my apartment at 12:30pm. I buzzed her into the front gate and told her where to go from there. She was at my door in minutes. When I opened the door Amelia was wearing a dress and it completely threw me to the left, but I tried not to show it. She hugged me and then asked if I was ready. I grabbed my purse and followed her to her car. She was just as beautiful dressed as a femme as she was a stud, but I didn't expect her to be one of those people who flipped and flopped.

Amelia and I rode in her car to a movie rental store. It took us forever to settle on a movie, so we picked up two new releases that neither of us had seen and some junk food that cost us an arm and a leg and then headed back to my apartment.

I turned on one of the movies and as the previews played I popped us some popcorn and made us some drinks. I set everything up in front of us so we could get comfortable. It seems like the previews went on forever, but Amelia wanted to see them all. I couldn't stop looking at her in her dress. I loved how she looked, but the curious part of me needed to know if she was one of those women who posed as a stud to get femmes who were strictly into studs and then changed on them once they fell in love.

"Can I ask you a question without you getting upset with me?"

"Yeah, ask whatever you want."

"What are you? I mean what do you identify as?"

"A woman."

"I know that, femme or stud?"

"Neither."

"Okay are you a stem?"

"What's that?"

"A stud and a femme."

Amelia laughed at me and sat her drink down then faced me. She didn't appear upset, but she looked disturbed.

"Why do I have to label myself?"

"I don't know it's just what I'm used to. It's normal."

"Normal to who? Gay and lesbian people? People who hate their own community, but fight for acceptance? Great source…"

"Well…"

She shook her head. "Have you looked up femme, stud, and stem in the dictionary?"

"No."

"Well you should because none of them describe who I am at all. For the word stem alone, you'll find about twenty-one definitions and none of them will say a woman who dresses both masculine and feminine. The only words that can be defined properly in WEBSTER'S Dictionary are gay, lesbian, transgender, transsexual, and homosexual."

"I didn't mean to offend you."

"I'm not offended. I was just giving you something to think about."

Amelia winked at me and turned to finish watching the movie. She laid her head in my lap and we both ended up falling asleep. When I opened my eyes, the credits were rolling and Amelia was gone. She left a note near the DVD case that read: *I didn't want to wake you because you were sleeping so peacefully. I had to rush and do something and that wasn't worth interrupting how beautiful you looked. You don't have to call me the instant you finish this note since I've been in your face most of the day, I'd just like for you to call me before you go to bed, so I can tell you goodnight. There are so many things I want to show you. ~Amelia"*

I stood and walked into the kitchen to pin the note on my fridge. I smiled just staring at it wondering what she wanted to show me. Amelia was so full of life and she always seemed so sure about everything. I envied her full spirit and the confidence she possessed. She seemed to be even more beautiful on the inside than the outside and I barely knew anything about her at all. I walked into my bedroom which was right behind the kitchen. My apartment was small. I flopped on the bed and saw that it was only 5:30pm. I decided to read a book and just take time to myself before I had to return to work in the morning.

I read a book until 9:30pm then I showered and grabbed my cell to call Amelia. She picked up on the first ring. "I've been waiting on you to call me."

I smiled. "Waiting? I must be someone special."

"You are. Are you in bed?"

"Yes, I am."

"You got to bed early."

"I have to work in the morning."

"That's what coffee was invented for."

"When do you sleep?"

"Whenever I find time I guess."

"Do you work?"

"No."

"Why not? Don't you want to?"

"Who would want to work if they had the option? I refuse to work if I can't do what I love and beside my grandparents left me a fortune so I'm just having fun."

"What is it that you love to do?"

"Draw."

"Why don't you draw?"

"I do, but you know what they say about careers in the arts."

"Yeah, so do you ever get bored?"

"Sometimes, but I've found something to keep me busy or should I say someone."

"Yeah, who might that be?"

"This girl I ran into leaving your apartment."

"Oh really? Was she pretty?"

"I'm kidding." She laughed.

Amelia talked for a few more hours, and I was trying my hardest to stay awake; but I wanted to hear everything she had to say. I was going to be tired when I woke up in the morning, but it was worth it. Amelia had so many stories to tell about places she had been and people she had met. She told me that things never got old to her and how she could find light in any dark situation. She told me that she never fell in love because she never had the time and she saw how it could destroy two sane people. She was afraid of it. Her words of how people complained about the problems in their life when nothing was ever actually that bad replayed in my mind as I laid in darkness wondering what I hated about my life and what I complained about. Everything.

~~*~*

My alarm clock went off at 5:45am and it was to get up and start my week. I hoped it passed by quickly. My eyes burned from the lack of sleep that I got and my head felt heavy. After ten minutes of just walking around and looking crazy my cell phone rang. "Hello" I said groggily.

"Good morning, are you awake and getting dressed for work?"

"I'm up, but I'm far from even attempting to get dressed."

"I'm sorry I kept you up, that's why I called. I would have felt guilty if you had overslept."

"Thank you. That's sweet."

"You're welcome. I'll let you go now. Have a good day."

"Thank you. You too."

I hung up the phone and got a text instantly that read 'XOXOXO'. Amelia was too good to be true. I dressed and left to report to my pieces of shit job. I was an office assistant to some of the rudest doctors I had ever met in my life. I had always saw doctors as friendly people until I started at my company. They seemed to only be nice to the insured people who could afford their services. I gave the nurses more of my respect because they did the majority of the doctor's job anyway.

Today was a busy day. The phones rang off the hook and people constantly walked up to my counter with forms. I was just waiting for the day to be over.

Lunch came and went and finally it was 4:30pm. I ran to the punch clock and ran even faster to my car where I could finally exhale. I turned the key in my ignition, but my car wouldn't start, the lights didn't flicker or anything. There wasn't even a click. After so many tries I gave up. I called Angelique, but she was busy or at least that was the lie she told. Calling Vince was out of the question since he didn't have a vehicle or access to one unless he needed to get somewhere. My friends were worthless. I called Amelia and she didn't hesitate, she was jumping in her truck as we spoke.

She pulled up in twenty minutes and knocked on my window. "Need a ride pretty lady?"

I was relieved to see her. I opened my car door and stepped out to hug her tightly. "I'm not having a good day."

"Well, let's see how we can turn it around."

She walked around me and popped my hood. She told me to try and start it again and then walked back to the driver's side shaking her head. "You're alternator is shot."

"I didn't know what an alternator was and at that Moment I didn't care. I just wanted to go home. I hopped into Amelia's truck and we were off. She looked at me every chance that she got, but I looked straight ahead. I was vexed.

"I'm sorry you had a bad day," she said while grabbing my hand.

119

"It's not your fault."

"Talk to me about it. Venting always helps."

"I just hate my job and my undependable ass friends."

"Screw your so called friends you have me and have you ever thought about quitting your job?"

"Every day."

"Why haven't you?"

"What would I do and I have to pay my bills."

"Your only reason for working is to pay bills?"

"What else would it be for?"

"To shop, travel, just live life and do things that you enjoy. You're job should fund that."

"It wouldn't be much fun doing all that alone."

"Do it with me. Quit your job. I'll take care of you until you figure out whatever it is that you want to do."

"You barely even know me."

"I'm getting to know you more every day. Will you just trust me?"

Amelia was sounding ridiculous to me, but she was far more serious than I was taking her. She told me to think about it before kissing my forehead and unlocking her car doors as we pulled up to my building inside my apartment complex. I opened my door and walked upstairs to my apartment, laughing at myself as I entered and turned on the lights. I shook my head because I was actually considering her ludicrous offer. I walked into my bedroom and undressed then I went into the bathroom to shower.

My mind ran wild as I thought about all the things I had always wanted to do in my life. How did I get so stuck and comfortable in this mediocre living? I wrapped my arms around myself and let the water hit my face. Amelia was right. I was living simply to exist and my life had become one big question.

Another day, another dollar, I walked outside to wait for the taxi I called to bring me to work and when I got to the bottom of the steps I spotted Amelia waiting for me in her truck. She smiled at me and yelled, "I figured you would need a ride!"

I smiled and ran to hop in on the passenger side. "How long have you been waiting out here?"

"Ten minutes maybe."

"Why didn't you call?"

"And miss out on seeing your facial expression just a second ago?" She winked and backed out to pull off.

Amelia always played the oldie but goodie station in her truck. We sang Midnight Train to Georgia by Gladys Knight and the Pips really loudly and off key, then we tried our damnedest to sing along to Patti Labelle's If Only You Knew. She was so much fun to be around. We pulled up in front of my building and the music was still blasting. I hopped out and she rolled down the window to the passenger side to sing in my direction If Loving You is Wrong by Luther Ingram really loudly. I laughed and covered my face. She yelled, "Have a good day," mid verse and then sped off.

I sat at my desk smiling and thinking about Amelia. My co-worker Ms. Thelma, an older lady who had been with the clinic almost twenty years stopped in front of me.

"What's his name?"

"Huh?"

"I haven't seen you smile like this in a year, so who is it?"

I tried to remove my smile. "It's nobody." I adjusted in my seat and changed the subject. "Can I ask you a question, Ms. Thelma?"

"Sure baby."

"If someone you barely knew, but you were getting to know offered to take care of you would you quit your job?"

"In a heartbeat."

"But, why?"

"How old are you?"

"Twenty-two."

"You know how old I am?

"Fifty?" I said to be flattering.

"Honey, I'm sixty-seven years old. If you aren't going to start taking risks now in your life when are you going to start? When you're my age? Now is the time for you to make stupid decisions, while you still have time to fix them." She sat down at her station.

"You're right."

"I wish I had done so many things with my life." She started down memory lane, but I cut in."

"Ms. Thelma?"

"Yes darling?"

"Can you tell them I quit."

I stood up and started gathering my things, while pulling out my cell phone to call Amelia. I felt crazy, but I also felt as though a weight had been lifted from my shoulders. I hugged Ms. Thelma and kissed her on

121

the cheek before heading for the exit. I called Amelia to pick me up and she was there in a matter of minutes.

She drove me back to my apartment and she smiled the entire time. She parked in her usual space and we went upstairs.

She looked at me. "So what do you want to do now?" Amelia asked.

"I don't know."

"Okay better question. If you could be anywhere right now where would it be?"

"A beach…"

"Florida?"

"Let's go."

~~*~*

Amelia and I got on the road the second she suggested Florida. We laughed, we talked, we played games; the sun came up and went back down. We were almost to the beach.

"Amelia why don't you ever tell me anything about yourself?"

"There really isn't much to tell."

"I'd beg to differ. Where are your parents? Do you have any siblings? Why haven't you tried to kiss me?

Amelia slowed down in the middle of nowhere and pulled onto the side of the road. She put her truck in park and unbuckled her seatbelt and then reached to unbuckle mine. She grabbed my hands and pulled them. She kissed my forehead, then my nose and each of my cheeks, than finally she kissed my lips. I melted into her passenger seat as her hands rested on each side of my face and her lips massaged mine. I didn't want to open my eyes once she stopped.

She whispered, "My parents died when I was six and my brother is in the Navy. We write and that's about it.

She turned and re-buckled her seatbelt and placed the car in drive. The rest of the ride was silent until we made it to Florida. We randomly picked a beach front hotel and Amelia covered everything. We slept for awhile and then went to shop and grab some food. Florida was going to be home for a few months.

Everything about Florida was beautiful. It was warm, the women were gorgeous, confident, and wore bold make-up and bright colors. The men, well, who cares about them. It felt like I could conquer the world with Amelia and I was starting in Florida. We sat down at a restaurant waiting for food. Amelia stared at me. "Did you go to college?" She asked.

"I did two years."

"What was your major?"

"Education."

"Why didn't you finish?"

"I couldn't afford it after losing my scholarship due to bad grades."

"How did you start failing?"

"I did more partying than studying."

"Would you go back if you had the money?"

"In a heartbeat."

"Is teaching what you always wanted to do?"

"You can say that."

"Teachers don't make any money."

"I didn't want to do it for the money."

The waitress sat our food down in front of us and we remained quiet until she left the table. Amelia dug more into my life, trying to figure out at what point I lost my drive and gave up on my dreams completely. She was determined to show me what life was all about. She leaned across the table.

"You should do something completely off the wall."

"Like what?"

"Marry me."

"What? Are you serious?"

"As death."

"Like now? Today?"

"Yeah, today. Let's do it."

Amelia and I went back to the room and logged onto gayfriendlybiz.com to locate a pastor that performed civil unions then we left to ring shop. She always seemed to have everything spontaneously planned out if that makes any sense at all. We both wore all white, she wore pants and I wore a dress. It was just us and the water on the ocean. It was beautiful and it felt right. We kissed after saying "I do" and then returned to our room to slow dance and sip champagne. We made love that night with the sliding door open. The sound of the ocean and my moans mixed well together. Everything was perfect. She was happy and so I was I. I was finally learning to take risks. I was ready to be myself again.

~~*~*

Both Amelia and I had cut off all of our hair and dyed it blonde, we got matching wrist tattoos that said live and love, she got to eat squid

123

and jet ski for the first time, we did speed dating just to be silly, we got our portraits painted, we sung karaoke, we danced at as many night clubs as we could; there was even a foam party, we went rollerblading and bike riding, and we slept when we found the time. Amelia had pamphlets of everything there was to get into and she made sure we dabbled into a little of everything.

I opened my eyes from another long night of partying and Amelia was sitting at the desk in our room, butt naked with her feet kicked up. She was holding a calendar and staring out at the beach. I sat up rubbing my eyes.

"What are you doing up already?"

"You know I don't sleep much. You want some breakfast? I can order room service."

"No, I'm not hungry."

She looked at me like she was seeing me for the first time. "You know we've only known each other for 180 days?"

"You've been counting?"

"Yep, since the night that we met in the club. I fell in love with you the second I saw you and I said to myself if I could have her I'd have everything I ever wanted in life."

"You didn't know me."

"I knew what I felt, that was enough. It was that strong."

"I make you happy?"

"More than you know…"

I sat up in the bed as she continued to speak.

"I didn't think people like you still existed."

"What are people like me?"

"Beautiful, smart, fun, honest, trustworthy…"

I blushed. "I feel the same way."

"Amelia smiled. "You love me?"

"Yes."

"Say it." She jumped up from the chair and into the bed, jumping on me and knocking me back. "Tell me."

My stomach tightened as I realized this would be the first time I uttered the words to her. Usually I'd question if it was too soon, but how can love be timed? "I love you."

She looked into my eyes. "I love you too." She kissed me and hopped back off the bed. "Let's go swimming."

"I don't feel like it."

"You can just lie on the beach and watch me then. Come on."

Amelia and I walked down to the beach. She ran into the water screaming and laughing, while I set up my big umbrella to block the sun and unfold my chair. I laid back and watched as Amelia threw herself into the waves. She swam around a little then emerged from the water, running toward me, waving and smiling. She made it half-way then fell down. I thought maybe she tripped, but it was taking her entirely too long to get up. I stood up and ran over to her, falling down to my knees to turn her over. She wasn't breathing. I screamed for help. I needed anybody with a cell phone.

~~*~*

I sat next to Amelia for four days, listening to her heart monitor, praying, and holding her hand. Her eyes didn't as much as flutter. I talked to her and begged her to come back. I read her a book and just before bed I'd tell her things she never knew about me, because I knew she could hear me. We had things to do. The doctor's wouldn't tell me what was wrong with her, not because they didn't want to, but because they had signed a confidentiality agreement with Amelia. The doctor walked into the room as I dozed off in my chair. He touched my shoulder. "I think you should go back to your room and get some real rest."

"I don't want to leave her."

"I don't think her condition will change much if you just take a break and get some rest, please I insist. We don't need you in here next." He gave me a warm smile.

I did as I was told, kissing Amelia on the forehead just before walking out of her room. I was coming back first thing in the morning. I went to the hotel and took a shower. I forced some fruit down my throat and watched television until I dozed off.

I jumped up out of my sleep. The television was still on. I looked over at the hotel clock. It read 2:45am. I got up and walked into the bathroom and flushed my face with cold water. I walked back into the room and saw the calendar that Amelia was holding the day she passed out. I picked it up and saw that today made 185 days that we had known each other and she even had 2:45am written in the calendar. I smiled. My cell phone went off and snapped me out of my Moment of happiness. It was the hospital. I answered quickly and listened as the doctor spoke. I held my hand over my pained heart as he told me that Amelia's organs had failed and she passed. I choked on my words. "What time did she pass?"

125

"2:45am. I'm so sorry."

I let the phone hit the floor and wasn't too far behind it on my knees, breaking. Everything hurt. I tried to hold myself, leaning down into the floor. I wanted this all to be a bad dream and I was ready to wake up.

~~*~*

Amelia had a lot of friends and distant family. Her funeral was silent. Her brother stood with me holding me close to him like he had known me all his life. He handed me a letter from his inside jacket pocket and told me to read it when I had some time alone. I sat on my bed back in my mediocre apartment and pulled the letter from my purse. It had my name on the front in Amelia's handwriting.

Hey beautiful,

Are you angry with me? I bet you are, but hopefully by the end of this letter you won't be. I hope you didn't think I'd leave without saying something to you and leaving you with unanswered questions so here it goes. I've been knowing since I was eleven years old that I would one day pass and waited every day after they told me that I had leukemia, which is just another form of cancer; heavy burden right? Yeah, that's what I said. I've been stuck with a million needles, had bone marrow transplants and every treatment you can think of. I fought as long as I could up until six months ago right before I met you. They told me that it was terminal. I was devastated. I started to think about my life and all the things I had always wanted to do and I realized I spent so much time being sick that I placed everything behind me and now I wasn't going to be able to accomplish any of it because death was knocking at my door. I wrote a list and I picked one thing to have from it before I went and that was love. The minute I saw you I started to live again. You became my strength and my new reason for not accepting defeat. You are my best friend and the love of my life. Celeste I died in love with you. Please don't hate me for not telling you. I just wanted to have a normal life without someone feeling sorry for me or trying to take care of me. I didn't want to be careful. You made me the happiest I had ever been in my life and I thank you for accepting all that I had to give in so little time. I need you to know that I'd give anything to kiss you one more time and tell you that I love you. No amount of money can buy what you gave to me. There are a few things that I would like for you to do; my brother is going to bring you my truck, everything is signed over for you and in the glove compartment there is a cashier's check for you. I split my inheritance from my grandparents, leaving my brother half and you the other. I know it's a lot of money, but I know you'll do the right things with it, go back to school and finish your degree and then have a baby maybe two. The next thing I'd like for you to do is to spread my ashes on the beach where we shared our love. I want to be there forever and I have one more task for you, look at your wrist. Can you do that for me Celeste? I love you. Forever...

Amelia

"Playing with Fire"

"When you <u>assume</u>, you make an ass out of you and not me."

I don't know what's worse, knowing that your partner is cheating or wondering if they are. Yari and I had not been happy with each other for some time now, but we had built too much together to just walk away from one another and to add more complications to our situation I had just given birth to our beautiful five month old daughter Constance. We figured it was the one thing we were missing in our life. Yari had been acting different since Constance had arrived. I was depressed and I needed her. I wasn't as confident about myself or my body after having our baby and I refused to even look in a mirror. Yari stopped complimenting me and she barely came home. She started doing all the suspicious things that cheaters did like answering her phone in another room, tilting her phone when she would text, keeping it on vibrate, and keeping her in and out box empty just in case I picked it up after she sat it down. We hadn't had sex in over eight months and it didn't seem like we would be fucking anytime soon.

Yari was working late again tonight and I wanted and needed some time to myself. I dropped Constance off at my Mother's house. I decided to treat myself to a drink or two at a local lesbian bar; maybe I would inhale lots of second hand smoke and kill over. I sat at the bar watching the basketball game they had playing on the flat screens and sipping on my cranberry and vodka. I played with the ring Yari had placed on my left hand three Yeahrs ago before the sugar between us went to shit. We weren't married. The ring was just a promise that we would never cheat on each other and if it got to that point then we would tell the other and leave. Fuck promises. Yari was not keeping her promise. I knew it. I couldn't prove it with physical evidence, but after loving someone that long you could feel everything they did. My eyes started to water and a single tear fell from my right eye as a woman took a seat next to me on a barstool.

She looked at me. "I'll have whatever she's having."
I turned to look at her and she smiled. "Rough night?" She asked.
I laughed a little and wiped my eye. "Rough months."
She reached out her hand to introduce herself "Nia."

129

I shook her hand. "Khanna."

She held onto my hand and turned it upwards to examine my ring. "Married?"

I sniffed and looked down. "No."

"Engaged?"

"No."

"Okay then, is this a don't talk to me I'd like to appear taken ring?"

I laughed. "It's a promise ring."

"What's the promise?" She still held my hand.

"To be faithful."

She moved closer. "Have you kept your promise?"

"So far."

"And your partner?"

Another tear fell as I whispered. "I'm not so sure." I pulled my hand back.

"I think you need another drink."

Nia motioned for the bartender to get me another drink as I threw back the one in front of me. She watched me intently. Her chin slanted down her lips were small, her eyes were hazel, a gap sat between her two front teeth, her skin was the exact color of sand, she had freckles on her cheeks so there was no way she was fully black, her hair was long, curly, and dark as long as she stayed from under the light. When the light hit it I could see that it was a reddish brown color that didn't come from a dye. She was slender and her hands were slightly bigger than mine. Her shirt was tight, but her jeans were baggy with a chain dangling from them. She couldn't be older than twenty. I'd be shocked if she was. The bartender handed me my drink. Nia paid her.

"Thank you." I said.

Her voice was sex. "You're welcome Khanna ."

"How old are you?" I asked.

"How old are you?" She retorted.

"Older than you."

"How do you know that?" She locked her fingers together in front of her and leaned on the bar.

"I can just tell so tell me."

"Twenty-one."

"Oh, my, God, you're a baby."

"You better be in your 30's or 40's"

"I'm Thirty-six."

"You don't look it."

"I try to take care of myself."

130

"Keep doing whatever it is that you're doing." She bit her lip and looked me up and down.

I smiled. "Are you flirting with me?"

"Maybe a little."

"I'm practically married."

"Practically, but not married…"

I watched her mouth move each time that she spoke. She was slick and her body language was slicker. She never took her eyes off of me. I blushed and batted my eyelashes like a school girl. It had been years since someone that young had hit on me and flattered me that much. I was sucking it up and taking it for more than I should, but it felt good. I would enjoy this little bit of time and attention before going home to be ignored.

We laughed a little more and talked about unimportant things. I teased her for being so young and she teased me for thinking I was old. Her youth was refreshing. She reminded me of how free I used to be before I became this person whom I didn't know: insecure, jealous, and timid. As she talked about her life I thought about all the things that I used to do that I didn't do anymore and all the things I said I'd do that I never did. It was refreshing torture spending this Moment with her. I checked my watch and saw that it was almost three in the morning. I needed to go. Yari and I always came in before three a.m. no matter where we were going or coming from. I stood from my stool. "I have to go."

She grabbed my wrist. "Why?"

"My girlfriend and child"

She released me. "Okay I guess I can let you go. I was really enjoying your company and conversation."

"Likewise"

"If I gave you my number would you use it?"

"I don't know."

She pulled my cell phone from my pocket. "I'll lock it in while you think about it." She pushed my phone back into my pocket.

I reached out my hand. "It was nice meeting you Nia."

"Likewise"

I laughed and walked away. I stopped at the exit of the bar and looked back at Nia. She watched me all the way out. Something about her piqued my interest. There was something about the way she told me everything about her while still telling me nothing. She was the baby of five and I was the oldest of five. Her Mother had passed because of cancer and my Mother was fighting cancer as we spoke. We both wrote poetry and Googled everything under the sun. We both preferred shopping online and we weren't flashy people. Neither of us had the best relationship with our Father even though we wanted it and we both loved to travel.

Our conversation played in my mind over the music that I blasted as I drove home. I laughed to myself at some of the things she said and the ways she flirted nonstop. I was home before I could blink. I didn't bother to raise the garage door and park my car because that door would wake the entire neighborhood. I had been telling Yari that it needed to be fixed for the longest, but of course she was too busy to bother with anything that had to do with me, us, or our home.

Yari was asleep on the sofa when I walked in. The television was still on. I grabbed the throw blanket from behind the sofa and laid it over her body then I picked the remote up from the floor and shut the television off. I pulled the pony tail that I wore down and let my hair fall around my shoulders. I undressed as I walked up the hall letting my clothes fall wherever. I turned on the light to the hall bathroom and cut on the shower. I needed to wash away the smell of second hand smoke and alcohol. I thought about Nia as I showered and I smiled. I needed her to wash away too.

I walked into our bedroom wearing my towel. I remembered that my cell phone was in my pocket so I walked into the hall and grabbed my jeans from the floor to retrieve it. I opened it and clicked contacts. I scrolled to Nia's name and walked back into our room and shut the door. I clicked on the delete option, but then hit the back key. What was I doing? I pressed call. The phone rang twice and I hung up. I had hoped it didn't ring enough to show as a missed call on her phone. I hadn't hoped fast enough. My cell rang loud and I picked it up as quickly as I could.

"Khanna" She said in her soft tone.

"How did you know this was me?"

"I don't just go around giving out my number. I see you made it home."

"Yeah, I did, but I don't know why I called you. I'm sorry."

"I'm happy that you did."

I was silent.

"What are you wearing?" She asked.

I sat on the bed. "A towel. I just showered."

"Where is your girlfriend?"

"Sleep in the living room"

"I don't understand."

I laughed. "She just fell asleep there…hey, I have to go." I hung up before she could say anything else or before I dug myself into a hole I wouldn't be able to get out of.

~~*~*

Constance slept peacefully in her seat as I pushed her around in my grocery cart and scratched off the items we needed at home from my handwritten list. I raised her blanket higher before walking into the section where the frozen food was to get some ice cream. I opened the freezer and grabbed cookies and cream ice cream and tossed it into the basket. I turned and bumped someone hard and when I pushed back it was Nia.

"We have to stop meeting like this." She smiled.

I held my hand over my heart to breathe. "I'll call this a coincidence, but next time I'll just assume you're stalking me."

She walked in front of my basket. "Is this your baby?"

"Yep, that's my Constance."

"She's beautiful, not that I didn't expect that." She looked up at me and winked.

"I have to get going."

"You're always in a rush." She stood in my way. "Stop for a second let me get a good picture in my memory of you.

I smiled. "What do you want Nia?"

"Your friendship."

"My friendship?"

She smiled. "That's all I promise, so will you call me?"

"Fine now get out of my way."

She stepped aside and I moved past her to go to the checkout line. She made my heart beat faster in my chest. She was charming beyond measure and the attraction I felt for her was far more than friendly. I paid for my groceries and loaded them into the car. I drove carefully and bobbed my head to Frank Ocean's "Novacane".

Yari was in her favorite spot on the sofa when I walked in. She stood when she saw I had bags. She carried Constance inside and placed her into her crib and then brought in the rest of the bags. She kissed my cheek before sitting back down. She could have kept that forced kissed. I didn't bother to pick a fight about it. I tried the nice approach. "How was your morning?" I continued to organize.

"It was cool."

"What time did you get back home?"

133

"About ten minutes ago."

"Long meeting?"

"Yeah."

"Are you going to get the promotion?"

"Maybe."

Yari had been working around lawyers too long. Her conversation was just as dull as they were. I didn't bother to ask another question and I suddenly wasn't in the mood to cook anymore. She would just take her plate and eat on the sofa anyway instead of the $1100 dollar wooden table with six chairs that we have sitting in our dining area that I sit at alone. I made a sandwich and went into our bedroom. I pulled my phone from my purse and texted Nia. I liked her conversations.

I took an hour nap and then woke up to shower and change. Nia had invited me over to her apartment for dinner and drinks. I had convinced myself that nothing was happening and I could beat any temptation. She was just a young girl who found me interesting there was no way that she could weaken me. I was smarter than her and more mature. I'd eat, talk, and come home. I hoped.

I was going to wear a dress, but dresses said too much and I didn't feel sexy enough for a dress. I hit myself in the head. I was being ridiculous trying to get all dressed up to sit around with someone who wasn't even my partner. I could not make this a big deal. I tossed on jeans and a t-shirt with some tennis shoes and put my hair back into a ponytail. I sprayed on some Victoria Secret body spray and grabbed my keys. I walked right past Yari. She was drinking a beer which meant she was in for the night. She could stay home with Constance for a change.

~~*~*

I hesitated at her door holding my bald up fist over the number 12 that was posted on her door. "Just knock Khanna" I said to myself. I knocked three times then turned to walk away. The door swung open. "Where are you going?"

I paused. "Uhh."

"Get in here."

I walked past her and examined her apartment. "Nice place."

"Compliments of my Father."

"I thought y'all didn't get along."

"We have a strictly financial relationship."

"I understand."

"You want something to drink?"

"What do you have?"

"Juice and beer."

"Yuck you drink beer too?"

"I'll take that as you wanting juice." She laughed and walked into her little box kitchen.

"Actually I'll have a beer."

She walked back into the living room and handed me my beer. She had already opened it for me. I drank it quickly and burped. She laughed. It was apparent that I was nervous. She walked over to her round glass table that had two chairs and motioned for me to sit. She pulled out a chair and patted it. I walked over and sat down in the chair.

"I hope you like spaghetti. It's the only thing I can really cook."

I laughed. "I love it. Do I get Texas toast too?"

"Girl you better know it." We both laughed.

She sat my food down in front of me then handed me a fork. She grabbed a napkin and pulled my shoulders back to lay it across my lap and I didn't say a word. She repeated the same things for herself. I went for my food, but she stopped me. "We have to say grace." I was impressed.

We ate slowly and talked back and forth across the table. She was interested in everything, but more passionate about politics than anything which was impressive coming from a twenty-one year old these days that really just needed their weed, money, and a new bitch every other month. I let her speak and I just listened. She liked jazz; I liked that too. She was a movie buff; so was I. She wasn't a big fan of the color red; neither was I. She felt kissing was more intimate than sex; I agreed. She was reeling me in with everything that dripped from her lips. She cleared the table and brought me another beer.

"Come sit with me on the sofa." I joined her on the sofa and she moved closer to me. "I've been talking all night. Tell me something about you. Anything..."

"Good or bad?"

"Hmmm...bad"

I exhaled hard. "I kind of have low self-esteem"

"I feel like you've been dying to say that to someone."

"I have. It's been on my mind since I never really had it before."

"You're gorgeous I don't understand why you do."

"I haven't felt the same since I had Constance."

"Child birth is beautiful."

"Tell that to my girlfriend."

"Give me her number."

I laughed. "Tell me something bad about you."

She bit then licked her lips and looked me dead in the eyes. "I always want things that I can't have."

I knew that by things she meant me. I blushed. I put my head down and she lifted it with her finger. "You're beautiful, Khanna." She kissed me.

I yelled at myself in my mind telling myself to push her back and leave right now. My body was doing the exact opposite and I pulled myself closer to her. She held her hand against my cheek and she swirled her tongue around in my mouth. She leaned away a little but I could still feel her breath on my lips. She whispered "This is that defining Moment. Do you want me to stop?"

My mind screamed yes, but my body said no as I initiated our next kiss. She pulled my shirt over my head and pushed me back. I was so lost I didn't have time to realize how insecure I was about my body until she removed my shirt exposing my stomach that still sagged a little because of the baby. I tried to sit up but she pushed me back again and planted kisses all over the part of me that I was disgusted by. I closed my eyes as she made me feel sexy. She unbuttoned my jeans and pulled the zipper down slowly. I watched her. She pulled my jeans from my body then my underwear. She gave my pussy a closed mouth kiss before coming back up to be face to face with me. "I bet you feel good inside." She whispered before parting my lips and sliding two of her fingers inside of me slowly. A slow moan eased from my lips as I ran my hands down her back and closed my eyes. It was too late to turn back now. I had crossed that line. She still fingered me slowly. "How far do you want this to go?"

I don't know." I whispered back into her ear.

"Tell me what I can't do."

"Just make me feel good." That was really all I wanted; to feel good since I hadn't felt anything in so long.

Nia removed her fingers and stood from the sofa and reached for my hand. She pulled me toward her bedroom and pushed me down on her bed. She stood in front of me and undressed while letting me know everything that she was thinking with just her eyes. I thought to myself *She's twenty-one Khanna, what are you doing?* I still didn't stop myself. She unsnapped my bra letting the straps fall loosely on my shoulders. She pulled the straps down and sucked on my collar bone. My nipples were exposed. Nia kneeled down and licked my panty line. This was pure torture, my pussy ached for her, but she refused to rush. She pushed

136

me back on the bed, telling me stay just the way I was. She walked away.

Nia returned wearing a strap. She put a condom over it right in front on me and then joined me in the bed, placing my legs on each side of her. She licked my inner thigh, getting closer and closer to my lips. I lost my mind completely when she parted them with her tongue and swallowed me like no one had before. I couldn't control myself. I pulled the sheets and my toes curled. She slid her finger inside of me once again, moving in and out teasing me and preparing me for the ultimate penetration. Nia wrapped her mouth around my breast and then slid inside of me.

My body tensed as she slid in slowly. I grabbed the headboard as she stroked me slowly. She whispered words into my ear, some I understood, and others I didn't because the pleasure was too intense. I held onto her iron headboard for dear life as she rocked me.

I pushed Nia onto her back and lowered myself onto her strap. She squeezed my breast with her hands as I rode her and moaned loud enough for the whole world to hear. She squeezed my ass and thrust upward to go deeper. I leaned down cumming on her strap and she wrapped her arms around me still pushing inside of me. She wasn't done with me yet.

She bent me over the bed and entered me from behind, gripping my shoulders and pulling me back into her. I felt my ass hit her pelvis with every thrust as she went deeper each time. She laid me back at the end of her bed so she could see me cum this second time as she moved faster and harder inside of me, while sucking on my toes. I tried to fight it, but it was impossible, my body was ready to release yet again. My promise was broken.

Nia had fallen asleep with her arms wrapped around me. I moved her best I could without waking her up. It was nice to see that she was a hard sleeper. I slid out of bed and walked into the living room to get dressed. She was out like a light. I eased out of the front door and made my way home. I checked my face in the mirror several times. My make-up was smeared and my hair was frizzy from the sweat of sex. I hoped Yari was asleep.

I tiptoed into our house and Yari wasn't on the sofa. I went to our bedroom and she was in our bed with Constance on her chest. I walked out and shut the door quietly. I went into the hall bathroom and the second I locked it I broke into tears. I held my hand over my mouth to muffle my sobs. I was a cheater. I flipped on the light and stood in the mirror looking at myself. I turned on the shower and pulled my shirt over my head. There were scratches on my sides and a hickie above my left breast. Shit.

~~*~*

Yari and I sat in the doctor's office waiting on the doctor to see Constance for her six month check-up. Yari's free arm was around my back and she held a magazine in her free hand. I wondered if she could feel the guilt seeping from my skin, the betrayal. I wondered if she heard me coming in last night and pretended to be sleeping. I wondered if she thought about where I was all that time. Paranoia was going to kill me. My phone went off in my pocket and I jumped. Yari turned her face up at me, "What's wrong with you?"

"Nothing."

"Why are you so jumpy?"

"I was just in deep thought and my phone scared me that's all."

She looked back at her magazine. I pulled my phone from my pocket and saw Nia's name on the screen. I didn't read the message. Yari was sitting to close. I voluntarily said, "Missed called".

She turned up her nose, "Okay."

The nurse called us before it could get awkward.

Yari walked ahead of me and I checked my phone while she wasn't looking. The text read: "You could have said goodbye." I texted back "I can't do this" and slid my phone back into my pocket. She texted right back "It's already done." We walked past a restroom and I stopped. "Babe you go ahead I have to use it." Yari waved her hand and kept going. I stepped into the restroom and called Nia. She picked up on the first ring. "Love me then me huh."

"Nia, it's nothing like that... I just...."

"Just what? I asked you if you wanted me to stop Khanna. Now suddenly you have a conscience and your girlfriend and daughter matter?"

"Nia."

"I want to see you."

I exhaled. "Nia I can't."

"Why?"

"You and I can't work."

"But we can fuck?"

"Don't say that."

"Its fine, I understand." she hung up.

138

Nia didn't call or text again for the rest of the day. Yari had put Constance down to sleep after we left the doctor and I stood in the kitchen making dinner to keep myself busy. I smothered pork chops, with baked macaroni, and string beans. I mixed a batter for yellow cake and sat out chocolate icing to smooth over it once it was baked. Yari walked into the kitchen and leaned on the counter. "What's wrong, Khanna?"

"How do you figure something is wrong?"

"You haven't cooked this much food since, hmm, I can't even remember."

"I could ask you the same question. You haven't said this many words to me since, hmm, I can't remember."

"I deserved that." She walked closer to me and moved my bowl from in front of me. She turned me to face her and stared into my face as if she were looking for something. I waited. She pulled me into her and kissed me. I had forgotten what her lips felt like. We kissed until we lost our breath. She leaned back "I'm sorry."

"For what?" I asked.

"Everything, I haven't been here for you since you had Constance, but that changes today."

I thought to myself "just fucking great" she apologizes the day after I let some young, tender chick with a slick mouth fuck my brains out. I looked at her. "Can I ask you a question?"

"Ask whatever you want."

"Why have you been so distant with me? Are you cheating?"

Her eyes opened wide and then she laughed. "Is that a real question?"

"Yes, answer it."

She grabbed my hands. "I made you a promise Khanna, I would never cheat on you and I'm keeping it no matter what."

I felt like someone had stabbed me twice in the chest after she said that. Suspicion had driven me into the bed of someone else. I hated myself. I wanted to fall out and die right now. I made a promise with myself in my head not to tell her. I told myself that I'd never see Nia again then I shamefully asked God for his help and forgiveness. Yari would be devastated if she knew that I had broken our promise. I couldn't take her hating me. I'd just deal with hating myself the rest of my life.

~~*~*

139

Yari and I had started to sleep in the same bed again. She was coming home earlier from work and helping more with Constance. She helped me cook and clean and today she volunteered to come grocery shopping with me. It was a major turnaround from what we had been going through. I guess I should have just been more patient. Constance was one now and she was walking. She talked her baby gibberish as Yari pushed her in the basket as I tossed in random items. As I read food labels I heard a voice call out my name. I turned to see Nia walking towards me. I tried not to look suspicious.

"Khanna, long time." She said hugging me.

"Yeah, long time." I said half-way hugging her.

There was an awkward silence then she spoke. "Constance is getting so big."

"Yeah she eats more than we do." I said moving closer to Yari.

She reached out her hand to Yari. "You must be the girlfriend."

Yari shook her hand. "That would be me."

"Lucky woman," Nia said with a hint of sarcasm. "It's nice to meet you."

"Same here I think," Yari said.

"Well I better get going. It was nice seeing you Khanna. We should catch up sometime."

"Yeah we should do that…" I said as I walked forward.

I hoped that Yari could not pick up on the tension between Nia and I. Yari was far from stupid and I knew that she felt something, but I didn't want her to question it. This is where knowing someone well became a downfall. Nia watched us as we walked away. Yari spoke in a low tone. "Who was that?"

"Nobody, baby."

"Don't insult my intelligence, Khanna."

"Just someone I met one night while I was out."

"You fucked her?"

"Yari!"

"Don't raise your voice. You know how I feel about public arguments. Answer the question. Did you fuck her?"

I swallowed back hard. "Once."

"Were you with me?"

I was silent.

"Be honest. Shit." She was losing her composure.

I whispered, "Yes."

We paid for our groceries and walked outside to load them into our car. I strapped Constance into her seat. I shut the back door and Nia was walking our direction again. I was not ready for this. She yelled out. "Khanna I wanted to make sure you had an updated number on me." Yari dropped the bags she had in her hand and ran toward Nia hitting her in the face. I ran to grab Yari, but they were already tearing into each other. I screamed for them to stop. The security officer ran from inside the store to help me break it up. Constance screamed from the car. The guard held onto Nia. She smiled with blood running from her lip. She looked at me. "It was worth it." She blew a kiss at me.

I grabbed Yari before I could she could run up on her again. She snatched her arm away. "Get in the fucking car." She snapped.

She hopped in on the passenger side and slammed the door. I jumped into the driver's seat and sped off. We were half-way home when it started to rain. I slowed down and turned on the wipers. Yari was still livid.

"I'm sorry." I made an attempt to kill the mood in the car.

"Fuck you. I'm out working so that you never want for anything and you're out laying on your back for a fucking child!"

She should have just hit me because her words hurt. She just called me a lazy ho in so many words.

"Pull over!"

"No."

"Pull the fuck over!" She grabbed the steering wheel. I slapped her hand away and pulled to the side of the road. She got out and slammed the door. She punched the glass and I jumped. I got out of the car. "Get back in the car Yari. It's raining!" I yelled.

"WHY, Khanna? We have one rough patch and you go fuck someone else!" She kicked the car and started to walk.

I wanted to walk behind her, but Constance was in the car. Maybe this was what she needed. I got back into the car soaking wet and I pulled off.

I carried Constance inside and laid her down then I tugged in all the groceries and put them away. I took off my wet clothes and threw them on the ground in the garage. One hour went by. Yari still had not made it home. I showered. I cleaned. Another hour went by. I cooked and cleaned some more. I stripped the beds and washed sheets and pillow cases. Here was the third hour. Now I was getting worried.

The door opened and Yari walked in dripping wet. I ran to her and wrapped my arms around. She didn't push me away. She wrapped her arms around me and cried. Her pain seeped into me as her cries got louder and her knees buckled beneath her. She sobbed into my ear "This hurts Khanna. It hurts!"

I held her tighter and rubbed her head. "Shhh…I'm so sorry baby…I know."

We sat by the front door and she cried until nothing was left inside of her. She stood and walked to our bedroom. I watched her. It was a painful silence. I heard drawers opening and the closet door slid open. I stood and walked to the back of our house. Yari was packing her things. I didn't stop her. We had both agreed not to make a separation between us ugly if the time had ever come and we both agreed that cheating was an unforgivable act because it broke trust and without trust there was nothing else left. I watched her move around the room throwing things into the three bags that sat on our bed. She took all that she wanted and then carried them out to the car. I followed her. We stood in the kitchen facing one another. Her throat was sore from crying.

"Umm, I'll pay the mortgage until you start working again and I'll send $500.00 a month to cover food and utilities. If Constance needs anything just text me, I guess. I'll come get her on the weekends."

I nodded my head in agreement as a single tear rolled down my face. She pulled her promise ring from her finger and sat in on the counter then she was gone. I locked the door behind her then slid down leaning against it with tears dropping faster than I could stop them. I picked myself up and walked into the kitchen opening the drawer that contained the cigarettes that I had stopped smoking a year and a half ago. I pulled one out and went into the dining room. I sat down and flicked the lighter to light it. I watched the flame. I had caused this. You play with fire and you get burned. I had traded a lifetime, a history with the woman I loved; the woman who was my caretaker for a Moment and it wasn't worth it. My assumptions made an ass out of me.

"Married to the Man"

I'm not going to sit here and tell you some sap story about me being raped, or losing my virginity to a man who didn't want me, and I just so happened to end up pregnant. I'm going to tell you the truth. I was a stupid teenager. I lost my virginity at the age of thirteen to the first boy who said *I love you* to me. I fell for his charm and his bad boy attitude and the next thing you know I was cutting class to lay on my back for him. I had no idea what sex really was then. All I knew was that it felt good and I wanted it often. By the time I had made sixteen I had ten sex partners. I was really popular with the boys. My Mom never told me not to have sex, because she believed children would do the opposite of what you said anyway, so all she would do is tell me to protect myself. One day four of the guys that I hung out with: Jason, David, Marvin, and Ricky, said they were all going to the park and then to smoke and drink afterwards.

I had a little crush on one of them so when they asked if I wanted to go I told them yes. I hopped in the backseat between two of them and they passed a blunt around. We got to the park and played around and talked about nothing. Jason, the one I liked stood off to the side by himself, so I took it as an opportunity to join him….

"Why are you being anti-social?" I said.

"No reason. I was really just being nosey," Jason responded.

"What were you looking at?" I asked.

He pointed to a house where a light was on in a window. It looked like two people were arguing. We both watched for awhile and then I moved in closer to him, wrapping my arm around his. He looked down at me and smiled. "You're really pretty."

"You think so?"

"Yeah, so are you coming over to my house to chill after we leave here, or are we dropping you off?"

"I'll chill, if I have a reason to."

"What reason you have in mind, *shawty?*"

"You."

Jason laughed and then pulled me back over where the other three boys were sitting.

"Y'all ready to drink?"

They answered in unison and then we all walked back to the car. I rode in the front with Jason. We glanced at each other every chance that we got, smiling and blushing like the stupid teenagers that we were. It took Jason about ten minutes to get to his house. His parents were never home and they always had a cabinet full of liquor. As soon as we got inside we all started throwing back shots in the living room while music blasted. I was wasted and horny. Jason stood up and then pulled me up to follow him. We went into his room and went at it as soon as the door shut. He pulled off his clothes and I pulled off mine. My mouth watered and my pussy throbbed at the sight of his hard dick. He bent me over his bed and pushed into me hard. We weren't even into it good when Marvin came busting in. Jason didn't stop fucking me and I didn't push him away. Marvin stood against the wall, pulled out his dick, and started to masturbate before walking over to the bed. I don't know if it was the alcohol or me just being greedy. Marvin sat in front of me on the bed and I took his dick into my mouth. Eventually David and Ricky joined in, each taking turns fucking me and getting their dicks sucked until they all came.

Fucking all of them had turned into a weekly thing for me until I popped up pregnant and none of them wanted to take responsibility. After that I was just a hoe in their eyes. They spread rumors about me and made threats, because all of them came from families that could be ruined with news like this. They all refused to be tested and I wasn't up for the fight because I had brought this on myself. My parents moved me away and I was stuck being a teen Mother alone. I did get to graduate and attend prom, but after that my life was over.

~~*~*

"I have a past and I'm not sure I'm the ideal woman for you." I said sitting across from Anthony and licking my ice cream.

"Did you hear what you just said?"

"Yeah?"

"Past. You can't compare the past to the present. I don't care what you went through or what you've done unless you just want to vent to me about it. I want you."

"You don't know me."

"I'm trying to get to know you."

Anthony Marsalis, one word, persistent. He was one of those men who wanted what they wanted when they wanted it and he wanted me to be one of those women who complied, but pending my history with men

I was reluctant to move forward with him. My Mother had been trying to get me to go out with him for months after he visited our church. All I wanted to do was live my life happily single and give my son all the things that I didn't have. Anthony wanted to change those plans the instant he met me. I don't know what it is with people and "the chase." I had turned him down for dates several times, but he would never give up. I couldn't take having him and my Mother hounding me so I had finally agreed to one date and here I was. I wondered what he would feel if knew the type of person I used to be and how I got to this point in my life.

He interrupted my thoughts. "Go ahead try to turn me off."

"I had Tavion when I was sixteen years old."

"Teen pregnancy is common now just like deadbeat Dads. Next."

"I wanted to have an abortion."

"But you didn't." He licked his ice cream.

"He was conceived through a gang bang and I don't know who the Father is…"

"Wow!" He almost dropped his ice cream.

"Still want to date me?"

"That depends. Would you sleep with any of my friends?" he asked sarcastically.

"No ass. I'm not that girl anymore."

"Well then. I want to date you. You were sixteen Tavia. We all do stupid things as teenagers."

"You don't have a baby."

"Are you calling Tavion a stupid decision?"

"Of course not."

"Then I'm not finding the flaw in this situation." He smiled. "So are you going to date me?"

I smiled.

Dating was exactly what we did. He made me realize that good men still existed and chivalry was not dead. Anthony was the first guy that I had met who appreciated my honesty. He didn't judge me and never even brought up my past. He was a very sweet, kind, gentle, and hardworking man. My parents loved him and he took my son as his own. We were married after seven months of dating and two years later I gave him Miri. We've been married now for six years and he's never asked me to do anything or for anything.

~~*~*

I felt lips pressed against mine and that meant it was 5:45 in the morning and Anthony was on his way out of the door. I had one hour left to sleep. He held his mouth against mine a little bit longer than usual. I raised my tired hand placing it on the back of his neck and kissing him back.

He whispered, "I transferred an extra thousand dollars into your account from the company account. Get yourself something nice today and buy something for the kids. I have a late day today."

"Baby, you didn't have to do that."

"I wanted to. I appreciate everything that you do around here and I want you to be able to treat yourself."

I smiled as he slid his hands over my breast beneath the covers. "Damn I wish I didn't have to go to work today."

"Can you spare fifteen minutes?"

"I can't be late. I have a lot of meetings today."

I sighed and kissed him once more trying to convince him to break the rules. "Okay baby. I'll sit you a plate in the oven."

"Thank you."

"Have a good day."

"You too baby now go back to sleep."

I shuffled under the covers trying to fall back to sleep, but it was pointless since I knew I had to be up in a few anyway. I would just lie there checking the clock every ten minutes to make sure I didn't oversleep. I decided to get up and just shower and watch the news rebroadcast. There was never anything positive on television anymore. I shook my head.

I walked into the room where Tavion, who was now eleven was sleeping and flipped o his light. "Time to get up baby…" he turned over like he didn't hear me. I'd be back in five minutes.

Miri was four now. I walked into her room and turned on her light. She was harder to wake up so I went over to her and picked her up and poked at her face. "Miri time to wake up sweetie." Her eyes fluttered and she wrapped her arms around my neck.

"Good morning, Mommy."

"You want cereal?"

She nodded her head yes.

"Come on let's go brush your teeth."

Tavion was up brushing his teeth and rubbing on his bird chest. I stood his sister next to him and plucked the back of his ear. "Put a shirt on boy."

"Ouch! Alright."

"Make sure Miri brushes her teeth properly. I'm going cook breakfast."

"Can I just have cereal too this morning."

"You sure can." I walked out of the bathroom.

Being a Mother and a wife was a fulltime job and this may sound horrible to you, but I'm tired. I do the exact same thing every day. I'm up every morning for six, I switch on the television in the living room and change the channel to *Nickelodeon*, I get my children out of bed and push them to the bathroom, so they can brush their teeth and wash their faces, I remind them to squeeze the toothpaste from the bottom of the tube. I make them breakfast and pack them some lunch. They watch cartoons as I look through the cabinets and the fridge to make a list of everything that I need to pick up from the store after I drop them off at school, I shop for the house, I re-cleaned the entire house, I do laundry, ironing daily for everyone, I pick the kids up, I help with homework, I run bath water, I cook dinner, I turn on the shower for Anthony as he walks in, I wait for him to join us at the dinner table, we discuss our day, and then off to bed we all go. I felt it was my duty as a housewife to ensure everyone's happiness and comfort. After getting Miri to fall asleep and checking to make sure that Tavion is pretending to be sleeping I'm too tired to do anything else. Sex is usually a luxury. It was a rare Moment when we both had energy and we took full advantage. We hadn't gotten back into our regular sex routine since Miri had been born. She had just stopped sleeping in the bed with us months ago. Now she crawls in bed with her brother. I wasn't complaining. The love between Anthony and I was still there and going strong, but it still just wasn't enough. I needed more of something, but I wasn't sure what.

My kids ate their cereal and I sat and watched smiling at how beautiful they both were. Sometimes it was hard for me to believe that they came from my body. I'd do it all again. They ate quickly and then ran to get their bags. I stood at the front door waiting as they ran past me to fight over who would sit in the front seat. Miri knew she was going to have to sit in the back because she wasn't old enough to sit in the front, but she just enjoyed giving her brother a hard time. They loved each other and hated each other at the same time. They were the highlight of my every day.

I dropped them each off to their separate schools and gave them kisses on the cheek before heading to Wal-Mart, Target, Family Dollar, Dollar Tree, and then finally the mall. I grabbed everything I needed for the house and got the kids some new clothes and shoes. I even grabbed some lingerie from Victoria's Secret to wear for Anthony and I got him a nice tie. I had some free time to spare so I decided to surf the web. I had convinced myself that I was just bored with my life and that's why I felt like something was missing. I figured I could take some online courses to add something extra to my life. I Googled to see what kind of certifications I could get in under a year or two and the two that stood out was accountant and massage therapist. I opened tabs on each one separately so that I could print out the information to run it by my husband. As I watched the pages print my cell phone vibrated on the desk next to the computer. I had forgotten that I even sat it there. Nobody really called me. The number to my son's school flashed on the screen and I picked it up immediately. "Hello?"

"May I speak with, Mrs. Marsalis?"

"This is she."

"Mrs. Marsalis, we need you to come down to the school for a conference. Your son just got into a physical altercation with another student."

"I'm on my way!"

I slid my feet back into my shoes and rushed to my car forgetting to grab my purse. I ran back into the house and then I was gone again. I was going to kill him. Fighting?! I taught him better than that and I knew his Father and I talked to him about violence not solving anything. This is exactly how it started. One fight and then who knows what happens after that! I had to calm myself down. I was being irrational. I pulled up to the school in record time and dashed to the school office. My son was sitting right outside of the door when I made it up the stairs. The other parent had already made it there. I grabbed him and they escorted us into the principal's office. The boy that my son had fought was much bigger than him. He looked like he had been held back a couple grades. It took everything in me not to laugh when I say that his eye was swollen and my son didn't have as much as a scratch on him. I directed my attention to the principal.

"What happened?" I asked the principal.

The other parent chimed in. "Your son clearly attacked mine!"

I wanted to jump at her ass, but I didn't. I kind of felt sorry for her because she looked so pitiful. Her clothes were too big and she wore her hair in a large afro. Somebody was clearly waiting on the revolution. I could tell that with a little make-up and better clothes she was probably something to look at. I gave her the benefit of the doubt in my mind that she was laying around the house when she got the call and this was cleaning clothes or perhaps it was laundry day.

"Excuse me. I do believe I was talking to the principal, *not* you!"

"I did not attack him! He tried to take my shoes!" My son yelled out.

I touched his shoulder. "Let Mommy handle this." I looked up. "See your little bully wasn't attacked. He tried to take something that didn't belong to him and he paid for it."

"My son doesn't have to steal." She replied.

I looked down at the little boy's shoes. "Clearly." I said with sarcasm.

The principal stood "Hey hey now we can all talk about this like adults. You two young men step out and let us adults talk." He said while reseating himself. "I'm suspending them both." He looked back and forth between us. "I'm giving Tavion three days since he was just defending himself and Jeffery gets five."

"Jeffery would not steal or start a fight!" The other parent yelled.

"Mrs. Henderson, I understand that we all want to believe that our kids can do no wrong, but this isn't the case here and I would like if you would just co-operate with reprimanding him. He clearly has some underlying issues that need to be discussed and I'd like to help any way that I can, but I can only do that if you let me."

Mrs. Henderson sat silent as reality sat in that she had a little trouble maker on her hands and my son was the one to finally tag that ass and put him in his place. I couldn't even be mad at my son. It served his little black ass right, trying to take something that he didn't work for. The principal talked with us a few more minutes and then we were released to take our sons. We walked out first. I wrapped my arm around Tavion's shoulder and whispered to him so they couldn't hear what I said as they trailed behind us to the parking lot. "You have a mean right hook huh?"

Tavion smiled. "Am I going to get punished?"

"No baby. I'm proud of you for standing up for yourself. Now had you come home without those shoes we'd have a problem. Mama would have to show you where she's from." I put him in a headlock.

We stopped for snacks and I bought him a new video game to play for the next three days that he would sit inside doing nothing. Those bitches wouldn't even give him the work he needed while he was out. I needed to find him a new school. It was kind of nice having him home with me since I was there by myself most of the day. I wanted those three days to drag.

Anthony got off early and picked Miri up from school. He came into the bedroom where Tavion and I were laying cuddled with each other watching television. I had called him earlier and told him about the fight. He jumped in the bed and attacked Tavion. "What up baby Tyson."

"Dad!" he laughed as Anthony playfully punched him all over.

"High five, big man.Us Marsalis men handles business!"

Tavion high-fived him and they engaged in male conversation. I rolled my eyes as Miri ran in the room holding her favorite bear and a picture she drew at school. She jumped into my lap and kissed me. She handed me her picture then explained everything that was on it. I loved my family so much. How could I still feel so empty?

~~*~*

I pulled up to drop Tavion off to school. It was his first day back. I parked to walk him to class. As we walked up to the side walk Mrs. Henderson and her son, Jeffery approached us.

I pulled Tavion close. "Good morning, Mrs. Henderson."

"Actually it's just Ms. and please call me Stacia."

I gave her my hand to shake, "Tavia."

"I'm sorry about what happened in the office a few days ago. I guess it's kind of hard to hear that your child was wrong, especially when you know that you've taught them better."

"I understand."

"Jeffery wanted to apologize," she pushed him. "Go ahead."

"I'm sorry for trying to take your shoes." he hung his head.

"It's cool, man." Tavion lifted his hand to dap him off.

I was proud of my baby. Stacia and I watched as they walked into the school together laughing. It had always been easier for boys to squash *beef*.

Stacia turned to me. "I was wondering if you would be okay with Tavion hanging out with Jeffery sometimes. We just moved here and I think he's just having a tough time with other kids and adjusting to being here."

"I wouldn't mind at all. What is he doing this weekend?"

"Nothing, I'm sure."

"Well, take my number. You both can come over Saturday. My husband will be out of town on business this weekend and my daughter will be with her grandparents. We can all get acquainted."

"You have a daughter too?"

"Yes, she's four going on forty."

We both laughed

"Well, I'll see you Saturday then? I'll give you a call for directions."

"Is there anything in particular that you two like to eat?"

"We're not picky people."

~~*~*

Tavion was excited about having company. He ran back and forth through the house waiting on Jeffery to arrive. We never really invited anyone over because Anthony didn't trust anyone in our house. We had a lot of expensive things and people would destroy your shit out of pure jealousy. I was happy that Anthony would be out of town this weekend because I wasn't really in the mood to get grilled about having a stranger over. I doubted seriously that this woman and her eleven year old son were capable of murder or armed robbery.

The day before, Tavion and I had gone to the grocery store and purchased lots of snacks for him and his new friend. It wasn't often that I let my children have junk food, so he had a field day running up and down the aisles, placing everything from chips to ice cream in the basket. He knew daggon well that he was not going to eat all of that in a day.

The doorbell sounded as I lay across the bed, reading about beauty tips in Jet magazine. I stood and Tavion dashed past me to open the door. I walked up behind him as he unlocked it. I slapped him on the back of the head. "Ask who it is before opening boy."

He rubbed his head, "Sorry."

I pushed him, "Move!"

I greeted Stacia and Jeffery with a smile. I opened the door wider for them to walk past us. Tavion and Jeffery instantly engaged in conversation.

"Mom, can he come to my room?"

"Yeah, go ahead."

They ran off and I offered Stacia something to drink. She wasn't thirsty just yet though. She looked much better than she did from our first meeting. Her bushy hair was now in double stranded twist and they hung a little bit past her shoulders. She wore a plain black t-shirt and some khaki pants with Sperry's. It was a step up from the disco era look that she was rocking in the principal's office. She wasn't very feminine.

"Would you like a tour of the house?"

"Yeah, that would be nice."

We walked out of the living room, and I showed her our five bedrooms, three and a half bathroom home. We had small talk about the boys after passing the room where they played.

"You guys live pretty far out."

"Yeah, my husband isn't a fan of cities."

"You're married?"

"Yes, almost seven years now."

"That's amazing. Most people don't make it past a year or two anymore."

"I got lucky I guess. Are you married?"

"Oh no, it's just me and my Jeffery. That's the only man I'll ever need."

I opened the door to the computer room and Stacia walked in ahead of me. She walked over to the desk and picked up the info I had printed a few days earlier.

"You're looking into massage therapy?"

"Yeah, I just need a hobby. Being a housewife can be kind of dull."

"That's what I do for a living."

"Really? What's the odds of that?" I laughed.

"I'll be happy to help you out once you start."

"I'd like that."

Stacia had a very different aura from most women that I met. She smiled a lot and she was very flirtatious with everything that she said or did. She seemed very comfortable in her skin. The confidence in her being, made me oddly attracted to her. Well, I wasn't exactly sure if it was an attraction or an admiration. I just knew that I liked it. We went back into the living room and took a seat.

"So how long did it take you to finish with massage therapy?"

"Roughly, nine months. The time frame varies from state to state."

"Do your hands get tired?"

She laughed. "No, I'm used to doing it and I enjoy the reactions I get."

"How can you tell if someone is tense?"

"I'll show you turn around. I mean if you want me to."

I turned quickly. "Oh sure, go ahead." I moved my hair to the side.

Stacia's hands were cold as she touched my collar bone and squeezed my skin. She rubbed her thumbs across the top of my back. I closed my eyes and dropped my head.

"You feel how tight you are?"

"Yeeaahh," I said as she rubbed.

She applied more pressure and my eyes began to roll, as I relaxed beneath her fingers. Before I could think about anything, I was moaning, as her hand traveled up and down my back.

"You don't get many massages, do you?"

"Huh?"

"You never go to a day spa or anything?"

"Oh no, I don't really have the time."

"I'm sure you could spare an hour. You should come see me in my office sometime this week. Your first massage will be on me."

"Okay, sure," I mumbled as she continued to massage. I just wanted her to shut up and rub. The instant that her hand ran up the back of my neck my eyes shot open. My pussy was starting to throb now and that couldn't be right.

"Are you... okay?" she asked alarmed.

"Yes, I'm fine. Do you want that drink now?" I jumped up.

"Yes, sure."

"What would you like?"

"Water is fine."

I hurried to the kitchen and took deep breaths before grabbing a bottle of water from the fridge. I walked back into the living room after getting my hormones under control and handed it to her.

Stacia and Jeffery stayed until seven that night. We played board games and watched television. Tavion wanted Jeffery to stay over but I told him no and promised him that the next time he could. I needed to run it by Anthony first, and I wanted him to meet Jeffery and Stacia for himself — to see that they were good people — because telling him over the phone that the boy your son had a fight with is spending the night, just wouldn't sound right. I took one of Stacia's business cards, and they were off.

I cleaned up our mess once they were gone and Tavion was in bed. I was exhausted. I showered and then lay across my bed completely naked. At about two in the morning, I felt warm hands run up my body. A deep voice whispered, "Did you miss me sexy?"

"Mmmm, Anthony?"

"You expecting someone else?"

I laughed. "No silly."

He slid his hand between my legs, splitting my pussy lips. "You're the only woman I know that stays wet."

"What are you doing home so early?"

"I missed you," he kissed my neck. "Are you sleepy?"

"Kind of, not really."

He turned me onto my back and opened my legs. His dick was rock hard. He leaned down, pushing himself inside of me. I didn't protest. He pumped slowly and kissed me. I closed my eyes and the first thing I saw was Stacia's hands on me. I opened my eyes quickly. Anthony's eyes were still closed as he kissed me. I tried closing my eyes again, but the image of her touching me was still there. I pushed Anthony onto his back and mounted him. I needed to concentrate. He held onto my ass, as I dropped down on him, and pressed my hands into his chest. I rode him until he came inside of me. This was the first time that I had had sex with my husband and I was just ready for it to be over. I didn't even care that I didn't cum. I lay beside him and we dozed off.

I sat at the desk, in the computer room, with Stacia's card in my hand. I ran my fingers across the printed words. A million thoughts shot through my brain, as I thought about her hands. *It's just a massage Tavia,* I thought to myself, as I picked up my cell phone to dial her number. It rang four times, and then the receptionist picked up.

"Relax Day Spa, Amber speaking, how may I assist you?"

"Is Stacia in today?"

"Yes ma'am, but she's with a client would you like to leave a message or schedule an appointment?"

"What openings does she have for Wednesday?"

"Morning or Evening, ma'am?"

"Morning would be nice."

"I have 8:30am, 10:00am, and 11am."

"I'll take ten."

"And what's your name ma'am."

"Tavia Marsalis."

"Okay, Mrs. Marsalis, I have you down for 10:00 am on Wednesday. We'll see you then."

"Thank you." I hung up.

I stood from my seat and went to pick up my kids from school. I sang loudly in the car as I drove, and I beat on the steering wheel to the rhythm of the music. Tavion was standing with Jeffery when I pulled up.

"Mom, Jeffery needs a ride today. Can we bring him?"

"Does he know how to get to his house?"

"Duh, Mom."

"Don't get smart, y'all will both walk."

They hopped in and then we scooped up Miri. Miri sat as close to Jeffery as she could get. He was about to get it.

"What's your name?" she asked.

"Jeffery," he answered with a friendly smile.

"What are you doing in my Mom's car?" she cocked her head to the side.

"She's giving me a ride."

"Where?"

"To my house."

"How does she know you?"

"I'm friends with your brother."

"Why are you his friend? He doesn't share."

Jeffery laughed. "He doesn't share with you?"

She shook her head no.

"How could he not share with you? You're so cute."

Tavion rolled his eyes in the front seat. Miri wore a big smile and moved even closer to Jeffery. I was going to have to watch her and boys.

Jeffery spouted off the directions and better than an adult would. We were at his house in a matter of minutes. His Mom wasn't home.

"Are you okay by yourself?"

"Yeah, my Mom will be home in a few."

"No, I'll wait."

We sat and waited for a half hour until Stacia pulled up. She got out and walked over to my car.

"You didn't have to bring him."

"It was no problem."

"You need gas money or anything."

"No, it's fine. He can ride with us anytime."

"I'm usually available to get him. One of my appointments ran over."

"It's okay. I didn't mind at all."

"Well, thank you."

Jeffery hopped out and I pulled off. I slowed and rolled my window down to catch her before she went inside.

You guys should have dinner with us tonight. I'd love for you to meet my husband."

"I think we'll take you up on that offer. What time?"

"Six?"

"Okay. I'll be there."

I got the kids home and helped them with whatever homework they had. Anthony was home, kicked back, sipping on a beer.

"Babe, we're having company tonight."

"Who?"

"Remember that kid that Tavion fought?"

"Yeah."

"Well, I've been talking to his Mom, and Tavion and her son have become great friends."

"Ha! Typical. Get your ass whipped and then be BFF's." he shook his head.

"He wanted him to spend the night, but I told him you'd have to meet him and his Mom first."

"Fine by me."

I went into the kitchen to prepare dinner. Tavion set the table for six instead of four tonight. Miri dragged her little kitchen set into the kitchen and pretended to be cooking too. She wore her little apron and stirred in her little plastic pots.

Stacia and Jeffery rang the doorbell just as I removed my pork roast from the oven. Anthony answered as I placed everything on the table. They walked in, as I placed the last food item in the center.

"What's for dinner?" Stacia asked

I smiled. "Pork roast, rice and gravy, and steamed broccoli, with the option of cheddar cheese on top."

Everyone took a seat at the table. We blessed the food, and then ate and engaged in conversation. Stacia and Anthony hit it off well. They both had a love for sports and cars. He was impressed with the fact that she was a twenty-seven year old, who owned her own spa.

"Babe, you should go and check out Stacia's skills one day, you deserve to relax."

"She gave me a business card, babe." I didn't want to say that I had already made an appointment for Wednesday; that could lead to a lot of other information being released. I hadn't told Anthony that she had been to our house before either. We shared a few more laughs and drinks. Stacia couldn't stay long since it was a school night for the kids. I escorted her to her car.

"You are an amazing cook."

"Amazing at following recipes from the cooking channel."

We both laughed. She got into her car and pulled off. I waved goodbye and went back into the house. Anthony met me at the door grabbing me. "Get in here woman its dark."

I laughed. "So, did you like her?"

"Yeah, cool chick. I think she's gay though."

I slapped him on the shoulder, "Don't say that."

"Baby, I'm no expert, but that chick likes chicks."

"Whatever," I kissed him and pushed myself away, "I have to clean up."

"I got it baby. You have to get up early."

"Aw, you're too good to me." I kissed him again and then turned in for the night.

~~*~*

I sat in the waiting area, waiting to be called. After ten minutes, Stacia walked out to the front and grabbed the clipboard at the receptionist desk. She looked up, surprised. "Tavia?"

I stood and smiled nervously. "Hi," I waved holding the strap to my purse on my shoulder.

"Why didn't you tell me you were coming? I would have cleared my schedule."

"It was really kind of, a last minute decision," I lied.

"Well, come on to the back."

I followed her. "Nice space."

"Thanks. It still needs some work."

"I think its fine."

"So what kind of massage do you want?"

"Oh, I don't know."

"I can do deep tissue, a back massage, Swedish…."

"What do you recommend?"

"That depends on how tense you are."

"I'm really tense." I lied again.

She walked over to me and handed me a towel and a robe. She stood closely and whispered, "Completely off the record, but if you're really tense, I'd be more than happy to offer you a *Yoni* massage."

"What's that?"

"Take off your clothes."

Stacia left the room. I sat my purse to the side and stripped down, wrapping the towel around my naked body and then the robe. I hopped up on the table that was in the room and sat waiting for Stacia. She walked in and shut off the lights. She lit candles around the room. She switched on soft music and then walked over to where I was seated. She placed her hand on each side of me and leaned in close to my face.

She spoke in a low tone. "Do something for me, okay?"

I nodded my head yes.

"Relax." She grabbed the tie to my robe and loosened it. "Lie back."

I lied back, as I was told, as she circled me checking every angle of my body.

She tickled my palm with the tips of her fingers as she spoke in a seductive tone. "*Yoni* is the ancient Indian word for vagina. This particular massage is used, to free women from sexual inhibitions, that may have been brought on by negative sexual or life experiences. It is used to free the woman's sexual energy and offer release of pent up energy".

Nervousness now stirred in my body.

"You have to trust me. This is not about sex or orgasm, even though that may happen. Just focus on the experience of touch, relaxation, pleasure, and release." She poured oil on my body. Stacia rubbed my temples, she tugged at my ears. She rubbed my shoulders, and pulled at each arm. She even massaged my fingers and toes.

I was completely relaxed. I hadn't even noticed that my towel was open and my breast and vagina were exposed until she ran her thumbs over my nipples and squeezed my breast. She slid her hands down my stomach and then dug her fingers into my hips. The instant she began rubbing my thighs, I knew that my *yoni* was next. Wetness formed between my legs just from the thought. I was ready.

She squeezed the outer lips gently between her fingers, sliding them up and down the entire length of my lips. She used soft, gentle, slow movements and she looked into my eyes, never breaking away. "May I go further?"

"Yes." I breathed.

She pressed against my clit, rubbing in clockwise, circular motions, then squeezing it gently between her thumb and forefinger. She was gentle. I moaned from her touch. "Should I stop?"

"No, please, don't." I could barely speak.

She slid her middle finger into my pussy and every part of me came to pieces. She moved in and out, as slowly as one humanly could. She would speed up and then go slow again. Stacia was…fucking me. My toes curled, as we watched each other the entire time. I tried to close my eyes.

"No, look at me," she whispered.

I felt her finger curve slightly inside of me. She was trying to *destroy* me. She massaged my G-Spot and I moaned loudly, hoping that no one outside that room could hear me.

"Sta-st-stacia!"

"Shhhh."

"Oh... my… gawd. Wha-What are you doing to me?"

"You're having an orgasm. Don't fight it. Come on."

I pulled Stacia into me and all professionalism flew out of the window, as she pulled my nipple into her mouth. My entire body felt as if it was going numb and my clit pushed forward as I released. Stacia removed her hand slowly, and I laid back to catch my breath.

No words were exchanged as I dressed and then left the building. I sat in my car in disbelief. My husband was right.

~~*~*

I avoided Stacia at all cost. She called, but I didn't answer. My husband was going out of town again this weekend and I was glad to finally have some time alone to think. Nothing had been the same since Stacia and I had that *moment*.

It was just Tavion and me. Tavion played his video games and I flipped through the channels and like usual there was nothing to watch. I decided I'd watch a movie. I went into the computer room to find a DVD and the doorbell sounded. Tavion ran past me. He opened it again without asking who it was. Stacia and Jeffery stood at the door. My body tensed up.

"What are you guys doing here?" I asked walking into the front room.

"Jeffery said,Tavion and him are having a sleepover."

I looked down at my son, "Tavion you didn't ask me about a sleepover."

"I asked two weeks ago, Mom. You and Dad said yes."

I tried to jog my memory. I had been so out of it lately; I had no idea which way was up or down. I pretended to remember. "I'm sorry baby you sure did. Well okay, you two go to your room. I'll make lunch."

They ran off.

"I'll return him in one peace."

"Tavia, are you going to keep ignoring me? Shouldn't we talk or something?"

"What is there to talk about?"

"I know you have thoughts or questions. Talk to me." She touched my arm and I damn near passed out.

"Let's talk in my room."

I shut the front door and locked it and then she followed me into my room.

"Did I do something wrong?"

159

"Yes, Stacia, I'm married."

"I understand that."

"You crossed a major line."

"You didn't stop me."

"I know and I'm ashamed of myself."

"Ashamed because you did it or because you enjoyed it?" She moved closer and grabbed me.

"Stop it." I pushed her.

"What if I wasn't done?" She pulled more aggressively this time and held me close.

"You didn't even let me kiss you."

"If I let you kiss me, will you leave?"

She shook her head no as she said it, "No." She pressed her lips against mine.

I closed my eyes and accepted her lips. She sucked on my bottom lip, sliding her tongue in and out of my mouth. "Let me taste you."

"Stacia, I can't."

"Don't you want the feeling that I gave you before? What he doesn't know won't hurt him Tavia." She escorted me over to my bed and laid me back, pushing my *nightie* up around my waist, and pulling my panties off. She gave my pussy a soft peck, before using her tongue to part my lips and wet up my clit. I moaned. I threw my head back as she savored the taste of my vagina. My room door swung open.

"Mommy, can we—"

"Close that door!" I jumped up. "Shit!"

Stacia and I rose quickly. She wiped her mouth and I adjusted my clothes. My son closed the door quickly and I could hear him running.

"You need to leave!" I yelled at Stacia.

Stacia called for Jeffery and he came running to her. She told him that they had to go and she'd explain later. I walked her out and slammed the door.

Shit. Shit. Shit. I paced back and forth in the living room trying to think of something to say to my son. Why couldn't I be stronger than temptation? I gathered my thoughts as quickly as I could, and then walked slowly to my son's room. He had his door closed. I turned the knob but he had it locked.

"Tavion?Baby? Open up."

"No!"

"Please."

"Leave me alone."

"Baby, let me explain what you saw."

160

I took a seat in front of his room waiting until he calmed down, but he never did. My eyes started to glaze over the later that it got. I leaned against his door and fell asleep.

I fell back hard as my son's room door swung open finally. "Daddy!" he stepped over me. Anthony looked down at me.

"Baby, why are you sleeping right here?" he asked.

I wiped my eyes, "Tavion locked me out." Tavion gave me a look that should have killed me, while latching onto Anthony's leg. I sat up.

"Dad, can we spend some time together today? Alone?" he looked at me out of the corner of his eye. I wanted to grab him and shake him. I was his blood Mother and I did everything to keep him happy and here he was, treating me like I was scum of the fucking Earth — ungrateful little bastard. I had to contain my anger and think about how I would feel if I was in his shoes. Anthony was the only Father that he had ever known. I thought Tavion and I had a stronger bond than that. I hoped he would at least let me talk to him. I was wrong.

"Yeah, what do you want to do today?"

"Anything, Dad. I don't care."

I interrupted, "Baby, can we talk before you two do anything?"

"What's wrong, baby?" Anthony looked concerned.

I had to let it all out. What I had to say would either help or hurt my marriage. I'd learn exactly what type of man Anthony was right now and I was hoping he was the kind that found girl on girl appealing rather than appalling.

"Faggolicious"

It never fails. Every time that I put my all into a relationship I get fucked over. I don't get some of these femmes. They complain about studs lying and cheating and some of them even hit their asses, but when they get someone like me who treats them the way they are supposed to be treated they don't fucking appreciate it. Some of the shit that I've been going through lately just makes me want to be asexual. I can see why studs are always yelling that they are done with women. Don't get me wrong I damn sure don't like men, but I'm starting to believe that I don't like women either.

Paula and I were doing great well at least I thought we were. I had finally found exactly what I was looking for in a woman. She was smart, beautiful, and aggressive. There was never a day that went by that she didn't tell me how much she loved me and how much she appreciated me. She had just gotten out of a bad relationship and I guess you could say that I was her superman. She had my nose so open after we made it official. I didn't even realize it was ending before it had begun. Paula would toss and turn in her sleep and I'd wake up from mine just to make sure she wasn't having a bad dream. I bent over backwards for her only to find out that the tossing and turning in her sleep was a result of her dreaming of her ex. The next thing I know I'm sitting in class and she sends me a text message saying that she loves me and I'm the most genuine person she's ever been with, but she feels as though her dreams mean that her and her ex aren't completely over. What pissed me off was the fact that she wanted me to understand. She wasn't even woman enough to say it face to face, a fucking text message!

I sat in my campus apartment day in and day out crying over that dumb bitch. I left to go to class and I'd eat in the cafeteria maybe once a day. She had me strung out completely. Say what you want about me crying, fuck you, I'm still a woman and what she did to me hurt. I hate being hurt, especially by love. It does more than destroy emotions. It hurts physically. That shit will make you sick. I wanted to call my best friend Andi, but I knew all she would tell me is *I told you so.*

Andi and I were complete opposites when it came to dating. She was rude and to her all women were bitches. I don't think she had ever been in love her whole life and if she did the chick must have fucked over her worse than anyone had ever done me. I knew I'd have to call her eventually or she'd come looking for me. It had been almost three weeks that I had been repeating the same routine over and over. I had not called anyone and I didn't answer anyone's phone call.

~~*~*

It was Saturday morning and the blinds on my window blocked out the brightness of the sun. I lay in bed unconscious when I heard someone banging on my door like the damn police.

At first I thought I was dreaming, but when the knocking didn't stop I sat up in my bed and forced myself to stand. The smell of my own breath caused me to open my eyes. That shit smelled like I had been eating garbage. I walked to the front door and opened it and there was Andi.

"What the fuck man? I've been trying to call you. All I get is the damn voicemail. Where that trifling bitch Paula at?"

"She's not here."

"I saw that ho in the mall with her ex and I've been trying to call you and tell you."

"She left me, Andi. They're back together."

"What the fuck? Why didn't you tell me? I could have whipped that bitch's ass."

"I'm over it."

"Nigga, you're too soft and you always falling for these bitches. Fuck and duck my dude fuck and duck. What the fuck have you been doing with yourself? Have you taken a shower? You look like shit."

"Thanks for the compliment."

I walked back toward my bedroom and Andi nipped at my heels with her *I told you so* speech. That was the exact reason that I didn't call her. I didn't want to hear that shit. I tried to lie back down, but Andi stood in my way. She pushed me toward the bathroom and handed me my toothbrush. I didn't even fight her today. I put the toothpaste on it and started brushing my teeth. Andi turned on the shower while I brushed.

"I'm going get you some clothes to put on. You're not sitting in this fucking room another day."

She stepped out and shut the door behind her. I started to remove my clothes. I wasn't in the mood to go anywhere and I wasn't sure I'd ever be. One painful relationship after another had finally taken me down. The nights I sat up and cried weren't just tears for Paula. They were tears for everyone that had ever hurt me. I was fed up and finally at my breaking point. I had even cut up all of their pictures, destroying their images made me feel a little relieved.

The water from the shower felt good against my skin. I had been washing the important parts, but I didn't have the energy to stand in a shower for minutes at a time. I scrubbed my skin like a skunk had shot its funk on me. After washing myself I just stood under the water, enjoying the temperature. I must have been in there too long because Andi knocked on the door, interrupting my thoughts.

"Come on!"

I stepped out of the shower and wrapped my towel around myself. I cracked the door so that Andi could hand me my clothes. I snatched them from her hands and then shut the door. If she hadn't been my friend since elementary I would have never even let her in to fuck up my miserable state. I put my clothes on and before stepping out I played in my bushy hair. It needed to be braided. I could do it myself, but I didn't feel like it.

Andi was sitting on my bed waiting for me. She stood up once I was dressed and we headed outside to her car. I jumped in on the passenger side and she hopped in on the driver's side. She looked over at me before pulling off.

"What we doing today?"

"I want my hair cut."

"Off?"

"Yep."

"Alright."

Andi backed out and then pulled off. She drove us straight to her barber. I thought I'd feel nervous once we got there, but I didn't. We got out of the car. I followed behind Andi because I had never been there before. She walked in and dapped off all the dudes in the shop that she knew. I took a seat at the front as she walked all-the-way to the back. She waved for me to come to the back and I stood up to meet her. I walked to the back and there was a stud sitting in a chair. Andi stood in front of her. They were looking at each other in a way that made me uncomfortable. Once Andi realized I was right next to her she snapped out of her love stare and introduced us. Her name was Deidra.

"What can I do for you today, Connie?"

"I want my hair cut off."

"Okay, how do you want it cut?"

"I don't know. I just want a new look."

"Okay, have a seat."

I watched my hair fall to the floor in bulk, with every piece that hit the floor I felt the weight of the world come off of my shoulders. I closed my eyes and let Deidra work her magic. Once she was done she turned me to the mirror and handed me a handheld one. She had cut my hair into a Mohawk and shaved designs on each side. It was actually very becoming. For the first time in weeks I smiled. Deidra smiled and I saw Andi smiling through the mirror.

"Very sexy."

"Huh."

"The haircut. It's sexy."

"Thank you." I twisted my brow. A stud had just called me sexy. Her words took me by surprise at first, but I just brushed it off. I stood up and went into my pockets to give her the money, but she pushed my hand back and told me not to worry about it. I insisted, but she refused to take my money. Deidra directed her attention back to Andi.

"You two going to the club tonight?"

"If misery over here wants to."

"Well, you should. I'll be there. You can buy me a drink and considerate it payment for the haircut."

"We'll be there," I said.

Instead of dapping Deidra off Andi hugged her and then she pushed me toward the door. I didn't bother to ask what that was all about. I was a little curious though, because it was the first time that I had seen Andi be that nice to anyone with a pussy and not once did she say anything disrespectful. Come to think about it, she barely said anything at all.

We got back into the car and I just sat there in silence. Andi didn't say anything either. She turned up the music and we hit the interstate. I had no idea where we were going next and I didn't care. I was feeling free with my new style and I wanted the world to see. I'm sure Andi had more than enough shit in mind to keep us busy.

~~*~*

Andi and I paid our money to get into the club. There was a femme on stage lip syncing to Keyshia Cole's song "Love." We posted up against a wall at the back of the club and just peeped out the scenery. There wasn't a single femme in there that stood out to me. My radar was reading them all: leech, ghetto, ex-drama, too many kids, bi-sexual...I just wasn't feeling any of those broads. I watched Andi out of the corner of my eye as she brushed off any femme that approached her. If they tried to make eye contact she would just roll her eyes. She had a serious chip on her shoulder about femmes and I was starting to wonder what it was.

Andi's face lit up and I turned to see what made her eyes do that. It was Deidra. She was headed straight for us. She spoke to me first, smiling from ear to ear. Then she spoke to Andi. She stood on the opposite side of Andi and I continued to watch the crowd. I was ready for a drink. I yelled to Andi and Deidra over the music.

"Y'all want a drink?"

They nodded yes and I walked off toward the bar. I pushed through the crowd, trying not to bump anyone. Ass was shaking everywhere. I grabbed girls around the waist to show I meant no disrespect by bumping into their asses. Some of them looked like they were pushing up on me on purpose. Once I made it to the bar I looked for an empty spot so the bartender could see me. Three people were served before me. I got our drinks and then walked all the way around to avoid the drinks from being knocked from my hands.

Andi and Deidra were standing close enough to kiss. They moved away from each other when I came over with the drinks. It was time for me to be nosey now. That was the third time today that some shit like that had happened. I didn't question her in the club. I just sipped my drink and grooved to the music.

I was feeling good, but then my whole mood was fucked up when I spotted Paula and her ex on the dance floor. I had hoped that she was just as miserable as me, but here this bitch was bumping and grinding and having fun. She was happy. I was ready to go after that. I saw Andi lean up off of the wall and I knew that she was seeing what I was seeing. I put my hand up to tell her to chill. She grabbed me and pushed me toward the door. We exited the club and Deidra followed. Andi told her she'd see her later and we left.

"I don't want to drive across town. You mind if I stay at your place?" Andi asked.

"You know you don't have to ask. You can stay over. You're welcome anytime."

We pulled up to my building. Andi pressed the code to the gate and we went inside. We walked to my apartment and went inside. Andi kicked off her shoes and placed them beside the door and went into my bedroom. I went into the bathroom to piss. She had turned on the television. I washed my hands and then went and joined her in front of the television. I sat at the other end of the bed and bucked myself up to get all into her business. I was her best friend, so it wouldn't kill her to tell me what was the deal with this Deidra chick?

"Andi can I ask you a personal question?"

"Yeah."

"Why do you hate femmes so much?"

"Because they nag and bitch and whine, they aren't aggressive enough for me, they act like they don't cheat or lie, and most of them just want to be fucked by the finest stud they can get their hands on."

"That's it."

"What are you asking, Connie?"

"I'm just curious. I never see you with a femme and you never have anything nice to say about them."

"Just ask what you want to ask."

"Who's Deidra to you?"

"My ex."

My mouth dropped. I just stared at Andi for a second. I wasn't sure how to feel about what she said. I asked more questions. "She is a stud right?"

"Yeah and?"

"I—"

"She's a woman," she cut me off.

"Andi?"

"What? Do I have to explain myself to you too? It's bad enough I get ridiculed by society for being gay and here you are looking at me like I got AIDS because I dated a stud. I'm stud for stud, a queer if you must know, Connie. Studs turn me on. I like the way they dress, the way they smell and I like fucking them and being fucked by them. Is that too much for your closed fucking mind? You're a woman too and femmes aren't the only type of women on this Earth. Here is a history lesson on s4s, it's not something new. Back in the sixties during all those feminist movements femmes didn't date studs because they thought we stood for everything they fought against as far as equal rights for women went. Studs dated studs. It's just becoming popular now and the whole community is in an ignorant uproar."

"I'm sorry. I didn't mean it like that."

"What did you mean then?"

"Nothing."

Andi and I sat in silence. I looked blankly at the television. Visions of Andi and Deidra played in my mind, them kissing and fucking each other. The thought turned me on. I was so wet that I thought it was going to go through my pants. Andi was right. They are women. I sat up at the end of the bed and Andi came down to the end with me. She placed her arm around my shoulder.

"I forgive you. You closed minded fucker."

"I would have never taken you for that type."

"You have to get past my looks." She stood and slipped off her shoes, unbuckled her belt to slide her jeans and boxers off and then removed her shirt and sports bra. "Can you see it now?"

We both laughed. I looked down to the floor and then back at Andi. I was stuck in her eyes and I saw her in another light as she stood before me stripped, exposed, vulnerable, and sexy. She leaned forward and kissed me. I kissed her back. We tore into each other like Thanksgiving dinner. She pushed me back on the bed and unbuttoned my pants. I kicked off my shoes. I had never in my life been touched the way Andi touched me. I was never the bitch in bed, but here I was moaning as she placed her hand in my boxers and played with me. I wanted more. She undressed me and kissed me all over. She sucked on places that I had no idea would arouse me. Andi's aggression turned me on and she had a touch of femininity. Her belly button was pierced and there was a tattoo right above her panty line on the left side. It had never crossed my mind that Andi was hiding that body beneath her clothes. She fucked me and I fucked her. After cumming over and over again and making Andi cum over and over again I knew that I was officially done with exclusively dating femmes.

~~*~*

Andi made me forget that I had a broken heart, being with her was like being with myself and she was easy to shop for her since she wore the same things as me. Yes, it sounds cheesy, but fuck it's real. There was no bullshit. She never disrespected me and she gave me my space when I needed it. I had my best friend, my homie, and my lover.

Paula had made attempts to get back with me after her second try at love with her ex failed. All of a sudden she was sorry and she didn't realize what she had with me. She wanted to try again, but all that sounded like to me was, I'm desperate, I'm feeling played, and I need you to numb the pain for me until another bitch comes along that I could leave you for. I was a lot of things, but stupid wasn't one at that Moment. I usually didn't even respond to her. She tried everything, even bringing in things that were happening with her family, because she knew I kept in touch with a few of them. Paula could swallow it, because I was on some new shit.

169

Andi and I decided to go out to the club since all we had been doing for the past couple of months was, working, sleeping, eating, and fucking. It would be nice to get out and dance or something. She showed up to my place at about ten, carrying bags with clothes and shoes in them.

"What's that?"

"Well, I was thinking we could dress alike."

"That's gay."

"We're gay."

"Um, I don't know about that."

"Man see, here you go. You just worried about people staring at us. You do this shit all the time Connie."

"It's not that, I just—"

"You just what? You're fucking a stud! So what?"

"You said yourself people are hard on S4S relationships."

"Yeah, but that's not going to stop me from being who I am. Don't worry about it. We don't even have to go."

"Baby don't do that, come on. I'll wear whatever you want me to, so you can see I don't care what people think. I'll even hold your hand too."

Andi teased me and started jumping up and down like a gay boy with a silly ass smile on her face. I just shook my head at her and laughed while reaching for the bags she was holding. I needed to shower and get dressed. Andi joined me in the shower and we had a quickie before we hit the scene.

The club was packed as usual. It's crazy how much time and money people put into clubs, especially gay people and then they wondered why they are always involved in drama. It took us a second to find a parking spot and as soon as we did I wasn't in the mood to go in anymore. I didn't say anything, because Andi had been looking forward to hanging out all week. She jumped out the car before me and headed for the entrance. I walked behind her unenthused. She paid our way in and I headed straight for the darkest corner.

Deidra spotted us and came over to speak. She obviously knew we were together because she acted different now. Andi leaned up against me and I tensed up a little. I don't know why it bothered me so much because she was still a woman. I shouldn't care if people stared. I had to keep repeating that to myself.

We left the club before they switched on the lights to put us out and by then I was drunk and unaware of anything. Andi held my hand and led me to the car. I heard someone call my name so I turned to see who it was, while still holding Andi's hand. It was Paula. She walked up to us slowly looking down at our hands. She spoke with caution.

"Hey Connie, what's up?"

"Nothing, we're leaving."

"Yeah, I see. I mean *what's up?*"

She was obviously waiting for a different answer, but she wasn't getting one since she was no one to me.

"What you want Paula?"

"Why haven't you answered any of my call or text?"

Andi glared at Paula, burning a hole through her head. Paula disregarded the fact that I was holding hands with Andi. Andi answered before me.

"You don't see me standing here?"

"I'm talking to Connie."

"And bitch I'm talking to you. I'll still beat yo ass, it's a bitch under these clothes ho."

"Connie? Is she for real?" Paula laughed a little.

"Yeah she's for real. We're together."

"So you've been brushing me off for this? A fucking stud? That shit is nasty."

"Paula get the fuck. Come on Andi."

I turned my back and I felt a hard push, knocking me down to the ground. I pulled Andi down with me. Paula kicked me and then spit in my face. I hoped she could run in heels. I stood and completely forget about anything that was going on around me. All I saw was Paula and a wad of her funky ass spit coming toward my face.

Paula was a bold bitch. She didn't even bother to run. I punched her so hard my knuckles cracked. I was going to make an example out of her ass. She would be the first and last to disrespect my relationship openly. Miserable bitch. We swung back and forth at each other, running each other into cars. I was trying to kill that bitch. I felt a hand grabbing me as I swung at her face, but they were not able to stop my rage. This bitch was going to sleep. Paula lost her balance in her heels and fell. I sat on top of her and hit her until I was picked up. I spit right back on her and adjusted my clothes so that I could go home with my girlfriend. If anybody else had something to say or felt some type of way about what Andi and I had going on I was sure they'd say it in their minds or they could get their ass beat too. People worry about the wrong things.

The T Boys

"Boys Will Be Boys"

"What is this?!"

"I've been meaning to tell you."

"When did you start taking this?"

"About three months ago."

"You promised you'd talk to me first. I don't know if I can handle this."

"What is there to handle, all you have to do is be there for me and support me!"

"How? Tell me how? I don't know what to say to you. It's not like you're having treatments for cancer or you're going through issues with your family. You're changing your entire sex! Don't you think that's a bit extreme and then you've been keeping it from me. I want a woman, not some fucking she-man!"

"Fuck you SanDrina. You've known since the day that I met you, that I was thinking about this."

"Thinking about it Vic, not doing it. You've been shooting yourself up with testosterone and not even telling me, was I just supposed to wake up to a fucking man one day."

"No! I can't believe you're tripping like this. I can't live in this body anymore. I need to start the transition, so that I can be who I really am."

"Feeling like a man doesn't make you one."

That was the last words that SanDrina had said to me before packing her things and walking out of the door. I don't know if it was me or the hormones, but her words hurt and my eyes watered as they sank into my brain. I thought she'd be the one who would stick by my side through all of this. My Mom broke down crying when she heard the news and my Father spewed his nasty remarks at me just before going out to numb it with a drink like he had done everything else in his life.

People can be so closed minded. Who was she to tell me what I was or wasn't? If she wouldn't have left on her own, I would have just asked her to leave because I didn't need that type of shit in my life. This was something I was doing for me so that I could feel complete. Call it a disorder or whatever, but it's who I am.

175

I was a man and I needed to look like one. Ever since my younger years I knew that I was a male. The breast and vagina that walked with me were in my eyes birth defects, but those would soon be nonexistent.

SanDrina flipped out after finding my needles and testosterone hiding in the back of one of my drawers. I was taking it to start the process of my transitioning to a male. I was growing facial hair, my voice was lowering, and my face muscles were beginning to shape into that of a more masculine image. She stomped into the living room as if she had found evidence that I was cheating. I should have known that she was just like the rest of the world. If she went off about the T-shots, I could just about imagine how stupid she would have acted when she found out I was going as far as having a hysterectomy and genital reassignment.

I was born Victoria Stephens a beautiful baby *girl* to Lance and Valarie Stephens. My Mother always had hopes that I would be this girly girl who was into boys and make-up, but unfortunately for her she got me, a wo**man** who wanted nothing more than to be accepted as one of the guys.

I had a friend named Erica who was just as much of an outcast as me. Her parents were lesbians. Parents had banned their kids from going within fifty feet of her, but not my Mom and Dad. I was free to do as I pleased.

Erica's Moms had gone on a cruise and she stayed over at my house. My Mom and Dad had left us at home with my oldest cousin, while they went to a game. My cousin paid no mind to us as she entertained her boyfriend in our living room. Erica and I snuck into my parent's bedroom to play dress up. I went straight to my Father's closet. Erica laughed as she watched me get all dressed up in the suit and tie. I stood in front of the mirror, staring back at my reflection knowing that was who I was really was. I was more than just the clothes. I was a boy.

After graduating high school I legally changed my name to Victor. It was the first step for me into manhood, even though I was known to most of my friends as Vic. SanDrina had been my girlfriend right after high school and all through college. I told her my feelings about my gender and she accepted them. We never talked about it much, because I didn't feel the need to, but I knew one day that I'd want to be a whole person, a whole man. I didn't think that she would walk out on me when that day had finally come.

It's been six years since that happened and I haven't been with a woman since. I didn't need another episode. I had a job that I loved and now my Mom cried a little less when she saw me. I'm completely independent and my transition is complete. It was rough with the surgeries and all, but I made it. It was not something I wanted to do alone, but I had no other choice.

The day of my chest reconstruction surgery, I waited alone and I dealt with the pain alone as the fluids drained from the wounds. I pumped myself with pain killers, but it did me no justice, so I stuck it out. I watched the doctors as he removed the bandages and I had to admit, he did a damn good job.

The T-shots weren't that bad, but it fucked with my sex drive some awful. Some nights I'd do anything just to have sex and others I was glad that I was single. I had hair in places that it had never grown before and a "period" was now non-existent. I couldn't be more happy with who I knew I really was. Every now and then I came across some asshole who would stare or make some remark, but that was the story of my life.

The real challenge would come with my genital reconstruction. I went over to my Mother's house the day before my surgery and my Father was sitting on the porch with his drink in hand. I attempted to walk past him like he wasn't even there, but he had other plans.

"Hey girl where you going? Don't you see your Daddy sitting here?"

I ignored him and continued to walk into the house. My Father and I had not had the best relationship, since he was a drunk and an abuser. Most nights I woke up in the middle of the night as he beat my Mother damn near to death, because he had had too much to drink.

"Don't you hear me talking to you girl. Oh, wait that's right, you don't answer to girl, but that is what you are."

If looks could kill, my Father would have died right there in that chair. I stopped to listen to his drunken words. I knew he had more to say. He always did. I made it a point never to answer him, because it would only make an already bad situation worse. I'd much rather have him yelling at me than punching on my Mother.

"Look at you. You're not my child. You're some fucking freak! You think people will accept you as a man? You'll never be a man. Not even the surgery will make you what I am you piece of confused shit."

His words hit me hard, but I didn't budge. I stood there like a man and took in all that he said, but not without my final say.

"With or without surgery Dad. I'll always be more of man and a better man than you ever were."

I walked inside and let the screen door slam behind me. He could sip on those words for some years to come. He was just a donor to me and God was my Father.

My Mother was sitting on the edge of her bed, which was her usual spot, sipping on coffee and smoking a cigarette. Her hair was pulled back with a satin cap over it and the news channel blared from her 16" television. She turned and gave me a weak smile. My Mother was old and lines covered her face, but you could still see that she was a beautiful woman.

"Hey baby."

"Hey mama." I walked over and kissed her cheek.

"Tomorrow is the big day huh?"

"Yes ma'am."

"Which surgery is this?"

"Genital reconstruction."

"I got one of your little cousins to look that up in one of those computers for me. It's a bit risky isn't it?"

"There are some risks."

"Vic, I've never tried to change you, even though it hurt at first I never tried. Do you really have to do this?"

"Mama."

"I just want you healthy baby and it just don't seem healthy. How about you sleep on it for me?"

I ended up backing out on my bottom surgery for the sake of what was left of my Mom's nerves. I was ok with just having my hysterectomy done. I still felt complete.

My job wanted me to relocate to another city because I was being promoted and my position was needed elsewhere. I was siked about it. I had a month to find a place to stay, everything else would be handled by the company.

I was flying out to go check out some property. I looked up real estate agents online and one company had emailed me back with the earliest date that they could schedule me to fly out to meet with a representative to view properties. I couldn't wait.

My flight was an hour and forty five minutes long and I slept the entire time. The flight attendant woke me up just as we were about to land. I pulled myself together and I was off the plane. I claimed my bag at baggage claim and then ran to find a taxi, so I could get to my hotel and shower before meeting this realtor.

It was one o'clock by the time I was done. I made it to the property before the realtor and I was relieved that I could finally breathe right. I stood facing the blue and white house, until I heard a car pull up. I turned and there she was, tall, fair skin, shoulder length hair with blonde streaks, and slender.

"Hi, I'm Erica..." she reached out her hands and then squinted her eyes, "...Vic is that you? Oh my gosh!" Erica dropped her hand and hugged me instead. She was not the same ten year old, shapeless, and toothless girl I had known over eighteen years ago.

"Vic, you...you finally did it."

"Did what?"

"The change."

"Yeah well...how did you know?" I looked confused.

"Oh please, I was your best friend. I knew *everything* about you."

Erica was the only woman who had seen my female parts and thinking of that now, made me feel a bit uncomfortable. It had been years since I seen Erica. She and her two Moms had moved because Erica was being bashed at school for having lesbian parents and that left me alone in the madness.

"So what brings you here?"

"A promotion."

"Seriously? Congratulations."

"Thank you."

"Well, I'm not going to get all in your business right now, but we have to talk later, over dinner maybe, let's get these properties out of the way," she smiled.

Erica showed me five different houses. I barely listened to anything that she had to say, because I was too busy staring at how beautiful she had grown up to be. The Erica that I knew was quiet in the public and that was mainly because after her teeth fell out, they acted as if they didn't want to grow back and she had enough of torture to deal with, having gay parents and all.

~~*~*

I sat across from Erica, watching her smile and push her hair from her face every couple minutes. She reached across the table to touch my hands.

"I can't believe you're here Vic, so tell me what's happening back home."

"Same shit different day."

"I knew you'd say that. How's your Mom?"

"She's making it. After my Dad died she hasn't really been herself. I've been the only man in her life."

"Mr. Stephens *died*? How?"

"A forklift ran over him at work."

"Damn, that's a jacked up way to die. I'm so sorry."

"Yeah, well, he was a fucked up human being."

She looked uncomfortable. "Well, tell me about you, how have you been making out with the new changes and all? I mean if you don't want to talk about it, we don't have to. I don't really know what to say and what not to."

"No, it's ok, I'm better than ever actually. After everything was complete, I felt like I had just got what I was missing my entire life."

"Not to be too personal, but did you...do...*everything*?"

"No E, I didn't do *everything*, but enough about me. What's new with you?"

"Well, I have a six year old daughter, I'm recently divorced and my Mom's are separated, but they are still really good friends. It was just too much drama. The custody battle was the worst when they decided to end it, but other than that, I couldn't ask for anything more."

"How long were you married?"

"Five years. It wasn't really working. He didn't want it to be over, but how much cheating and lying can one person take? The day of the divorce he was so dramatic, making it seem as if he wasn't going to live without me. Every time that he comes to pick up our daughter he wants to talk."

"I guess it's like that old saying goes. You never know what you have until it's gone."

Erica and I had talked about old times all through dinner. After asking me about my transition once, she never asked anything else. She accepted me as a man. She fell into the habit of referring to me as *he* and *him* with ease. She was still the same old Erica.

Erica's daughter was with the Father, so I asked her if she wanted to be my company for the rest of the night and she was more than glad to join me. She drove us to the hotel and valet parked her car.

We called room service to bring us drinks and then we ordered a movie while we sat in the bed and talked more.

"Vic?"

"Yeah."

"Would it be weird if I asked to see your chest?"

"Why do you want to see it?"

"Because I'm amazed at what you've been through. Can I?" Erica eased her hand to my shirt to unbutton it and I slapped her hand away playfully. No one had seen the surgery, but me and the doctor. My slap did not faze her. She buried her head into my neck and began to lick and suck on it, while unbuttoning my shirt. Erica touched me like I was a man. She stopped to stare at my chest before stroking my "dick" through my pants.

"Victor I haven't made love to a man in so long will you make love to me?"

I pushed Erica back on the bed and kissed her deep and passionately. I loved the way she said my name. She opened her legs for me to lay in between them. Erica rubbed my back as I sucked on her breast.

"I wanna feel you Victor. I want you inside of me."

I pulled out my "dick" and filled up Erica's insides. She moaned loudly as I moved in and out of her. Not once did she make me feel like a woman. I felt like a man, fucking a woman, who wanted my dick inside of her. Her moans made me go faster and harder as she dug her nails into my back. Erica knew how to please a man. This man.

~~*~*

Erica and her daughter moved in with me eight months after I moved. She was everything that I needed and when the time was right I was going to make her my wife. Her daughter Adrian had started to call me Daddy, since her piece of shit real Father was too pissed that Erica had moved on to be bothered with his own daughter. He had vanished. I was glad to take that place. I gave Adrian everything that she could want.

Even though Erica worked she still had dinner on the table every night and put Adrian to bed. Erica accepted me and after that night we spent in the hotel together she never mentioned my transition again, to her I was a man. Erica did not see herself as a lesbian, she saw herself as a heterosexual woman in love with a man. She was proud to show me off to her friends and family. Of course no one could tell I was born a female anyway unless they saw my original birth certificate. I kept that information locked away in my desk drawer at work.

My boss needed to see me in his office today and I had no idea why. My palms were sweating as I waited on his assistant to call my name. What the hell could he possibly want? I jumped as my name was called.

"Victor he's ready for you now."

I walked into his office and took a seat. He looked at me as though I had mud on my face.

"Have a seat Vic. We need to have a serious talk."

My boss went into his desk drawer and pulled out pictures from my surgery and my birth certificate.

"You care to explain this?"

"Sir I—"

My boss cut me off before I could say a word. He went on and on about honesty and about how I hadn't been honest with him about who I really was. He talked about how I lied throughout my entire career. I sat there and took in every word. I couldn't cry because I couldn't seem weak. Apparently, I had not locked my drawer after leaving work one day and his assistant had went into my office looking for some files for a client while she was working late and turned them over to my boss. I couldn't believe this was happening.

I lost my job and I had to go home to face Erica. So many things ran through my mind as I drove home. Could they really fire me behind this? This was an invasion of privacy and discrimination. I'm going to sue!

Erica's car was parked in front of the house instead of in the driveway; she always parked her car in the driveway. I went inside and called her name, but she never answered me. I checked every room, but she wasn't there. Where the fuck could she be? I called her cell phone, but it went straight to voicemail. This just wasn't like her.

My cell phone rang in my coat pocket and I went over to answer it. I saw Erica's name on the caller ID and felt relieved.

"Baby where are you"

"Dyke bitch!"

"Who the fuck is this?"

"I got my wife and my daughter you fucking pervert. They wouldn't come willingly, but I managed. Did you think no one was going to find out? Amazing what money can get you. Make sure you thank your boss's assistant for me you fucking faggot."

"What the fuck did you do with them?!"

"Come find out bitch!"

Erica's ex-husband slammed the phone down in my ear. I ran outside to check Erica's car and there was blood all over. I knew the nigga was obsessed with her, but I never thought it was this bad. I couldn't think.

I hopped into my car speeding down the highway. I didn't know where I was going, but I had to do something. Red and blue lights flashed behind me as I turned up a dark road. I pulled over. The officer's walked up to my car. I had tears in my eyes.

"Sir you in a rush?"

"My...my...I..."

"Slow down boy. What is it that you're trying to say?"

Right now I had two strikes working against me with these white cops. I was black and identified male. They saw the blood on my shirt and asked me to get out of the car, but I wouldn't, because I needed to get to anyone who could help me find out information on Erica's ex husband. My refusal to get out, caused then to pull me out of the car. I fought back. The officers beat me until I was semi-unconscious. I'd never get to Erica and Adrian now.

~~*~*

They placed me in a holding cell and were going to try and pin resisting arrest on me, but another cop decided to hear me out. I told him as much as I could while leaving out details of my transition. My head was spinning wondering if Erica and Adrian were okay. The officer pushed my paperwork through as quickly as he could and I was released. I was so happy that Erica had pushed me to get the gender marker on my driver's license changed, because this could have played out differently and been a lot worse than what it already was. I was funky and had blood on my clothes, but that did not matter to me.

I got back to my car and went to our house to see if I could find anything with Erica's ex-husband's address on it. That woman did all she could to be rid of that man, so I knew it would be close to impossible to find anything. I pulled the door down to our attic and my boss's assistant popped into my head after replaying what Erica's ex-husband said on the phone "thank your boss's assistant for me." She had to know something. I ran to the kitchen and grabbed the cordless phone and called my now previous place of employment. Emily answered on the second ring.

"Mr. Watson's office."

"Emily, this is Victor. I need some information from you."

183

"I'm real busy right now."

"Look, I already know you were bribed. Don't make this get ugly. You'll be fired too."

"Where are you? I'll meet you."

"Go to the book store down the street from your building. I'll be there in ten and I'm serious."

Emily was standing to the back of the store when I walked in. We stood on the last aisle and she told me everything. Erica's ex-husband was an old high school friend of hers and he came to her as if I was breaking up their "happy home" and offered her money to dig up information on me. She gave me his number and address after breaking down into tears once she learned that Erica and Adrian had gone missing and could possibly be hurt or worse, dead. It amazes me the fucked up shit people will do for some change. He only gave her a thousand dollars and I could bet that was gone in a few days. I put it on my life that if anything had happened to Erica or Adrian, Emily would pay with her life.

I put Erica's ex-husband's address into my GPS and pulled off from the book store. Dude lived seven blocks from us, which only showed me that he had been planning this shit for awhile. Everything around his house looked normal. I popped my trunk and pulled out my jack and walked around the back to break a window so I could get into his place. My heart stopped when I saw Adrian tied to a chair in the room where I broke the glass. She yelled "Daddy!" I ran over to her and hushed her. She started to speak in a whisper.

"I knew you were coming Daddy. I was waiting."

"I'm sorry it took me so long. Are you hurt?"

"No." Her eyes started to water.

"Where is your Mommy?"

"I don't know."

"Will you wait here for me and stay quiet?"

"Yes Daddy, but be careful. He had a gun."

I didn't untie Adrian just yet because I knew she wouldn't listen and stay behind. I kissed her forehead and eased into the hallway. It didn't seem like anyone was at home, so I figured he had gone to work just to keep up his normal routine. I searched every room. I stopped in his kitchen and placed a knife under my shirt just in case he was in there somewhere.

I found Erica tied to the bed in the master bedroom. Her face was swollen and bloody and she was naked. It instantly pained my heart to see her that way. I ran over to her to make sure she was still breathing and she was. She tried to speak through her swollen lips.

"Don't, don't touch me," she said weakly.

"Baby it's me, Victor." I tapped her face.

Her eyes were swollen shut. I pulled my cell phone from my pocket and called the police. I didn't have a gun and I could take the risk of trying to get Adrian and Erica out of here and her ex pulling up to kill us all. Those two ladies were going to live a long happy life. He could kill me, but not them. I searched the room for the key to the handcuffs that held her arms up on the bed, but I didn't see it anywhere. As I walked back over to her I heard a gun cock.

"Looking for this?" he held up the key and smiled.

Rage was in my heart as I laid eyes on Erica's ex. He pointed the gun at me and I charged at him. His gun went off and we fell to the floor. I could never remember being that angry in my life. I hit him over and over again. It was the rage of the young boy in me who wanted to beat my Father for abusing my Mother. Cops rushed in pulling me off of him and cuffing me. This was the second time I was being cuffed in less than twenty-four hours and I was sick of it already.

The bullet that was fired from the gun had hit Erica. The ambulance rushed in to remove her from the bed. She had already lost a large amount of blood and was barely alive. They carried Arian to the front and she jumped from the cops arms when she saw me in cuffs. She ran up on the cop, hitting him in the legs.

"Let my Daddy go!"

I looked at her, "its ok baby girl, Daddy will straighten everything out."

She wrapped her arms around my neck as I kneeled down. "Let's go home Daddy. Where's mama?"

"Mama needs a doctor, just go with the officer. I'll come get you in a few, I promise."

She hesitated to let me go as the officer pulled her toward the door. She watched me with tears in her eyes until she couldn't see me anymore.

~~*~*

Adrian jumped into Erica's lap while I grilled ribs and chicken for the whole family who was about to be on their way over to see Erica.

"Look Mommy. I drew you a picture."

Erica smiled and hugged Adrian. "It's beautiful baby."

185

"Mommy when are you going to be able to walk again?"

"Soon baby."

"I don't mind that you can't. I really kind of like your wheelchair."

Adrian was a chatty little person. I yelled for her to leave her Mother alone and go to wash her hands. Erica's family had started to arrive from both sides and when I say sides I mean both Moms. I hugged one of her favorite male cousins Carter and he took my tongs and walked over to the grill. I walked over by Erica and kneeled down in front of her.

I touched her face, "Hey you."

"Hey," she half-way smiled.

"How you feeling?"

"Okay, I guess."

"You need me to do anything?"

"You've done enough Victor, thank you," she leaned over and kissed my forehead.

Erica's family and I did all that we could to make sure that she enjoyed herself at her welcome home barbeque. I knew that she wasn't feeling like herself and there was nothing that I could do to make her feel better because she had endured a lot. Her family left around eight o'clock after helping me clean up. Her Mom put Adrian to bed for me and I gave Erica a bath and rolled her into our bedroom. She placed her arms around my neck and I lifted her from her wheelchair and placed her under the covers, making sure she was comfortable before laying in bed next to her. A month and a half of sleeping with her felt like an eternity and let's not count my night in jail. I lied down facing her.

"What's on your mind?"

"I'm just thankful."

"And you have every reason to be."

She placed her hand on my cheek. "I love you so much. You know that?" A single tear fell from her eye.

"Shhhh, stop that. I love you too and that's forever. I mean it."

"You still want to marry me?"

"More than ever."

"Even if you have to push me up the aisle?"

"I'll get a matching chair."

She cracked a smiled and I pulled her closer, so that she could place her head in my chest. The quote anything worth having is worth fighting for took on a whole new meaning in my life. I wrapped my arms around Erica, kissed her forehead one last time and closed my eyes thinking I was about to doze off, but Adrian popped into our room.

She whispered. "Daddy?"

"Yes?"

"Can I sleep with you and Mommy?"

"Come on."

She slid between the both of us and we wrapped our arms around her. My whole world was right here and there was no other place I'd rather be.

"Promiscuous"

"Kyla!"

"Yes."

"Bring Daddy some water!"

"Okay."

I ran down the steps inside the townhome that my Father rented for us over two years ago, when my Mother ran off. I tripped over the long white nightgown that I wore and instead of catching myself, I latched onto the pink teddy bear that my Mother used to place in bed with me every night. I missed my Mother and the sound of her singing voice just before I would doze off at night. I wanted to touch her coconut skin and lay on her chest as she rocked me back and forth. I wanted the scent of her perfume in my nose. I knew that mama missed me too, but she wouldn't dare come back here to Daddy. This was just a prison to mama. She couldn't come and go as she pleased and as Daddy would say; her only place was in the kitchen and the bedroom. Mama would always scream at Daddy, telling him that this wasn't the life she wanted and she was too young, but he would just slap her mouth shut. Daddy was evil and after mama left he really lost his mind. I had to cook and clean the best way I could and just keep quiet enough not to upset the old man I called my Father. I was seven when mama left and with everyday that went by, her voice faded, but never her face since I was an exact replica of her, only fairer.

Daddy lightened my skin and softened my hair with his Caucasian blood. I hated him for making mama leave and sometimes I hated her too for not being strong enough to stay at least for me. I prayed every night and asked God to send her back, at least to take me away too, but she never came. Daddy saw me as mama's replacement. I was his half-nigger slave child.

I picked myself up from the floor and continued to run into the kitchen to get Daddy's water. I walked back upstairs, being careful not to fall backwards since both hands were occupied and I couldn't grab the rail. Daddy had the door to his bedroom door open and the only light came from the television. I walked in slowly to hand him the water, then I stepped back, glancing at the walls covered in pictures of my Mother. I wondered if she still looked the same.

189

"Took you long enough, girl."

"I'm sorry."

"Sorry? You don't mean that. What do we say when we mean it?"

"I apologize."

"That's right, now go turn on that light for me and come here."

I switched on the light and walked over cautiously to my Father.

"You're getting real big there. Come a little closer." Daddy pulled me by the waist, "You look exactly like your mama, beautiful, just like her. I tried to make her happy, ya know, but she never was. Daddy makes you happy, right?"

"Yes."

"Yes what?"

"Yes sir."

"Stand still."

Daddy put his mouth to mine and his tongue felt like sandpaper pushing through my tiny lips. He closed his eyes and grunted. I stood very still with my eyes wide open. I couldn't cry since this wasn't the first time he had done this to me. Daddy pulled out his private and began touching himself and he stopped kissing me.

"You see that? That can make you feel good. You might as well get used to looking at it. This is what makes the world go around and it's all women are really wanted for. You want to touch it?"

"No."

"Yes you do, go ahead and don't be afraid of it. It's for pleasure. Grab it and do what I'm doing."

"Daddy I don't—"

Daddy snatched my hand and placed it on his ugly man part. He guided my hand up and down. I turned my head now starting to cry. I looked at the pictures of mama and wondered if this is why she ran away. Daddy lifted my gown and placed his hand between my legs, moving my panties aside so that he could rub my dark area.

"Stop crying, Daddy would never hurt you. I love you too much, just like I loved your mama. She never loved me much, but you love me, right?"

I started to shake just then. He was doing more to me than usual. I never liked any of it, but who was I supposed to tell? That night Daddy took what was left of my innocence while my teddy watched and it hurt.

The next morning, I awoke to the screams of our next door neighbor Ms. Nelson, who had been coming to dress me every morning for school ever since mama left. Daddy worked early mornings so he couldn't do it himself and I never walked to the bus stop alone. I sat up quickly to see what her screams were for and noticed my own blood staining my white sheets.

Ms. Nelson pulled my clothes from my body and looked at me with a puzzled look and tears in her eyes.

"Are you hurting? What's wrong?"

I shivered from the thoughts of Daddy. I cried not knowing if I should tell Ms. Nelson or not. She shook me hard asking me the same thing over and over as I cried. Ms. Nelson dialed 911 and I never saw Daddy again.

~~*~*

Twelve years later

This life was getting old. Here I was on a Greyhound bus to Washington, D.C. I was getting closer and closer to where I really wanted to be, New York. It was just taking me a little longer than I planned since I couldn't get a job. I had no work history, no high school diploma, and my living situation was always temporary. My life was a complete wreck after being bounced around from foster home to foster home and transferred from school to school. I had quite the reputation. Sex got me everything that I wanted for awhile, but I had to take the good with the bad and sometimes the bad resulted in other girls who wanted you beat half to death for blowing their boyfriend or girlfriend.

I sat back watching the trees and reminiscing about the last two years of my life and the people I had left behind. Robert, Dana, Gerald, Mike, Karen, Samuel, and Kevin were all from Florida my original home. Xavier, Shantel, Ashton, Terrance, and Celia were my Georgia victims. Barry Everett, Hannah, Vince, Ferrah, and Jonas were my addictions in South Carolina. Ivory, Lance, Mark, Quinton, Natalie, and Onya satisfied my needs long enough to keep me in North Carolina. Yancy and Zora were all I needed in Virginia, because between the two of them my vagina stayed busy and it got me a ticket to D.C.

I couldn't remember how I felt about any of them outside of fucking them. I just knew that I enjoyed the passionate sex of a woman over that of a man who would barely do foreplay, which was almost needed in my case because I never kissed anyone. They all provided shelter and food, which was all I really needed. I took clothes and money too, but I never stayed anywhere long enough to carry much else.

The walk from the bus station to the shelter I found online before departing was a long one, but I managed. I was used to my life not being

191

a walk in the park. A lot of people would argue that I made my life this way and they would probably be right, but this was my life and it worked for me. I'd be in New York soon and then I could get discovered for something spectacular. What that thing would be was unbeknownst to me, but I was good at a lot of things. I could sing, dance, act, and I was very beautiful so maybe I could be a model. The one thing that I appreciated my Father for was his height. Between him and my Mom and the rest of the family I had never known, I grew to be 5'10 with a slim frame, but healthy build. My ass and hips sat exactly where they were supposed to and when I wore heels, I had the world at me feet. My 36C cupped breast introduced themselves to any room before I said a word and my legs well, I told you I was 5'10" didn't I? Straight women hated me, lesbians wanted to fuck me, and men would go for broke just for a Moment of my time.

I got to the shelter doors just in time. They were getting ready to shut everything down for the night. They gave me a hot meal and a room. The rest I'd get in the morning. D.C. was filled with foundations that helped the homeless and I was going to take full advantage until I found my temporary sponsor and collected enough money to hop to the next state or maybe enough to go straight to New York. I really wasn't interested in what was going on in Pennsylvania.

I dropped everything I had on the floor in my room and it was lights out for me.

I opened my eyes at 6:30am. My stomach was growling as if I had not just eaten before bed. I knew they were serving breakfast and if I wanted to beat the thousands of people sheltered there as well, I had to get out of bed. I hopped up and grabbed my toothbrush from my bag. I stepped into the narrow hallway and spotted the restroom. I freshened up and headed downstairs. I grabbed my tray and utensils then headed to the line that was forming fast. It was hilarious standing in line with a bunch of homeless picky people. The nerve of them to have nothing and be particular about what you fed them. I watched a few turn up their noses, while others complained. I laughed silently to myself and then gave myself a week to be out of there.

One of the men standing behind the table looked like he was about 6'4 and he looked like he struggled to serve all the shorter people who held their tray damn near to his waist. He was handsome though as he greeted everyone with a smile and made small talk with others. He had the straightest and whitest teeth I had ever seen up against pecan colored skin. He wore a plain white shirt, and let his jeans sag just enough to say I have class, but don't test me I can still be hood. He didn't look like the kind of man that would wear flip flops, but he was definitely rocking them and he was cleanly shaven. If this was a different time or place then he could most definitely get me, but I never dated anyone who knew exactly how I lived. Pay phones and meet up places were my secret to keeping them wondering. Pay phones were becoming more and scarce these days, so eventually I would have to find an idiot that would pay a monthly cell phone bill for me.

When it was my turn to be served, the gentleman smiled wide at me as I held my tray higher than everyone else. I gave him a half smile and decided to flirt a little.

"I thought I'd help you out."

He spoke with a deep tone that sent chills through me. "Thank you I appreciate that."

"I'm glad that I could *pleasure* you."

I winked at him and then walked to the next person. I couldn't hold up the line. Homeless people were antsy as if they had some place to be. His eyes followed me down the line and to my table. I laughed at his admiration, but I was flattered as well. I was used to attention. I ate slowly so that he could have an extended amount of time to stare before he never got to see me again, but just as I finished my food he walked over to my table with juice.

"I saw that you didn't grab anything to drink."

"Well, aren't you observant."

"This is going to be very awkward, but can I ask what you're doing in a shelter?"

"Now why would that information interest you?"

"You just don't seem like someone who would be in a place like this."

"Well, we all make our choices and this is mine. Where else should I be?"

"I can name a bunch of places. If I give you my card, will you call me, maybe I can help you."

"Help me? Sure you can help me? Tell me where one of those places is that you could see me in? Am I wearing clothes?" I rolled my eyes.

He stepped back and smiled. "Look, here is my card and if you need anything just call me ok."

I drank the juice quickly, picked up his card, tossed out my food, and walked away without saying bye. He just stood there as I walked away. His card read Amir Hayden, Photographer and Graphic Designer. I was going to trash his card until I read it. I placed it in my back pocket and headed to my room to get dressed. I wanted to get familiar with the area that I was in before I started my short lived experience in D.C.

~~*~*

My day wasn't productive at all. Everyone in DC was an ass, which didn't bother me much, but it would make it harder for me to get things done. People in the South were much more giving. I should have just milked one of those fools for everything they had. All they wanted was a piece of ass anyway. I went back to the shelter exhausted. I didn't want to be there, so I pulled out the card that Mr. Photographer man had given me at breakfast. I went downstairs to see if anyone had a phone I could use. One of the volunteers let me use their cell phone, which was the nicest anyone had been to me all day. I dialed the number on the card and after four rings Amir picked up.

"You got me, so speak."

"That's how you answer your phone?"

"Hey, who's this?"

"Kyla, the young woman from the shelter this morning."

"Wow, I can't believe that you actually called."

"Yeah, me either."

"So, what can I do for you Ms. Kyla."

"I really just kind of wanted to get out and get into something or someone."

"Oh, um, do you have clothes?"

"Yes, if I need them."

"Okay, just grab everything you have and I'll be there in about twenty minutes."

Amir hung up without saying bye; maybe he was getting me back from earlier. I handed the phone back to the volunteer and ran up the stairs to grab my things. Today wasn't great, but maybe tonight would be better.

Amir pulled up in front of the building. I felt weird having someone pick me up from a shelter, but I shook it off and hopped into his ride and he sped off.

"What do you want to do?"

"It doesn't matter, whatever you have in mind."

"You should watch who you say that to."

"Why? I'm just saying it to you. Do you bite? I like that."

Amir pulled up to his house. It was all white, but lined in blue trimming. His driveway curved at the front and his grass was cut neatly. He stopped right in front of his door and reached for my bags.

"I can get them sir."

"Ladies don't carry bags around me, sorry."

I didn't argue with him, but I did give him a look of confusion. I followed him through his wooden, front, double doors and looked around. His home was nicely decorated. There were black and white portraits of random women hanging along his front wall, a staircase was in front of me, which I assumed lead to bedrooms, the living room was to my right and the kitchen to my left. Amir had put my bags away and came into the room with his camera.

"Uh, what are you going to do with that?"

"What do you do with cameras?"

"I can think of a few things."

He started snapping pictures of me and circling me to catch every angle. I laughed at how serious he was and the fact that he took pictures of me while I looked a horrible mess.

"Follow me."

"Ooooh, where are we going? Your bed?"

I followed him to a room with lights and props everywhere. I assumed that was his studio from the set-up and the back-drops. He instructed me to stand in front of a black back-drop and I did like I was told. Amir walked over to me and pulled the hair tie from my hair. My hair fell past my shoulders and he teased it lightly with his fingers.

"Do you know what you could do with this face of yours?"

"No, you want to show me?"

"Stop that, Kyla."

"Stop what?"

"Turning everything into sex. There are people who want nothing from you. I don't know where you come from, but I can tell you where you might end up throwing yourself at people like that."

I felt stupid and embarrassed. Amir had to be the first person who was resistant to anything I threw out. He looked at me like I was disgusting. As light as I was I was sure that my face was now red. I could no longer make eye contact with him as he continued to adjust my hair and clothing. I found everything to stare at but him. Once he was finished he turned on the lights that were connected to stands and umbrella covers and shut off the overhead light. His camera flashed over and over. I shifted my body each time he flashed because I was sure he didn't want the same picture of me on his camera repeating. He stopped to grab a spray bottle. I closed my eyes as he wet up my hair and it waved a little, then he started snapping again.

Amir handed me a towel to wrap around my damp hair and then motioned for me to follow him back into the living room. We both flopped down on the sofa. He had his laptop and the thumb drive from his camera. He inserted it into a slot and pictures began to upload. I watched in amazement as pictures of myself uploaded slowly.

"You're a natural. The modeling industry would love you. How old are you anyway?"

"Twenty-two. How old are you?"

"Twenty-eight."

"You don't look it."

"I know," he grinned.

He clicked from picture to picture, explaining to me what made each shot so beautiful. I was lost in myself. If that was half of what people saw when they looked at me then I could understand why they did as much as they did. I looked at the time on the computer and thought it was a little late for Amir.

"You should probably bring me back."

"Why you have a curfew?"

"No."

"Are you meeting somebody?"

"No, I just didn't want to wear out my welcome."

"You can stay here as long as you like and before you can say anything I have extra bedrooms, so you won't be in mine." He smiled.

"You're an ass." I smiled back.

"Where are you from?"

"Florida."

"You're a long way from home."

"I've never had a home."

"Why do you say that?"

"I never stay anywhere long enough to call it home."

"Well, how long will you be in the D.C. area?"

"Until I can get a ticket out."

"You should stay awhile and let me show you around. You don't have to make up your mind now, just sleep on it."

"I'll do that."

~~*~*

Six Months Later

I could not believe that I had stayed somewhere more than three months. Amir never asked me to leave and I never tried to. He helped me to get my portfolio started and launch my modeling career. He wanted me to get my GED, but I couldn't find the time to take the classes because modeling kept me busy. He never asked anything from me, but I did small things to show my appreciation, things that I would have never done for anyone else. Whenever I shopped I'd buy him shirts and colognes that I thought he would like. I kept his house clean, so he didn't have to, even if he left his bed unmade before he left, I would make it for him. I even went as far as cooking sometimes. He was a great person to the public and an amazing friend to me. There was no reason for him to be single or not have any kids, but that was not my business. I was just forever grateful to him.

Amir and I spent a lot of time together. He took me to jazz clubs, poetry clubs, dance halls, parks, museums, foam parties, hip hop clubs, and book readings. He loved to read. Whenever he wasn't snapping pictures he was buried in a book somewhere in the house. I wasn't much of a reader so I never even bothered to ask what he read about.

I did however enjoy the poetry clubs that we visited weekly. The laid back atmosphere was always calming to me. I could sip my drink and snap my fingers to the music. It was all love in one room. Color did not matter, size did not matter, gender did not matter, and orientation did not matter. I recalled a poet on stage by the name of Priss the last time that we went. The first thing she announced was that she was a lesbian and the crowd went wild. She recited a piece that excited everyone in the room, male or female:

"This piece is called divided sheets."

I'm gonna show her my bad side tonight
Show her what goes on in my mind when I close my eyes
Show her how slippery it can get in between these thighs
If...she...can handle it...
No need to proceed with caution
Because I want...to...fuck...until we exhaust, exhaustion
You can lick here and suck there
Place my legs anywhere
I only submit to you
And do all the things you want me to

All we need is you and me
As I pull you in deep
Releasing soft screams
I'll say your name if you make me
As my body is shaking and my back is arching
I still want more of you
I...just...can't...get...enough
So we fuck and we fuck and we fuck
And you just won't let me cum
Until you say that we're done
More shit talking
Ass slapping
Hair pulling
Back scratching
Face riding
Tongues sliding
And I'm slowly losing my mind
Losing every bit of myself in you
Letting you know who this pussy belongs to
I'm moaning and groaning
Desperately wanting to please you
I want you to feel what I feel too
And you will
Just be still...
Because tonight you and me
Are dividing sheets

That night I opened up to Amir about my sexuality. He asked me what I preferred, but that was a hard question for me to answer since I really just liked people and I learned a long time ago that pleasure comes from everywhere. I was attracted to their personality and certain physical features may jump out at me, be it their hair, their hands, their eyes, their lips, and so on. I just needed a nice human body up against mine. Amir told me that I was pane-sexual and he went on and on about it all night. I had no idea why that excited him so much. That was the most interesting night I had with him.

"I'm always telling you things about me. You should share something with me."

"Be careful what you wish for," he laughed.

"Seriously tell me a secret."

"Alright, now don't flip out on me."

"Promise," I crossed my heart as if I were a child again.

"Do you know what transgendered means?"

I laughed hard. "Amir?Seriously? I've been homeless all my life. I know exactly what it means. I shared rooms with a lot of gay, lesbian, and transgendered people."

"Yeah, well, I can imagine, people don't take well to us."

"Us? Are you...?"

"Yes I am. I'm transgendered."

"Wow. So you...?"

"No I don't have a penis and yes I was once a female."

"I don't believe you."

"Why would I lie about that?"

"Why didn't you tell me before?"

"Would you have looked at me the same?"

"Yes."

"I don't believe you."

We both laughed. Amir didn't have to explain a thing to me and I never asked because I didn't care.

~~*~*

We had crazy schedules. I was always doing a shoot or a video and he was always shooting and volunteering at various shelters. Today was one of those days that we could finally just sit in the house. I woke up early to cook us breakfast. He was lounging in the living room reading as usual in his favorite recliner as I walked by. I stopped to shake my head at him and he looked up.

"Hey, good morning ma'am."

"Good morning."

"What are you about to get into?"

"I was about to cook us breakfast."

"Come here for a minute. Come lay here."

I snuggled as close to him as I could as he wrapped his arm around me. He began reading out loud from the book in his hand, which was "Their Eyes Were Watching God," by Zora Neale Hurston. His voiced vibrated through my ears "*Ships at a distance have every man's wish on board. For some they come in with the tide. For others they sail forever on the horizon, never out of sight, never landing until the Watcher turns his eyes away in resignation, his dreams mocked to death by Time. That is the life of men. Now, women forget all those things they don't want to remember, and remember everything they don't want to forget. The dream is the truth. Then they act and do things accordingly..."*

I lay there just listening to him and his heartbeat. I thought to myself that that had been the first time that I felt safe since the last time I laid in my Mother's arms and stared into her eyes. I closed my eyes and sunk into his chest as he read. Amir and I had gotten close, but I wasn't sure what type of close it was. We stood on that line between best friend and play brother, either way it was a line that I didn't want to cross because he was the first person to genuinely care for me. I shared with Amir very intimate details about myself, the countless people I sexed, my Father and what he did to me, and all the places I laid my head if only for a night. Instead of rejecting me, he embraced me. He told me about his family and his upbringing. His parents had passed away a few years ago and left him the house that we lived in. He was an only child and he held two degrees that he cared not to use since photography had been his only passion. He lived to please his parents since they came down hard on him when they realized he was transgendered. Amir was fully transitioned by age eighteen with the help of his Mother who secretly paid for everything because she refused to disown her only child. His Father was against it, but he never spoke openly about the issue nor did he acknowledge the physical changes. To Amir his parent's death was bittersweet. He would miss them dearly, but he would never have to hear his birth name again. Amir would tell me anything until I talked about relationships. He always changed the subject on me and I respected that.

I loved these days. Amir read until he was hungry. I finally got to cook us breakfast and we sat up watching television until that bored us to death. We went out for lunch and then took a walk. He never left home without his camera. He didn't want to miss a thing. It always seemed like he took more pictures of us and me than anything else, but it made him happy. The skies started to grey and that was our cue to go back home. It was pitch black outside by the time we made it home. Amir went straight for his laptop and stereo system. Music blasted through the house as he uploaded his pictures from today. I showered and then joined him. We looked at pictures and then danced in the middle of the floor just laughing at one another when we did something crazy. Amir could not dance to save his life, but it didn't stop him from trying. He never danced in public, but at home, he acted a fool. I loved seeing that side of him. The mood of the room shifted when the song changed. 24/7 by Kevon Edmonds blared from the speakers. I lifted my finger to walk away, but Amir grabbed my arm, swinging me to face in his direction. He pulled me close to him and we began to dance. I was naturally a leader so I thought I was going to control the dance, but Amir had other plans for that.

"Let me lead, just dance with me. Relax."

I cleared my throat and tried to get comfortable. I had almost forgotten that I had a pussy until Amir's pelvis thrust into mine and my pussy jumped. It had been months since I had sex with anyone. My life had been so busy that sex had fallen to the bottom of my priority list and most of the people I met, strictly used me for business and not their own selfish pleasure. My life had taken a major turn. I was the person I didn't expect to be for another couple of years. Amir had opened a serious door of opportunity for me.

We swayed to the music. I found myself lost in Amir. His hands rubbed up and down the small of my back. I was getting too comfortable so I stepped back a little bit and shifted my body. Amir wouldn't let me go. I looked up at him and he looked down at me. He knew that I wanted to move.

"I can let you go…"

"Then why don't you?"

"I don't want to…"

"Amir."

"What? Do you really want me to let you go, Kyla? Stop running. Let me keep making love to you."

"How?"

"How am I making love to you? I haven't touched you since I've known you and still I made you stay here with me. You've been getting fucked all your life, don't you see the difference?"

"I—"

Before I could say a word Amir kissed me. He was the second person to press his lips against mine in my entire life other that my piece of shit Father, but this time I wasn't completely repulsed. His lips were soft and his tongue was warm as it intertwined with mine. I hoped that I wasn't too bad at it since I never kissed anyone. Amir's hands moved down to my ass. He squeezed it and I held on to him tightly. I couldn't do this. I pushed back and stopped. He stood with a puzzled expression.

"I'm going to go to bed."

I ran up the steps to my room and closed the door behind me. I looked at the large picture of myself that hung above my bed and leaned against my door. I had so many thoughts running through my mind and so many feelings running through my body. I had been numb to people for so long I had no idea what to do. Should I go further or just leave now?

I dozed off thinking about Amir, but loud thunder and hard rain woke me up from my sleep. I jumped because I hated thunder. I gripped my sheets tight and curled up in my bed, and then lightening flashed. I hated lightening even more. I jumped out of my bed and dashed to Amir's room, where he was knocked out. I slid under the covers and grabbed his arm to wrap it around me.

He spoke groggily. "Are you upset with me?"

"No," I said in a whisper.

He held me tight and I just closed my eyes as more thunder roared through the sky. Amir ran his fingers through my hair and started singing a silly lullaby. I laughed because I knew that he was just trying to shake my fear from the thunder. I turned over to face him and I wrapped my arms around him.

"Why are you so good to me?"

"Because I love you."

I shivered from his words. I didn't know if I should say it back or if I had any idea what love was, so I kissed him to avoid having to respond. Amir squeezed my thighs and slid his hand under my shorts to grip my ass the way he had earlier. This time I accepted his touch as he pushed our pelvis's together. I felt something poke me so I looked down.

"What is that?"

"What do you think? I am a man."

I didn't ask any more questions. I smiled and continued to kiss him. I was addicted to his lips. I could kiss him all night if he allowed me to. He pulled my body beneath his and before kissing me again he just looked into my eyes.

He whispered. "You are so beautiful." then he stroked my face.

I lifted my finger to trace his lips and he pulled my finger into his mouth sucking on it. I took a deep breath because his gesture aroused me more that I would have imagined. He sucked each of my fingers and I could feel my pussy soaking my shorts. Amir leaned up to remove his shirt revealing his toned body and smooth skin. He removed my clothes next. He slid his middle finger between my pussy lips and licked off the juices.

"Damn," was all he said.

Amir sucked on my nipples one by one. He licked down to my navel and from there he traced my panty line with his tongue. He teased me in the worst way. There was nothing I could do but moan and bite my bottom lip as he made his way to my pussy. He used his tongue to repeat what his finger had just done, starting from the bottom, he parted my lips with his tongue alone and stopped at my pearl. My body shook as he hummed on my pussy and slid his finger in to massage my g-spot. He had to hold my legs apart or I was going to suffocate him. It was the first time I could not handle the amount of pleasure my body was receiving. I shook a little harder and then I felt myself about to cum. I tried to push Amir's head away, but he wanted me to cum in his mouth, so I did. I pulled his face up to mine so that I could lick my own juices from his lips. My tongue was abducted into his mouth as he sucked on it the same way he sucked on my clit. Amir sucked on my lips before tracing my chin and jaw line with his tongue. He licked the outside line of my ear and sucked on my neck and before I could open my eyes he filled my walls up with his dick. I moaned loudly into his ear and called out his name. He prodded in and out of my walls, driving me completely insane. I scratched his back and bit into his shoulders when he stroked me hard. Amir had invented love-making. He pulled out just before I could come again and grabbed my ankles flipping me onto my stomach. I leaned up on my knees and he pushed me back down and then inserted himself into me from behind. I screamed into his pillow. It was so intense I began to cry. Tears covered my cheeks and Amir kissed my face while still stroking me. I banged on his headboard.

"I-I-I'M CUUUUUMING!!!!"

"Yeah cum for Daddy…cum on my dick."

I moaned louder as my body shook and shivered from the sensations running through my body. Amir pulled out of me slowly and planted kisses all over my back. I lay there exhausted, trying to catch my breath, staring off into nowhere. He lied beside me and pulled me over to him and just before dozing off he whispered "stay with me".

I laid with him for another hour or so, but my mind got the best of me and I decided I had stayed too long. I eased out of bed and went to my room to pack my things. I loaded as much of my stuff as I could into the car that I was able to purchase from modeling. Amir deserved better than me, someone who could actually love him, because I had no idea how. I left a letter on his favorite chair that said 'thanks for everything' and then I was out. New York here I come.

*~*Amir*~*

I reached over to wrap my arms around Kyla only to discover that she wasn't there and the side where she lay was cold. I sat up thinking maybe she was downstairs in the kitchen making breakfast. I wanted to believe that's where she was even though I had another feeling that she may not be here at all. I stepped out of bed grabbing my boxers and T-

203

shirt from the floor to cover my chilled skin. I walked out of my room and followed the handrail that lead to the room where Kyla slept for the last six months. The room was empty and the bed was made as usual. I checked the closet and all her drawers; everything was gone. The only thing that lingered was her scent. I just stood there staring at what was left of her face, a stupid black and white photo that hung above her bed. I thought I did everything right to make her stay.

I walked out of the room and locked it. I never wanted to go in there again. I walked down the stairs and into the living room to grab my laptop. Kyla had left a note on my chair. I waited to unfold the small piece of paper. I hoped that it was an 'I'll be back soon' note or some type of explanation why she would just up and leave, but of course that kind of shit doesn't happen in real life. All I got was a "thanks for everything." I was pissed, no I was beyond pissed. I balled the paper up and threw it as hard as I could.

"Thanks for everything? THANKS FOR EVERYTHING?" I yelled.

I felt myself losing my composure as my voice echoed through the house from me screaming out loud. This was not who I was. I took a deep breath and balled my fist, just squeezing my frustration inside my hands. My jaw clenched and my heart beat fast. I would not let another woman push me over the edge like that. This was the last time I'd open my arms, my doors, and my heart to a female.

*~*Kyla*~*

It took me about four and a half hours to get to New York. I don't know why I had it set in my mind that it was further away than it really was, I could have left sooner. The GPS system in my car, lead me straight to the hotel that I called to reserve a room. $1500.00 for a fucking room was so damn ridiculous, but then again this was New York. I may as well get used to the prices, because I would probably be paying that in rent alone, not including utilities. I had saved a lot of money from the jobs I did in Maryland, thanks to Amir paying for everything.

I tried to drown out thoughts of him as I drove. I blasted the music, I sang along with the songs I knew, and I avoided anything slow or about love. I couldn't be in love, because I had no idea what that was and I would have just disappointed Amir eventually. It was time to do what I did best, move on.

I grabbed a few things that I would need and then handed my keys to valet. I walked into the lobby of the hotel and checked in with no problem. After that long drive all I wanted to do was wash away Amir's scent and sleep. I wasn't hungry and I had some busy days ahead if I was going to be a famous model in New York. The competition here would be gruesome, but I was ready.

~~*~*

It took me two and a half months to land a job. The people here were ruthless. They were picky and critical. If I was one of those sensitive bitches I would have given up a long time ago. The first go see that I had, the man actually said to me "Honey, yes, you are pretty, but there are a lot of beautiful women in the world, so if that is all you have, we don't need you, because being beautiful is no longer special. I have twenty girls waiting outside who look just like you...NEXT." His words played in my head over and over after that day. I had to find a way to make myself special and I did exactly that, by doing whatever I was told to do. I had to drop my inhibitions.

I hadn't gotten signed with a major company yet, but I had ran into a few people who wanted to do some paid shoots with me. Today was my first photo shoot for a magazine spread. I walked into the studio with my little duffle bag and went straight to get my hair done. I was shooting with two other girls. Once my hair was finished they dressed me and I walked over to the photographer. He turned and recognized me instantly. Ryan and I had done a shoot together back in Baltimore. He was a well-known and respected photographer all over the world and just a cool down-to-earth guy.

"Kyla?"

"Ryan?"

"What are you doing in New York?"

"I thought I'd come to see what the big city had to offer, I forgot you lived here."

He hugged me. "It's good to see you, stay after the shoot, so I can give you my information, we must keep in touch or hang out sometime."

It took five hours to finish the shoot and I was exhausted with all the changes and posing. My body ached badly. If posing does not hurt, then, then trust me, you are not doing it right. I didn't bother to remove my make-up or brush out my hair. Ryan walked over to the station where I was gathering my things.

"What are you doing tonight?"

"Nothing, I don't think."

"Have you been anywhere yet?"

205

"No, I don't know anyone."

"Well, I can fix that. Give me your number; we're hitting the streets tonight. Umm is your boyfriend here with you?"

"My boyfriend?"

"Yeah, Amir?"

"Oh no, he uh, he didn't want to come."

"Tell him I said hello, when you talk to him."

"Yeah, I'll uh, I'll do that, so what time should I be ready?"

"Be ready for nine, we'll have some drinks first. Do you mind strip clubs?"

"No, not at all."

Ryan had put Amir on my mind again, just when his smile had stopped plaguing me. I still dream of him often when I slept and the last night that I was there and the way he made love to me. The thought always made me cringe, but in a good way. I had gotten my day to day thoughts under control, only thinking of him when something reminded me like Ryan just had done.

~~*~*

Ryan was at my place for 8:45 p.m. on the dot. I buzzed him up while I put some finishing touches on my make-up. I didn't know exactly where we were going, so I did what all women would do in doubt. I put on a simple black dress that clung to every curve on my body and leopard print heels, which was simple enough for any occasion after nine o'clock.

Ryan and I left my apartment as soon as I was done. He had a limo waiting outside. I was so excited because that would be the first time that I had been inside of one. The driver opened the door for us to climb inside and he closed the door behind us. I sat just looking around. There was so much space to do nothing. Ryan could tell that it was new for me.

"You're welcome to do anything that you like, but I would advise you not to stick your head through the sunroof. People see that shit on TV and think the wind blowing is fun, but I can tell you that plenty of women have been upset after sitting back down and looking into the mirror."

I laughed at Ryan, because I knew he was referring to their hair being ruined. I admit that my first idea was to stick my head through the sunroof, but I spared myself the embarrassment. I settled for pressing buttons and drinking up his champagne. I felt like a child and Ryan just laughed.

We pulled up to a strip club and got out. The guy at the door let us in without paying a cover charge. Ryan and I sat right by the stage. The girl that was dancing was nothing to look at. She was high yellow with no ass and tattoos covered her body. Ryan ordered drinks for us and I sat back and sipped.

After about an hour or so I was buzzing and feeling good. The girl dancing now was killing the pole and I couldn't take my eyes off of her. Her stomach was flat and her thighs were thick. She had a tattoo right above her ass and small tattoos trailed down her left leg. She had smooth caramel skin and honey blonde hair. My eyes were glued to her. Ryan noticed the trance I was in and leaned over.

"You like her?"

I nodded still sipping on my drink, "Uh huh."

"You want her?"

I turned to look at Ryan and he winked at me and leaned back in his seat. He had a grin on his face that told me he was up to something, but I was too fucked up to figure it out. As soon as the stripper that I was temporarily in love with walked off stage, Ryan got up from his seat. Ryan returned, pulling the stripper that was just on stage by her hand.

"Bubbles this is my good friend Kyla, Kyla this is Bubbles."

I looked Bubbles up and down. That bitch was a stallion. My mouth just dropped. She would make bank if she were an eye candy model and it would be better than shaking her ass and taking her clothes off for change. Bubbles grabbed my hand and lead me to the back of the club where there were private rooms. She gave the guard a signal and he looked the other way. Ryan followed us with a smile. She led me into a dark room with nothing but a long sofa along the wall and red light. Ryan stood by the door as Bubbles pushed me down on the sofa. She danced slowly to the music. I felt as though I was frozen in place as I watched her sway her body. She licked her lips at me before kneeling down in front of me and running her hands up my thighs. Bubbles lifted my dress with her teeth and pulled my lower body toward her by my legs. My pussy was directly in front of her face and I wasn't wearing panties.

Bubbles blew air onto my pussy and my clit jumped. I threw my head back as she wrapped her full pink lips around my clit. I felt the tip of her tongue ring hit my clit and it started to vibrate. I gripped the sofa as Bubbles held my knees apart and my juices flowed into her mouth. Bubbles sucked my pussy until nothing else came out and then backed up with a smile. I lay there tipsy and exhausted. Bubbles kissed my thigh before getting up and then walked toward the door. Ryan went to hand her some cash, but she pushed his hand back and whispered something to him before leaving the room without the money.

~~*~*

I felt like shit the next morning. I remembered everything that happened up until after we left the strip club. I had no idea how I made it home. I sat up in my bed with my hair all over my head and my breath was straining my nostrils. I fanned my hand in front of my face and then rolled onto the floor to get myself out of bed. I needed coffee bad.

I brushed my teeth, showered, and then got dressed to find the nearest *Starbucks*. New York was always busy no matter the time or the place. It was taking me forever to adjust to the quick pace and the people. The line at Starbucks was atrocious. It was a Monday morning and there were suits everywhere. I had nothing to do and nowhere to be so I just waited.

I walked back to my apartment and my phone rang as soon as I walked through the door.

"Hello?"

"I can't believe you're awake?"

"Yeah, thanks for getting me home safe."

"No problem. I wouldn't let anything happen to you."

"What are you doing tonight?"

"Sleeping."

"Nope, you're coming to a party. All the celebrities will be there. It'll be good exposure for you."

I was dog tired, but I knew that I couldn't say no to someone like Ryan. He could make or break my career. I exhaled and tried to sound as excited as possible while agreeing to attend the party with him. We chatted a little while longer and then hung up the phone.

I still had some stuff in bags that needed to be put away. I had been so busy trying to get my name and face out there I hadn't gotten around to it. I randomly grabbed a bag and the minute I opened it, I saw *"Their Eyes Were Watching God"*. I had taken Amir's book from his shelf. It was the first book that he had read to me and I wanted to keep it. I wondered if he noticed it was gone.

*~*Amir*~*

Five fucking months and STILL she was on my mind. I was losing it. I tried ripping up pictures that I had taken of us, but that only resulted

208

in me removing them from the trash and taking the time to tape them all back together. I never went into her room; I barely ate or slept and worried everyday if she was okay. I was trying my hardest to man up and go back to living the life I had before she even existed in my world. All I wanted was for her to feel safe and to show her a different way of living and I still got left. Why the fuck was I suffering? I was the good guy. The best man! I would have given her anything. I had to go and fall in love with a ho. *Damn. Ok I take that back. I didn't mean that.* I wanted to be mad at her, but every time I thought something degrading about her; I beat myself up. I know the person she was in her past, but that wasn't who she was with me. I fell for the best part of her.

I needed to get my mind off of Kyla and it needed to happen now. I could think of nothing better to do, but read a good book. I walked up the steps to the room that I was turning into a miniature library to find a book that I had not read yet. I was going to read a book and blast my music. My eyes roamed the shelves and noticed a section of books that were leaning, so that meant that one was missing. I always placed my books back on the shelf. I went to my room to retrieve the notebook where I had recorded all the books I owned by author and title. My books were lined by height and width so I had to write them down. *"There Eeyes Were Watching God"* was missing. I stood there for a second just staring at the shelf. I pondered on why she may have taken that book and then it hit me; maybe she was scared and she really loved me. *She took it to have a piece of me, right?*

I raced down the steps to get my car keys and my wallet. I had been sitting here sulking all these months and I refused to continue to do it. If she wanted us to be over then she would have to tell me to my face whenever I found her. I wasn't going to just let her walk away and end something that was barely starting. Her heart was safe with me.

*~*Kyla*~*

I sat in the VIP section of one the top clubs in the city having the time of my life. Ryan had really gotten me out there. A waitress brought us another round of drinks and I leaned down to do a line of coke before throwing back a shot of vodka. I felt like my life was perfect. I could walk into any club I wanted, people knew my name, and I had bitches and niggas at my feet.

Bubbles had become one of my closest friends and by close I mean, we shopped together, clubbed together, and fucked each other when we felt the need to. Ryan would always watch and just smile. He supplied the drugs and alcohol and we put on the show.

I threw back one more shot and then I looked at Bubbles. I wanted her so bad. I motioned for her to come over to me. She uncrossed her legs and stood to come in my direction. She could hush a room of niggas anywhere. I leaned back in my chair and she straddled me. I grabbed her ass as she eased her weight down on me. She placed her hands on each side of my face and then slid her tongue into my mouth. Bubbles was the only other person that I kissed without a problem besides Amir. I pulled the string she had tied behind her neck and let her shirt fall. Her titties were exposed to the entire VIP section. We both laughed as I pulled one of her nipples into my mouth and massaged the other one with my hand. Bubbles pushed my head back and stood up.

"Let's go!" She yelled over the music.

I didn't protest. I stood and she tied her shirt back up. We left the club and got into Ryan's limo. Of course, Ryan wouldn't miss out on some girl on girl action, so there he was right behind us. Bubbles started removing her clothes as soon as she was inside. I followed suit and removed mine as well. Ryan sat on the far side and decided to beat off while Bubbles and I ravished each other. Bubbles lay back so that I could lick her lower lips and just as I bent down Ryan was on top of me shoving his dick inside me. I screamed for him to stop, but he didn't. I tried to push myself up, but Bubbles grabbed my hair and held my head down as he fucked me. Struggling was getting me nowhere, but punched and damn near smothered. I didn't have much strength being high and drunk, but I tried until I couldn't try anymore.

*~*Amir*~*

Kyla had made quite a name for herself in New York. Her face was everywhere. She had no privacy whatsoever. I showed her picture to a few people and they led me right to her apartment building. The guy at the front desk gave me a hard time and wouldn't let me up so I stopped an old woman out front who was getting ready to walk into the building and asked her if I could walk up with her. She looked at me crazy and for a minute I thought she was going to hit me with her purse. I thought fast and pulled a hundred dollar bill from my pocket and then she was happy to assist. It's all about the Benjamin's in New York. It was the reason I never wanted to live there. The people I always ran into wouldn't do something for nothing. It was a city of hustlers. I started on the second floor once inside. I knocked on four doors.

"Who is it?"

"Um, my name is Amir and—" I heard the door opening.

"Who the fuck are you?"

"I'm sorry to bother you; I'm looking for a Kyla."

"Kyla Nash?"

"Yes."

"She lives up on the fifth floor. Door 504."

"Thank you!" I grabbed the guy who answered and hugged him.

I ran to find the stairwell and then rushed up to the fifth floor. I was all out of breath by the time I reached her door. I took a minute to get myself together and think of what I was going to say. I knocked hard, but no one answered. I don't know why I grabbed the knob, but I did and it was unlocked when I turned it, so I walked in. The apartment didn't have much of anything in it and things were everywhere, which wasn't like Kyla at all. I looked over and my heart sped up as I looked at Kyla laid out on the sofa beaten and her clothes were ripped. There were lines of coke on her coffee table and she was missing a shoe. I ran over to her.

"Kyla!Kyla!" I tapped her face lightly.

Her eyes fluttered open and she was obviously still high. She smiled at me a little, but I wasn't sure if she even recognized who I was. She lifted her hand to touch my face.

"Daddy?"

"Kyla, it's me, Amir. I need you to keep your eyes open."

"Amir?"

She fought to keep her eyes open. There was a cup of water on the table so I sprinkled some on her face. I didn't know shit about people on drugs, but I refused to sit here and do nothing. I carried Kyla to the bathroom and removed her clothes. I turned on the shower and stepped inside with her in my arms and started washing the dry blood from her face. She opened her eyes again and this time she was more alert.

"Amir?"

"Yes, baby, it's me."

Amir," she started to cry. "I'm sorry Amir. I'm so, so, sorry." she cried harder.

"Shhh, it's okay, I have you and you're safe now."

Water soaked my clothes and Kyla clung to me just sobbing. I held her as the water washed away whatever had happened to her. She kissed me deeply and she refused to let me go. I reassured her that I wasn't going anywhere and she definitely wasn't leaving me again.

~~*~*

One year later

Kyla had finally confessed to me what happened in New York. She showed me where Ryan's office was and I paid him a visit. I beat the shit out of him and then called the police on him and his little accomplice Bubbles for preying on Kyla. The trial was rough, but she won her case and I got off without a domestic charge. Ryan was sentenced to nine years and Bubbles and the driver of the limo got off with a yeahr each. They would be eligible for parole in six months for testifying against him. It turned out that Mr. Ryan raped models often, but none of the other girls cared to come forward because of their fame.

Kyla didn't want anything from her apartment. She just wanted to put everything behind her and be with me. Once we returned to Maryland, she placed *Their Eyes Were Watching God* back on the shelf and she enrolled into GED classes. She did rehab every now and then, but she stayed cleaned, no alcohol and no drugs. She wanted to try and live life the simple and sober way for a change and I couldn't be happier.

It didn't take her long to get her GED and get herself back on track. Sometimes she had nightmares and she would wake up in cold sweats, but I'm always right there to hold her close to my chest. She volunteers with me sometimes at shelters for the homeless and she'll share her story with young girls to inspire them. She enrolled to take up psychology after she got her GED and she keeps pushing me to share my life as a transgendered man, but I'm not quite there yet. I hold her close to me every night and sometimes I wonder if she will leave again and if I would go after her again. I just give her all my love for now and hopefully after her graduation, Kyla won't just be my girlfriend, but my wife.

"Straight girl Crush"

(Feature story by: Trixie V.)

"Mama, what's a dyke?"

I stared at my five year old daughter wide eyed in shock. As she looked up at me from her coloring book I had nothing to say. I stared back into her eyes trying to think of a way I could explain what she had just asked me.

Nothing came to mind.

The only thing that stuck out first was my sophomore year of college. I heard the word "dyke" and "bull dagger" more than any person should. My parents used it as casual as the word mustard or ketchup.

The memory goes back when my mind was unchained by Nietzsche and Aristotelian thought. Those kinda things weren't in summer vacation bible study when I was ten so you could imagine what my term papers looked like...

My parents were Christians. No, I take that back. They were the worst *kind* of Christians; Catholics. They told my brother he would go to hell for touching himself and made us give all of our peers "Christian side hugs", as they called them, as to not provoke any urges that frontal hugs beckoned.

This is the reason I chose out of state college.

People's first thought is to always call the Christian girls and the preacher's daughters the biggest freaks. I come to you with the simple answer of: Yes, yes we are. I didn't wild out the second I stepped foot on campus. However, when I discovered my first frat party I didn't hesitate to explore my horizons.

I was well into my sophomore year and I hadn't gotten a bad reputation because well, I was downright scared of lying to my parents about the technical stuff. It was bad enough I conjured up some imaginary boyfriend that pretended to woo me with the word in order to have my virginity. They still question whether or not he was real. Personally I think they prefer that lie better than the *actual* events I'd come to confess to them.

"Hey Eliza, are you going to that new bar they opened on campus?" my friend Robyn whispered to ask me as we studied in the quiet area.

213

"Hell yes. When?" I whispered back. I never passed up a good time.

"It's this Saturday. I hear *everybody's* gonna be there." she smiled.

"I would say so seeing as how it's gonna be right here on campus. You know we're about to kick up some real trouble." We both giggled dapping each other and being shushed by a fellow studier.

Robyn was my roommate my freshman year. And agnostic, so I didn't have to worry about her judgment. She pretty much lived the life I was shielded from as a kid. If my Mother had met the real her she would say "The devil placed her here to sell you this lifestyle dressed in rubies and gold." If that was at all true, then I was sold the second we met. She was the one that helped me peel layers of awkwardness off to reveal my 5'5 175 pound body of hips and honey dips. The day she gave me a makeover she said, "If God really is real, when you get to heaven you should ask Him why He made all that and *not* want anyone to touch it."

Robyn and I called it a day with studying and went our separate ways for the day. I headed to my anthropology class like I always did. Readying myself to question my entire existence like I'd been doing since the beginning of the school year, I sat in the back of class in the same spot I took day after day. Then she walked in. She had fair skin with long brunette hair down to the middle of her back. Her eyes were green and she had full cherry stained lips. She was short but slender. I couldn't keep my eyes off of her. I saw the professor handing her things and talking with her.

Of course, she was new. I would've noticed her sooner.

The sound of my ancient professor's voice shook me from my stupor. I still spent the entire class time taking notes and watching her undecidedly pull all of her hair from one shoulder to the other. She was so graceful in everything she did. The way she held her pencil and leaned over to write, the way she held her hand under her chin when she was paying close attention, even when she burped from drinking her Coke too fast between notes. I was baffled.

I wasn't gay.

When class was over, I shot out of the door to not stare at her anymore. I felt crazy for feeling like that about a girl. The second I got to my room I asked Robyn to come with me to the student life center.

"Have you ever kissed a girl?"

"On a dare when I was in high school but it was short lived. Why?"

I shrugged. I'd never kissed a girl. I never wanted to. Not until I saw her anyways...

"You're not about to come out to me are you?" she asked me laughing.

214

"Huh? No. I just was curious."

"Oh well I was going to say if you are it's cool but it comes at an unfortunate time because Jared asked about you."

"Jared?" my eyes bugged and she nodded. "Star of the basketball team, six foot nothing, tall drink of water in a desert *Jared*?"

"Yes and he asks about you every time I leave my room."

"What did he say?"

"He wanted to know if you were single and if you were looking. So you know what that means."

"That means I need to move on your floor." We laughed.

Jared was the cause and the solution. Everything a girl dreamed of in a guy and then some.

And if I planned on getting any kind of close to him I'd better just recognize the situation for what is was: Amanda was a pretty girl and I admired her. Nothing more, nothing less. Besides, I was straight. There's nothing we could do with each other.

The next day my classes didn't start until noon so I went over to the student life center to watch some plasma TV and pretty much slack until class started. Jared walked in looking my favorite sin in basketball shorts and a t-shirt with his book bag with no books in it on his back. I was strewed across one of the sofas wearing yoga pants and a school shirt. My short cropped hair was behind my ears and I was fully engaged in a music video I had seen a million times from this same spot. I was putting up a front so he would come to me. Something Robyn taught me.

"Any room for me on that couch?" Jared came and stood in front of the TV.

"Hey you," I smiled. "Yeah, come sit with me." I played cool. I tried to move but he pulled my legs over his.

"What are you doing in here so early?"

"My classes start late today. Just thought I'd hang out. What about you. Shouldn't you be practicing for something?"

"No," he relaxed himself under me, "I'm always in here. You're on my stomping ground."

I giggled saying whatever.

"So are you going out this weekend?"

"I thought about it," I lied casually. "Me and Robyn were thinking of stopping through if we weren't doing anything else. Why do you ask?"

"Well, I wanted to tell you about that bar that's opening up this weekend. It's run by a friend of mine. It doubles as a club. There's bull riding and karaoke. You should come."

"Oh I see. Shameless self promotion." I joked.

"No," he chuckled, "I just wanted to know if you were gonna be there. I'd like to dance with you." He smiled.

I wanted to burst at the idea but I kept my cool. "I guess so." I said half smiling.

"Don't be like that with me. I see how you look at me sometimes." He pulled me onto his lap.

"Maybe," I said. He started to whisper to me when I saw her walk by. She had on light gray sweat pants and a wife beater. Her long hair flowed behind her as she took her dry cereal to a table full of friends. I watched her smile and walked over joining in the conversation from a small distance. It was as if everything started moving in slow motion. She sat down and picked at her cereal one grain at a time. Laughing and rocking in to the conversation and onto the back of her chair. She turned and looked at me for a second smiling then turned back to her friends.

She noticed me.

"So, are you in?"

"I'm sorry, what?"

I totally forgot that Jared was acting as my chair and whispering apparently unimportant things to me.

"Saturday, you down?"

"Yeah, I gotta go." I got up grabbing my bag, "Tell Rob to give you my number. We'll talk." I walked away heading in the direction of first class of the day. I wanted to chalk this whole thing off as a crush but every time I saw her I became so completely unraveled.

I anticipated Anthropology like a kid awaited Christmas. I even showed up super early to get a closer seat. I wasn't brave enough to sit next to her considering how I stared like a maniac so I just sat a seat closer behind her. Which is not creepy at all... She came in late as usual still wearing her earlier attire. I tried not to stare too much and I didn't have to. Her perfume was oddly compensating for the visual I got a fix from.

Once class was over she left before me not taking a second look back.

I needed to figure out what was going on...

Saturday

"You ready?"

"Yep." In true club fashion, I had chosen to wear ankle length tights, boots with a vest. No shirt, no bra. Robyn wore a barely there dress and the highest pair of heels in her closet. Since I'd told Jared I may or may not be going we dipped in and out of other local clubs

216

before actually going to the bar. We wanted the fresh smell of beer and other venue on our breath.

This new bar was *happening*.

It was huge. The bar was endless, there were two pool tables, a stage with the gigantic bull, and a screen for karaoke like Jared said and the dance floor was huge but packed with every student face I'd ever seen in my two years in college.

Robyn's goal for the night was to bag a student athlete. They were famous for hanging in clubs and bars. Now that there was one on campus her quest wouldn't be so difficult. She pulled me to the dance floor and proceeded to dance on me in case anyone other than Jared tried to. This technique also doubled as advertisement for her. As we danced and got sweaty some bulky guy who obviously was a football player caught her attention. Perfect timing for me to take a bathroom break. I wandered aimlessly through the sea of dancing people looking for the bathroom only to end up in some weird drunken freshman sandwich. These kids obviously were first year and had never been to a house party. Someone grabbed my hand and pulled me out and wrapped their hand around my waist yelling "She's with me now back the fuck off." over the music. I was pushed by the person to the bathroom and inside. Finally I would be able to see my savior and thank them.

I turned to see her standing behind me in a tight black dress with a skinny light brown leather belt around her waist; her long hair ever flowing like the red sea holding a corona in her hand.

"Thank you," I couldn't smile. I was too stunned.

"No problem. My friends and I have been saving girls all night. We're sitting right out in the booth where they're claiming victims." She turned towards the mirror to check her makeup, puckered her lips twice and turned to me. I was still staring like an idiot. "Hey. Aren't you in one of my classes?"

"Yeah? I mean, yeah." I stammered. "Anthropology."

"Anthropology, Yeah." She smiled. Her teeth were impossibly white. "So did you come here alone…" she squinted her eyes turning her head to the side indicating she was trying to guess my name.

"Eliza," I said extending my hand.

"Eliza. I'm Amanda. Excuse me, I'm a little shit faced." She giggled taking my hand.

"It's fine. And no, my friend Robyn is… somewhere in here."

"Robyn? I think I know her. Do you wanna come hang out with us at our booth?"

"Uh Yeah, just let me see where my friend is and you could meet her." I smiled. She smiled nodding then turned to check her face again.

I texted Robyn 'Where are you skank?' and pretended to check my twitter as Amanda sat her drink down and combed through her beautiful hair with her fingers and swung it from side to side. Robyn texted back:

'Don't wait up. See you later :p

"Great." I dropped my hands by my side. I stuffed my phone back in my vest safely as Amanda turned to me concerned.

"What's wrong?"

"My friend ditched me."

"Oh cool," she smiled. "Then you get to hang out with me."

Her friends partied like no one I'd ever seen party before. They drank until every bit of their insides was out, they danced until they were sore, and they shared their love freely if you get my drift. I came out of the bathroom from my third liquor expulsion. Apparently Amanda and her friends were rich and could buy drinks with Daddy's credit card all night. Amanda was on her fifth beer standing in between another one of her friends' legs who was sitting up high on the top of the booth seat. As she chugged her drink, the girl stuck her hand down in the top of Amanda's dress. Amanda didn't jerk away or smack the girl's hand. She just finished her beer and pulled the girl down and proceeded to give her the most inappropriate tongue kiss I'd ever seen anyone give. The girl slid her hand under Amanda's dress and up over her breast. Amanda followed suit by pulling her half shirt down a little more feeling on her chest as well. I didn't know what I was seeing. I'd seen lesbians before but never like this. Without alerting them I just left. I went back to my room and tried to decipher my feelings. I was wedged between confused and turned on.

I needed to face this demon head on.

Monday morning we had an exam so the initial awkwardness of me not staring at Amada was silenced. Besides, she was so hammered Saturday I doubt she even remembered...

The test given was supposed to be four hours but of course it never takes that long. It was our midterm before Spring break so after this I was going pack and sulk about having to go stomach my Mom for a week.

I was done with my test in an hour, our genius professor decided to give material that wasn't covered in class. On my way out of the building I stopped in the bathroom. As I was washing my hands the other person that had come in came out to wash their hands.

"Hey you."

I looked up to see Amanda smiling rubbing soap up to her wrists. "Hey Amanda." My very breath was taken away. "How do you think you did in there?" she shook her hands and placed them under the dryer and I followed.

"I did ok. Wasn't expecting some of the questions he put."

She snorted agreeing. "What happened to you Saturday? We all went out to eat after. We were looking for you."

"Oh," I drew my hands back and held the sling of my purse, "I wasn't feeling well so I headed out early. You guys know how to drink." I giggled nervously.

"Yeah," She laughed. "Well, we're all getting together in my room before everyone leaves. You should come. And if you aren't busy bring your invisible friend." She joked.

"That sounds nice but I kinda have to leave early. The only flight I could get leaves early in the morning."

"Oh Yeah? Where you headed?" we both walked out of the bathroom to the building exit.

"Connecticut."

"No way, that's where I'm going. I was just gonna party it out and sleep on the way there." we both laughed. She was gorgeous. Too gorgeous for words. "If you want we can cab together in the morning. You should really come by my room."

All I could think of was my Mom telling me how lesbians prey on other people because they "work for the devil". I really wanted to say no but I really wanted to hang out wither her. She was really nice and fun and funny. I couldn't let something as little as her sexual preference get in between what could possibly be the best friendship I have other than Robyn. What have I learned in college?!

"Sure. Why the hell not." fell out of my mouth before I could stop it.

"Nice, let's do it."

I went to my room and grabbed my pre-packed bags while Robyn sat on my roommates bed watching.

"And you just met her Saturday?"

"Yeah. She wanted to meet you but you were busy."

She smiled. "Yeah I was wasn't I... Anyway that's not the point. You spent all night with her and Jared was looking for you."

"How would you know? You were too busy ass to pelvis with football boy."

"Yeah, I was wasn't I?" she smiled. "Well you better go see him before you leave and go play sleepover with your new buddy." She got up and left the room.

I didn't bother telling her about what happened. I wasn't sure of what she would say about me hanging around a girl I liked who just so happened to be into girls. Amanda and her friends were hanging around the only way they knew how; smoking and drinking beer listening to 'Hey' by the Pixies.

"Hey, you made it." I drug my bags in her room. She reintroduced me to everyone. They all remembered me and offered me things. We pretty much spent the night buzzed and talking about Spring break plans.

Turns out Amanda and I grew up in the same town. We had never met because her family lived in the upper part where the richer people lived and my working family lived in the ok area. After some friends had left and others were asleep we laid in her bed just talking more. We had a million things in common and agreed on almost everything. I'm not sure of what impressed me more about her; her looks or her brains.

My alarm on my phone woke me up to her spooning me and her long hair all over the pillow and her shoulder. She was the prettiest girl I'd ever seen in my life and I think I wanted her. Her alarm went off shortly after mine and we both got up as if we hadn't just been cuddling. The cab ride was silent seeing as we both were too tired to muster up conversation. We spent the flight laughing and talking. She fell asleep on me a couple times which gained some questionable looks from older people on the plane. When we landed Amanda couldn't get in touch with anyone to come pick her up, she was pretty upset about it.

"It's fine. I'm sure my Mom wouldn't mind having an extra girl in the house." I smiled.

"Are you sure?" she asked sitting on her luggage upset.

I pulled her up and pulled her towards the shuttle. I called my Mom and let her know we were having an extra guest and of course she was excited. Any reason to keep up appearances and use her good towels and table wear. When she heard it was a friend from school she made sure to go into super Mom mode which was ridiculous...

"Ladies!" she greeted us at the door, "You both look exhausted. Come let me get your things. Ezra!" she called for my brother who had taken the road frequently traveled by staying home for college. He came running down the stairs and straight to the door when he saw Amanda. 'Get these young ladies bags will you?"

He grabbed Amanda's bag smiling at her leaving me to tow my own. Amanda smiled at me and grabbed my bag for me. At dinner we made proper introductions and proceeded to talk about everything I didn't care to listen to. Things like Amanda's religion. Dinner wasn't so bad with her there. She kept the light in the room with her humor and how she kept shooting my idiot twin brother down.

After dinner I showered while Amanda called her parents to see how long it would be until they came to pick her up. She was pouting when I went into the room.

"Still no answer?"

"No. I know my Dad's just working. He's always working…" she looked down.

I sat next to her and put my hand on hers, "Well look at it this way, it's more time we get to hang out together." I smiled. She looked at me smiling back. She flipped her hand up to grasp mine and rubbed my face with her other hand.

We locked eyes for a Moment.

She stroked my bottom lip with her thumb slowly then leaned in to kiss me. I jumped back once the peck left my lips.

"I'm sorry." She said quickly.

"No, no. it's fine." I looked away sliding away from her on the bed.

"I just… I thought…"

"No, really, it's ok." I smiled waving it off.

"You do… like me, right?" she asked confused.

I just looked up surprised, "I do but… I don't know what to do with those feelings. I've never been with a girl."

She moved closer to me and took my hand. I was a bit tense, "It's ok." She smiled, "I don't bite." She rubbed my hair and kissed me again. I relaxed my nerves and let her take control. She had the softest skin anyone could have. We moved closer to each other as our kiss deepened. I didn't know what I was feeling. Something in me was excited she was kissing me but a very strong part of me wanted to stop. We wrapped our arms around each other and squeezed our bodies together.

There was a tap on the door and we quickly separated.

"Are you both alright in here?" my Mom poked her head in.

"Yeah, Mom, we're good."

"Okay." She smiled, "Goodnight, see you all in the morning."

We both said our goodnights and she left out. Amanda touched my leg and I stood up.

"Did I do something wrong?"

"Yes… I mean, no. I mean… I don't know. Don't you have a girlfriend?"

"No."

"What about that girl from the bar?"

"Denise? I was drunk, she was drunk. Surely you've had one of those nights."

"I don't know if this is right. I mean, if I'm right."

She stood up and came over to me tucking my hair behind my ears, "It's only right if you feel it. And I feel that you like it when I touch you. I like you. I feel that you like me too. If I'm wrong please tell me to stop." She leaned into me and kissed me again.

I closed my eyes to see if I could feel anything. To see if I could feel whatever it is she spoke of.

She took my face in both her hands and planted kisses all over it. She sat me down on the bed and lifted my shirt over my head tossing it to the floor. She smiled at me before laying me gently on my back kissing me slowly. She was so soft and smelled of honey and almond. I ran my fingers in her hair and looked into her green eyes. "Trust me." She whispered. And I did.

I laid next to her in silence thinking about what just happened. I didn't know if I was more ashamed of the sex or the giggling.

The next morning we woke up to the sound of several stomping feet. I wasn't up fast enough because the door swung open and I could hear my Mother gasping.

"My God, Eliza! Who have you brought in my house?!"

"Mom let me explain!" I held the covers over my bare chest and Amanda tried to cover herself.

"Explain?! Explain what! No child of mine will be or be associated with the homosexual lifestyle." She shut the door and ran somewhere unknown in the house. We both frantically got up and got dressed as Amanda apologized a million times.

"It's ok. She makes everything into a huge production."

Her and my brother came into the room tossing holy water all over the place slinging a rosary and yanking the sheets off the bed. My Mother went over to Amanda placing her hand on her head repeating Hail Mary's rapidly.

"Mom!" I ran over to her grabbing her hands. She was pushing down on Amanda so hard she could barely move. "You're hurting her!" I tried to move her hands but she directed her rosary and crucifix towards me."

"You've been possessed by those demons at that school. The Eliza I know would've never done something like this!" she proceeded to press the old wooden cross on my head. I smacked it across the room when it contacted with my skin. My Mother gasped watching it fly to the other

222

side of the room. She looked at me then drew her hand back and slapped me. I held my face as she covered her mouth. She tried to comfort me.

"No!" I yelled at her, "The only person in here that's possessed is you! You talk about God and judgment. You've been judging everyone your whole life. You're no different from anyone else. You just want others to feel bad about living because you never did." I helped Amanda off of the floor and grabbed her suitcase. Her aunt was able to come get us and take us to her house. I stayed with Amanda for a couple days until my Mom cooled off and was ready to talk. Amanda tried apologizing to me again but I stopped her.

"It's ok. I should've warned you about my Mom before I invited you to stay. You're ok though right?"

"Yeah, I'll be fine. I just hope we'll still be able to see one another after all this." She smiled.

"We will." I hugged her. "Promise." She let me go and held my hands. She kissed both my cheeks before letting me go.

My Mom was waiting for me in the car outside. When I got in I didn't look at her and she didn't say anything. She took the short way home. This indicated she was mad. When we got to the house she sat on the sofa and looked at me. I sat next to her settling in the sofa cushion. I was about to muster up some kind of apology slash explanation but she held her hand up.

"First I wanna say I realize this was because your Father and I sheltered you as a child. I apologize for my part in that."

"That's fair," I stated.

"Secondly, I just wanna tell you that I'm not upset with you about…what happened. I'm not disappointed or hurt. However I am very disgusted. I want to tell you that you are to complete out this semester at your school but after, you're moving back home."

"But Mom—"

She held her hand up again, "You will do as I say and come home or I will be forced to let you go."

"Disown me?!"

"Yes. No child of mine will live a lifestyle that isn't pleasing to God."

I couldn't argue with her. I couldn't fight with her for Amanda's sake. What would I do? I was only a child with no idea about love or life so I took the coward way out and agreed.

When I got back to school I made sure to avoid anywhere she would be. I didn't know what to say to her. I didn't tell any of my friends about what happened. I just continued on campus like it never happened. One day before the semester was over I was having lunch with Jared. Someone tapped me on the shoulder.

"Hey," Amanda said.

I turned to see her smiling face, "Hey."

"Can we talk?" she looked from me to Jared.

"Uh Yeah. Sure." I told Jared I would be right back and followed Amanda off to the side away from everyone else.

"How have you been?"

"Good."

"That's good. I haven't seen you around in a while. I was beginning to think you were avoiding me."

I didn't confirm or deny it. "So... About what happened over spring break..."

"No need. I figured things got ugly considering how things turned out the morning after." she joked but I could tell she was hurt.

"True. But I just want you to know I didn't regret it. And I'm not sorry for it."

She smiled and stroked my cheek. "Well I just wanted to say hey. I saw you and thought I'd say good bye and good luck. See you soon." She turned to walk away from me.

"We're still friends though...right?" I called to her.

She turned to face me and smiled. "We never stopped." She waved and went to rejoin her friends. I watched her walk away feeling a little hurt. I knew somehow this wasn't the right decision. But in that Moment, I didn't have a plan.

"Mama?" my daughter called to me again.

"Huh?"

"What's a dyke?"

I blank a few times remembering where I was. I looked upon my waiting daughters face. I opened my mouth to speak but Amanda rounded the corner with our glasses of lemonade, "It's not a very nice word." She answered for me. I smiled as she sat down next to me handing me my glass.

"Where did you hear that word anyway?" I asked.

"At school. My friend Tyler told me that his Mom said we couldn't be friends because you were a dyke."

Amanda and I looked at each other. "Well baby, if he's not willing to stay your friend over something as silly as his Mother saying so then he isn't your real friend." She told her.

That's right. Real friends stick together." I smiled at Amanda.

"So, what does it mean?" she still inquired.

The room went silent.

"It's an ugly way for people to judge two Mommies that love each other," Amanda explained.

"Oh, well, if he says that word again I'm gonna tell and then he's gonna have to eat soap."

We both laughed as she continued to color. Amanda snuggled closer to me and continued to watch TV as our daughter colored.

I couldn't protect our baby from the judgment of others but I refuse to shield her from the world and have her grow up in ignorance.